Public Sector Reform in
the Middle East and North Africa

Public Sector Reform
in the
Middle East
and North Africa

Lessons of Experience
for a Region in Transition

Edited by
ROBERT P. BESCHEL JR.
TARIK M. YOUSEF

BROOKINGS INSTITUTION PRESS
Washington, D.C.

The Brookings Institution is a private nonprofit organization devoted to research, education, and publication on important issues of domestic and foreign policy. Its principal purpose is to bring the highest quality independent research and analysis to bear on current and emerging policy problems. Interpretations or conclusions in Brookings publications should be understood to be solely those of the authors.

Library of Congress Control Number: 2020947435
ISBN 9780815736974 (pbk)
ISBN 9780815736981 (ebook)

9 8 7 6 5 4 3 2 1

Typeset in Electra

Composition by Elliott Beard

Contents

Preface

RAMI G. KHOURI

IN THE FIRST HALF of the twentieth century, the Arab region completed impressive state-building processes that steadily improved citizens' quality of life and forged national identities where none had existed before. Jordanians, Kuwaitis, Lebanese, Saudi Arabians, Libyans, and other citizens of new states emerged onto the regional and international scenes. The newly made states and their new citizens worked together and established an unspoken pact whereby both state capacity and citizens' quality of life improved.

In the second half of the century and the first decades of the twenty-first century, most non-energy-rich states have seen their state-building momentum slow, stall, or even reverse as state financial resources could not keep up with the needs of growing populations. Erratic economic and social development after 1990 saw most non-oil-financed governments unable to improve or even maintain the quality of life of large swaths of their populations. The states' retreat from some quarters of society allowed non-state organizations or the private sector to pick up the responsibilities of providing citizens the basic services, protection, opportunities, and political voice they needed to remain loyal citizens. Many citizens lost confidence in their states and their national identities. Some turned to other identities, including religious and tribal ones that long predated modern states. A few Arab regions even broke away from the central state (Yemen,

Sudan, Iraq, Islamic State), and some populations or regions remained inside the state borders but mostly relied on other forces to serve and represent them (Hamas, Hezbollah, Ansarullah-Houthis, and others).

This trend of state fragmentation may be accelerating now due to current pressures from recent oil price drops, geopolitical tensions, and COVID-19 pandemic-related economic slowdowns. The UN today says that 70 percent of all Arabs are poor or vulnerable, and that figure is rising daily due to severe economic slowdowns. The relationship between state and society is emotional and psychological at some levels, but mostly it is manifested in how governments and citizens interact on a daily basis to access essential resources like water, health care, reasonably priced food, education, job opportunities, and security.

For this reason, the civil service's interactions with citizens on a daily basis is probably the best indicator of the status of state-society relations. It is the flash point where citizens and state meet in person every day. This is also an important setting where citizens can experience either respect or injustice at the hands of the state. Dignity is measured in the material provision of services but also in the manner in which all-powerful officials treat individuals at that all-important window where one submits applications and forms. This is where individuals see whether the state respects them or disdains them.

When things go well, citizens feel they are treated with dignity. When they do not go well, citizens feel humiliated. Humiliation is the first step to losing faith in the system, and in the most extreme cases, that can lead to losing faith in the legitimacy of the state and its institutions. If the existing political system offers no credible avenues for redressing grievances, citizens become desperate and often turn to other identities and actors for support. Some citizens depart permanently for other lands, better identities, and more secure futures for their children. Some break away from the state to form new states, though the experiments of secessionist states tend not to go so well (South Sudan, Kurdistan, South Yemen).

This is why reforming the public sector in the Middle East and North Africa (MENA) is such an important challenge. This book is essential because it is necessary to pause and assess where and why some public sector reforms in MENA have succeeded and others have not.

Few people in our region have had as much sustained direct experience with these issues as Tarik Yousef and Robert Beschel Jr., and they have done us all a service in compiling these case studies of public sector reforms. As these case studies demonstrate, public sector reform requires the convergence of strong leadership, sustained political will, and resources for strategic planning and implementation. These variables are always vulnerable to erratic regional and global economic trends, volatile local politics, and, ultimately, the collective sentiments of the public. The smallest and biggest forces in our world—microscopic viruses and cosmic deities— also play a role, but people interested in exploring public sector reforms in the MENA region should focus on a force we can easily gauge every day: the sentiments of citizens and the equitable organizational capacities of state institutions. This book is an excellent starting place to understand the complexities involved in analyzing this issue, which will only become more important in the years ahead as much of the MENA region becomes an arena where increasingly marginalized citizens battle police states on the street.

Or, if you like on-the-spot research, you could go to any government passport or driving license renewal office in any MENA country and watch how states interact with their citizens. For example, when attempting to renew my passport in Jordan decades ago, I observed an old man who had been waiting in a slow-moving crowd for nearly an hour on a hot summer morning be told to come back another day with more signatures from other government agencies. He exploded in anger at the clerk's haughtiness and his own helplessness. A few years after that experience, the Jordanian government unleashed a whole battalion of super-efficient public servants, many of them from the police and military branches, who radically reformed the passport and national ID card offices, the car and driver licensing departments, the tax department, and many other government departments. I assumed, from my discussions with many colleagues and senior officials in Jordan at that time, that the reforms happened because some people in the political leadership recognized that citizens were routinely humiliated in their daily encounters with the state, causing cumulative anger and stress in society.

When I renewed my passport ten years later, I walked into the same office and thought I was in a Swiss bank. The spacious room was air conditioned, with neat rows of comfortable benches and seats. I pushed a button on a machine at the door to get my number. A few minutes later, my number was called, I approached my designated counter, handed in my papers, then was asked after two minutes to pay the fees in the cashier window next door and wait to be called again. I did that, and after just twenty-five minutes they called my name, I picked up my renewed passport and walked out of the office with a pleasant and unusual sense that we have the proven ability to transform a citizen's pain into pride. Policymakers in the MENA region would do well to recognize that how state institutions deal with citizens actually matters very much. This book is a most useful and timely place to start pondering this.

Acknowledgments

WE ARE GRATEFUL TO several institutions and to a much larger number of individuals who have helped in the preparation of this volume. First and foremost, we are indebted to our case writers—Mark Ahern, Fatema Alhashemi, Adele Barzelay, Mhamed Biygautane, Tristan Dreisbach, Khalid El Massnaoui, Khalid Elashmawy, Tony Goldner, Okan Geray, Deepa Iyer, Fadi Salem, Andrew H. W. Stone, and Simonida Subotic—without whose tireless efforts we would not have been able to capture the fascinating studies that form the core of this book. We are also grateful to Nithya Nagarajan and Khalid Al-Yahya for their many important contributions earlier in the drafting process, and to Khalid for writing the case on the SADAD bill payment system within Saudi Arabia. We are grateful to Fatema Alhashemi, who managed the project over the past three years, overseeing the completion and updating of chapters, and to Anna Jacobs, who provided superb editorial and technical support as we prepared the volume for publication.

Their efforts, in turn, would not have been possible without the active collaboration of the governments and individuals featured in these cases. We very much appreciate their willingness to share their experience, both positive and less so, with a broader audience. It is our hope that this effort will mark a modest but important step toward greater transparency in identifying, documenting, and sharing experience with public sector reform in the countries throughout the Middle East and North Africa region, from which all will benefit.

We are particularly appreciative of the efforts of a number of individuals whose support and good will were essential to this project's success. This book has been supported by a number of World Bank managers and staff, including Manuela Ferro, Guenter Heidenhof, Renaud Seligmann, and Hisham Waly. From the Brookings Doha Center, we acknowledge the support of Fatema Alhashemi, Anna Jacobs, Nadine Masri, Ghadeer Abu Ali, Rawan Dareer, and Seyda Aydin. Our peer reviewers were Nick Manning, Edouard Al-Dahdah, Hana Brixi, and Mike Stevens. In addition, valuable feedback, advice, and assistance was received on individual chapters by a number of commentators, including Muhyieddeen Touq, Marwan Muasher, Firas Raad, Hala Bsaiso Lattouf, Salam Fayyad, Saddek El Kaber, Ghassan Khatib, Mahmoud Mohieldin, Charles Adwan, Lydia Habhab, Hala Hanna, William Crandell, Salvatore Schiavo-Campo, and others. Lida Bteddini helped at various stages in the preparation process, as did Lina Badawy and Mavo Ranaivoarivelo. Alexandra Sperling and Rebecca Hife provided valuable assistance at numerous junctures as well. A number of the cases drew upon interviews of senior officials by Rami Khouri conducted as part of the World Bank MENA region's broader governance effort.

Robert Beschel is particularly indebted to the support and encouragement he received from a variety of Kuwait-based colleagues during the production of this volume. Abhijit Barve provided invaluable inputs and went well above the call of duty, as did Alya Al Hamad and Haya Al-Qassar. Zeinab El-Bakri, Bader Al-Saif, Haitham Haddadin, Ayaz Ahmed, Talal Al-Saleh, and Mohammed Al-Zuhair provided comments on various sections, and Amani Nayif has helped at numerous points, as well. Nadir Mohammed has been a major source of encouragement and insight along the way, and his many valuable comments on earlier drafts are deeply appreciated.

The authors are grateful to Professor Jennifer Widner of Princeton University's Innovations for Successful Societies program for permission to use the two cases on document processing in Jordan, as well as the program's support in drafting the Tunisia case on Right to Information. We are also grateful to the case writing program at Harvard University's John F. Kennedy School of Government for their flexibility regarding the use of the Saudi Arabia SADAD case.

Funding for this effort came through the Norwegian Governance Trust

Fund at the World Bank, along with the World Bank's Global Governance Practice in the Middle East and North Africa Region and the Brookings Doha Center.

Above all, we would like to thank our families, who have borne with the production of this volume with patience and good will.

Robert P. Beschel Jr. | *Tarik M. Yousef*

Public Sector Reform in
the Middle East and North Africa

ONE

The Challenge of Public
Sector Reform in MENA

ROBERT P. BESCHEL JR.
TARIK M. YOUSEF

IN ALL COUNTRIES, GOVERNANCE and public sector reforms are driven by
a complex set of interacting and occasionally conflicting dynamics. There
are political pressures to respond decisively to exogenous shocks, ranging
from wars and financial crises to natural disasters and pandemics. There
are ongoing pressures to deliver high-quality services quickly, equitably,
and responsively to the citizenry. There are pressures to ensure transparency and predictability in regulatory policy to attract domestic and foreign investment. There are fiscal pressures to restrain expenditures and
to achieve efficient and effective spending outcomes, as well as contradic-
tory impulses to both expand revenue and to avoid the political stigma
associated with higher taxes and user fees. There are informal pressures to
maintain networks of patronage and power, as well as to assuage important
constituencies, such as staff, unions, suppliers, corporations, and civil society organizations.

Throughout the Middle East and North Africa (MENA) region, the
challenges are even more complex. During the Arab Spring, the political

landscape and governance reform agenda became topics of intense hope, concern, and uncertainty. Subsequent conflicts in Libya, Syria, Iraq, and Yemen, as well as the rise of Islamic extremism, have heightened geopolitical volatility and placed a premium on political stability. High levels of unemployment and population growth create ongoing challenges for job creation, which have historically been met through public employment—resulting in lax productivity, weak accountability, uneven service delivery, and some of the largest public sectors in the developing world. At the same time, the sharp drop in hydrocarbon prices since 2014 and their further fall in 2020 has placed serious financial pressure on many countries, as even non-oil producers are affected by the decline in remittances and transfer payments.

Expectations of greater political participation, transparency, and social accountability in the aftermath of the Arab Spring have now largely given way to the resurgence of what some scholars have dubbed the "new authoritarianism" and what others have characterized as a full-scale "counter-revolution."[1] Yet beneath this broader headline, the picture is often more complex and nuanced. Even in authoritarian states, there is often a strong reformist impulse, especially in response to crises or in pursuit of popular legitimacy. Saudi Arabia's Vision 2030, for example, envisions a host of far-reaching changes under the rubric of effective governance, including delivering "the highest standards" of transparency and accountability; managing finances efficiently and effectively; creating agile public organizations; and implementing effective performance tracking.[2]

While this authoritarian resurgence must be seen as a setback for the aspirations of 2011, new protests in 2019 have again raised the prospect of an "Arab Spring 2.0," as a few observers have framed it.[3] Unlike the initial Arab Spring protests, which focused on ousting longtime autocratic leaders, the most recent round were heavily focused on the "good governance" agenda, including combating corruption, eliminating vested interests, opening up the political and economic space, and improving the quality of service delivery.[4] Protesters view the lack of economic opportunity and poor government services as stemming directly from corrupt governance arrangements, whether driven by military domination in Sudan and Egypt or by sectarian political bargains in Lebanon and Iraq.

Cycles of Stability and Upheaval

An honest reckoning would note that the governance reform agenda in the MENA region has waxed and waned for much of the last century in tandem with the cycles of economic boom and bust. World Wars I and II were periods of fervent nationalist activity, as Arab publics looked to throw off external rule and move to self-rule. However, expectations were thwarted first by the assertion of European colonial rule and subsequently by the ascension of a series of native autocrats and dynasties.

More recently, these cycles appear to have shortened and intensified. The period from 2002 on was initially a heady time for proponents of good governance, catalyzed by the reverberations of the September 11 attacks and the emergence of transnational terrorism as a global concern. External forces were pushing for governance reform, most notably the United States through the "Freedom Agenda," which sought to promote democracy around the world. So were internal voices, captured in the analyses of the Human Development Reports from the United Nations Development Program (UNDP) and a variety of declarations, from Alexandria to Doha, which all underscored the imperative of democratic political reform.[5]

Just prior to the Arab Spring, this agenda appeared to have lost momentum. Lebanon's Cedar Revolution became mired in a perpetual constitutional crisis rooted in the contradictions of its confessional politics. Palestine's 2006 elections, widely regarded as fair and free, had unleashed a stream of events that left the Palestinian state divided and deadlocked. After nearly descending into civil war in 2006 and 2007, Iraq had emerged as a more hopeful but still fragile polity, only to shortly thereafter be confronted by the rise of the Islamic State group (IS). Elsewhere in the region, the ruling elite appeared to be every bit as well-entrenched as they had been before, if not more so. The stability and longevity of the region's authoritarian governments was once again widely assumed, accepted, and perhaps even favored by the international community.

Yet beneath the apparent calm, it was clear that underlying political, economic, and social dynamics were at work that would make the existing political and economic arrangements in many countries untenable. Summarizing the state of play regarding the region's governance agenda during the summer of 2009, we argued:

> The status quo is unlikely to continue for much longer. A variety of factors are putting pressure upon these regimes to change. MENA is

on the cusp of a generational transition, and many leaders currently in their 70s and 80s will be forced by reason of death or ill-health to give way to a younger generation of rulers. Many large public sectors are at their breaking point, and the traditional strategy of using public sector employment for patronage and to soak up excess unemployment is no longer viable. New technologies and media will erode traditional monopolies on information. The growth of an educated middle class will create additional pressures for an expanded political voice commensurate with its growing economic clout.[6]

Just over ten years later, the octogenarians are gone, yet much of the analysis remains relevant. While it was certain that change would come, everyone failed to anticipate the strength of the backlash and the tenacity of entrenched interests. The forces that oppose comprehensive governance reforms have proven to be powerful and resistant to any adjustments to the status quo. The pace and speed in which political reform would arrive, as well as its nature and content, also remained very much open-ended questions. In the end, those were the elements that really mattered. Few would have predicted that the unrest would have started in Tunisia, whose national security apparatus had long been one of the most ruthless and effective in the region, or that the sparks would begin with an act of extraordinary desperation by a street vendor, whose sacrifice reflected the marginalized voices of a generation of youth across the Arab world.[7]

The revolutions of 2011 and the subsequent protests of 2019 shared a common assessment of the region's governance failings. Political and economic power is overly concentrated in the hands of a narrow ruling elite; the rule of law is not adequately respected; and corruption is a serious problem.[8] With the possible exception of e-governance metrics and reforms to encourage private sector growth and investment in a limited number of countries, most global indicators of governance have not significantly improved over the past decade.[9] Parliaments and judiciaries remain relatively impotent and ineffective in challenging executive power. Access to information is limited. In many countries, governments have repressed independent media and civil society. In states rife with conflict, institutional degradation and loss of human capital is rampant.[10]

Budgets, Technology, and Protests

While the dynamics underlying the status quo are powerful, strong countervailing factors continue to press for change. Chief among these are growing financial constraints, technological expansion, and citizen mobilization. The recent COVID-19 pandemic will also exert a powerful influence that will create both threats and opportunities for the broader MENA governance and public sector reform agenda. Figure 1-1 provides a breakdown of Brent Crude Oil prices—a standard international benchmark—from 2010 to 2020. It captures the collapse in oil prices from 2014 through 2015, followed by a limited recovery that preceded the most recent collapse of prices in 2020. While prices have enjoyed a modest rebound since their nadir in April 2020, the long-term future of fossil fuel is uncertain. In the near term, the COVID-19 pandemic will continue to suppress the demand for automobile and aviation fuel, while the medium to longer term is clouded by concerns about capping carbon emissions and the growing cost-effectiveness of green energy alternatives.

The volatility of oil prices and the uncertain future of fossil fuels has

FIGURE 1-1. Brent Crude Oil Prices, 2010–2020

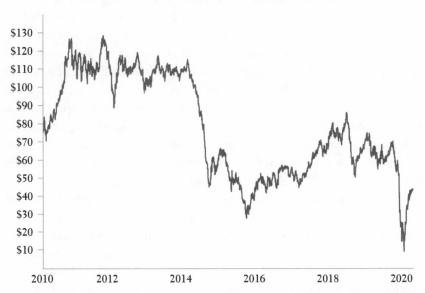

Source: Macrotrends, "Brent Crude Oil Prices—10-Year Daily Chart," 2020, www.macrotrends
.net/2480/brent-crude-oil-prices-10-year-daily-chart.

pushed governments to focus their energies on reform. The impact of the oil price collapse after 2014 was felt throughout the MENA region with the emergence of double-digit fiscal deficits in oil-exporting countries and spillover effects to neighboring economies, leading to a growth slowdown, heightened financial vulnerabilities, and uncertain economic outlooks. As a result, IMF-supported stabilization efforts have been reintroduced to shore up government finances and to incentivize reforms. But with the recent oil price collapse and the COVID-19 shutdowns, the region is projected in 2020 to face the biggest economic contraction in decades. This will place severe limits on available fiscal resources to cushion the socioeconomic impact and support a recovery. As of July 2020, the weighted average price for a barrel of Brent crude oil was around US$44—a marker that would allow only Qatar to cover its current government expenditure.[11] Most countries are now cautiously looking at ways to enhance domestic revenue mobilization, with the understanding that efforts to introduce taxes may provoke citizen demands for a greater say over how these resources are allocated.

A second dynamic transforming the broader governance landscape within MENA is the rapid growth in information and mobile technologies. Many countries, particularly those in the Gulf Cooperation Council (GCC), have effectively utilized these technologies to improve governance, especially the provision of public services.[12] By the end of 2018, nearly half of MENA countries had mobile phone subscriber penetration rates of 70 percent or more, as compared to a global average of 66 percent. United Arab Emirates (UAE) and Qatar now have the highest global penetration rates of social media, which has become the primary source of news and interaction for growing shares of the MENA publics.[13] The region continues, however, to lag behind international trends in legislating free access to information and ensuring transparency. Worse still, a variety of legal instruments, including national security provisions and criminal defamation laws, have been used to dampen free digital expression.

Not surprisingly, these developments are now influencing traditional governance arrangements in new and dynamic ways. Mass protests have made a comeback in recent years against economic austerity measures, deteriorating public services, and perceived government corruption in Algeria, Egypt, Iraq, Jordan, Lebanon, Morocco, Sudan, and Tunisia. These demonstrations coincided with these populations self-reporting some of the lowest levels of life satisfaction and optimism of any region in the world.[14] Drawing upon mobile technologies, these protest movements are amorphous and leaderless, which offers both advantages and disadvantages. In 2019, protesters in Algeria and Sudan adopted slogans from the 2011 Arab Spring uprisings, demanded systemic governance reforms, and toppled incumbent leaders. This led to tightly managed, but uncertain political transitions.

The COVID-19 pandemic is likely to impact the region and its governance agenda in complex ways.[15] As of mid-2020, the region has yet to experience the high number of fatalities per capita that have plagued other regions, such as Europe and North America and South America. Yet few would argue that the threat has peaked, and the danger of mass fatalities remains very real should the virus break containment and ravage through underserved communities and refugee camps. Early assessments of the socioeconomic fallout suggest a significant impact on livelihoods due to increased unemployment and poverty.[16] The dislocation could also severely disrupt the flow of remittances that account for between 8 percent and 14 percent of GDP in Egypt, Jordan, Lebanon, and Palestine. Together with heightened uncertainty about the timing and speed of recovery, these conditions could fuel the spread of social unrest and undermine stability. On the other hand, the fiscal pressures generated by the pandemic could accelerate ongoing reform plans to diversify economies, strengthen social protection systems, and enhance the performance of the public sector, as seen recently in the improved quality of intergovernmental coordination.

MENA's Development and Governance Agenda

Through the haze of these dynamics, three points are clear. The first is that MENA is currently facing daunting economic, social, and developmental challenges. Demographically, the population of the Arab world is expected to grow by 40 percent over the next two decades, adding a figure equal to the current population of Egypt, Iraq, and Morocco combined. These young and increasingly educated cohorts will require jobs, yet the region has maintained one of the highest youth unemployment rates in the world for decades.[17] Furthermore, the region has historically been far less adept than East and South Asia in attracting private investment to spur growth and generate employment. Demographic pressures will, in turn, create major challenges to provide adequate housing, infrastructure, education, health care, and water—services that Arab public sectors will be called upon to deliver in whole or in part.[18]

The return of large-scale protests has underscored the emergence of a new and more complex set of socioeconomic problems in MENA. There is growing evidence, for example, suggesting that the size of vulnerable populations in non-oil exporting countries has risen significantly in the past decade. Conditions of heightened economic vulnerability facing the lower middle class, due to failing social protection systems and emphasis on selective and targeted subsidies together with rising income inequality and limited intergenerational mobility, are contributing to the spread of political discontent.[19] These challenges require addressing long-standing questions about the very social contract underpinning state-society relations to mitigate growing social tensions while expanding the benefits afforded by markets and technological change.

Second, issues of governance and public management will form an essential part of any solution to these problems. Governments in the region provide critical services, such as public health and education. They intervene and redistribute on a scale unrivaled elsewhere in the world. They regulate—indeed, in many countries over-regulate—the private sector. They make the bulk of investment decisions and provide basic infrastructure. Governments are often the largest employer and exert a disproportionate influence over the broader labor market. They control the instruments of state coercion and closely manage the available space for public information and consultation. With limited exceptions, MENA governments wield an extraordinary influence over the lives of their citizens and the development trajectory of their economies.

Any major effort to reorient the region's economies toward private sector-led growth, to pursue more inclusive development strategies, or to improve the quality of service delivery, will, almost by definition, be an effort to translate developmental aspirations into concrete plans for public sector restructuring.[20] Ultimately, these transitions will need to be broken down into the nuts and bolts of legal, institutional, and regulatory reforms to gain traction. Otherwise, they will remain forever at the level of slogans and aspirations. Once they enter the realm of public management, they become subject to a myriad of bureaucratic constraints, tradeoffs, frictions, and inertia that are common to all countries.[21] The ability of future reformers to navigate these challenges will play an important role in their ultimate success or failure.

Third, as noted, the impetus to reform is not new. Governments have been struggling to implement improvements in how they organize themselves; make critical policies and decisions; allocate human and financial resources; collect revenue; improve the quality of their services; and spur private sector growth and development. They have adopted reforms most eagerly in response to severe economic downturns and political crises. Most of these reforms have been technocratic in nature, although a few have supported greater transparency and social accountability. Some of these reforms have been quite successful; others were dismal failures; and many ended up somewhere in the muddled middle.

Filling the Gap in MENA Cases

For the past two decades, governments in MENA have grappled with how to structure, manage, and deliver public services. Through the prism of eleven case studies, this book addresses the general dearth of knowledge about public sector reform and aims to make a significant contribution to our broader understanding of the challenges to pursuing it in this region. We have sought to understand not only the types of reforms that were undertaken but the underlying decision processes that shaped the reform agenda; how they were structured and implemented; who supported them and who resisted them; how the reforms were managed and how resistance was overcome; as well as where things went well and where they did not.

In the study of public administration, the case study method has become a widely accepted approach for evidence-based analysis, capturing noteworthy examples in a focused and structured manner and drawing lessons for policymaking.[22] Hundreds of cases have been drafted on a wide variety of experiences within national, state, and local governments. Most of this experience is America-centric, reflecting the more pragmatic and managerial orientation of Anglo American administration. (Continental administrative traditions have historically placed a higher premium on law and legal training.) Fortunately, over the past few years, Harvard's Kennedy School of Government—perhaps the leading exemplar of the case study approach—has made a conscious effort to diversify its library and expand the number of cases from overseas.

However, very few have been developed for the MENA region. Of the roughly 2,000 cases in the Kennedy School's database, fewer than five directly address managerial and administrative challenges in Arab countries.[23] In 2010, the Organization for Economic Cooperation and Development (OECD) published a series of cases that focused on policy reforms. While the study highlighted the initiatives that MENA governments were pursuing at that time, it paid less attention to examining the implementation and results of these reforms.[24] Princeton's Innovations for Successful Societies program has probably come the furthest in filling this lacuna, and over the past decade it has produced several case studies on reforms in MENA. Yet few scholars, practitioners, and analysts would dispute that much more needs to be done.

The Cases Selected for This Study

The cases in this study cover a range of countries, issues, and reform strategies. Five look at reforms in core systems and procedures within government, including cabinet reforms in Jordan; public financial management reforms in Palestine; efforts to reduce the cost of the wage bill through a voluntary retirement program (VRP) in Morocco; reforms to strengthen meritocracy in human resource management in Lebanon; and e-governance reforms in Dubai. Taken together, they address many of the key cross-cutting functions any government must perform, including coordinating policy; allocating financial and human resources and managing them effectively; and utilizing technology to deliver products and services.

The sixth cross-cutting case, Tunisia's right to information (RTI) reforms, is different in that it sought to improve transparency in the wake of the Arab Spring. Many have argued that transparency plays an essential role in both combatting corruption and advancing social accountability. Yet the MENA region remains among the least transparent when measured by metrics such as RTI legislation.

The remaining set of five reforms looks at various efforts to improve the performance of line departments. One case examines Egypt's reforms to improve its business climate and attract foreign investment by streamlining procedures for opening a business—a critical priority for many countries in the region. Another looks at Egypt's efforts to enhance revenue collection and improve the business environment by reforming its tax policy and administration. A third case reviews Saudi Arabia's initiative to improve service delivery and bill collection by setting up an automated payments system. A final set of cases looks at two highly effective efforts to improve document processing within Jordan.

Not all of these cases were successful. Jordan's efforts to reform its cabinet structures made some modest improvements but fell well short of expectations. Lebanon's efforts to restructure its human resource management practices were a clear failure, although an instructive one; the aspiration still survives in some quarters and may be revisited at some point in the future. At the other end of the spectrum, by any measure, Jordan's largely home-grown efforts to restructure its document processing were a striking success and resulted in far more fair, efficient, transparent, and customer friendly service.

A number of cases fall somewhere in the middle because they represent solid but imperfect efforts to improve public administration. On the one hand, these initiatives enhanced performance, improved transparency, streamlined business processes, reduced opportunities for corruption, and delivered services more efficiently. On the other hand, the results of these programs were mixed. Morocco's experience with its VRP exemplifies this trend. The program's financial returns were positive. However, its impact on the broader functioning of the public sector was problematic. The program was unable to avoid the problems of adverse selection typically associated with such exercises, and many of the "best and brightest" ended up leaving the public sector. Tunisia's experience with RTI legislation is another such case, in that it underscores the complexities of trying to strengthen transparency and social accountability in countries without a strong tradition of civil society engagement.

Taken together, these cases represent many of the most interesting and important sets of public management reforms attempted in MENA during the last two decades. All were serious efforts in which the credibility and prestige of senior officials were directly implicated. Several were among the region's more impressive and far-reaching success stories. Some have endured the test of time, while others have faded. The final chapter reflects on the experiences gleaned from these cases, as well as their broader implications.

As we enter the third decade of the twenty-first century, public sector reforms will be on the agenda of incumbent autocrats and new governments seeking to respond to the growing demands of their citizens.[25] As countries slowly emerge from prolonged conflict, they will need to contemplate rebuilding institutions and infrastructure. Public sector reform will be at the heart of this process. For these reasons, we believe the lessons learned from these experiences, both good and bad, will be highly instructive for future reformers in both MENA and beyond.

Notes

1. See Marc Lynch, *The New Arab Wars: Uprisings and Anarchy in the Middle East* (New York: Public Affairs, 2017); and Shafeeq Ghabra, "The Arab World at a Crossroads: Rebellion, Collapse and Reform," Arab Center Washington, DC, 2018, http://arabcenterdc.org/research-paper/the-arab-world-at-a-crossroads-rebellion-collapse-and-reform/.

2. See Vision 2030, "An Ambitious Nation," 2020, www.vision2030.gov.sa/en/themes/4. Kuwait Vision 2035 was launched in 2017 and Oman Vision 2040 in 2019, both of which target ambitious public sector reforms; Morocco and Jordan also announced reform agendas for 2020.

3. Marwan Muasher, "Is This the Arab Spring 2.0?" *Carnegie Endowment for International Peace*, October 30, 2019, https://carnegieendowment.org/2019/10/30/is-this-arab-spring-2.0-pub-80220; Paul R. Pillar, "Will There Be an Arab Spring 2.0?" *National Interest*, November 21, 2019, https://nationalinterest.org/blog/paul-pillar/will-there-be-arab-spring-20-98527.

4. Rami G. Khouri, "Comprehensive, Contentious, Convulsive, and Continuing: Some Observations on the 2010–2020 Arab Uprisings," *Journal of Middle East Politics and Policy*, 2020, https://jmepp.hkspublications.org/wp-content/uploads/sites/17/2020/03/Khouri.pdf; Arab Barometer, "What Arab Publics Think: Findings from the Fifth Wave of Arab Barometer," 2020, www.arabbarometer.org/wp-content/uploads/Arab_Barometer_CEPS_Presentation_Public-Opinion_2020.pdf.

5. See, for example, UNDP, "Arab Human Development Report 2002," 2002, http://hdr.undp.org/sites/default/files/rbas_ahdr2002_en.pdf; World Bank, "Better Governance for Development in the Middle East and North Africa: Enhancing Inclusiveness and Accountability," MENA Development Report, 2003, http://documents.worldbank.org/curated/en/558101468776955399/Better-governance-for-development-in-the-Middle-East-and-North-Africa-enhancing-inclusiveness-and-accountability; and Bibliotheca Alexandrina, "The Alexandria Declaration," 2004, www.bibalex.org/arf/en/Files/Document.pdf.

6. Robert Beschel and Tarik Yousef, "Governance in the Middle East and North Africa: A Survey of Major Issues and Trends," in *Legatum Prosperity Symposium* (United Kingdom: Brocket Hall, 2009).

7. See Navtej Dhillon and Tarik M. Yousef, editors, *Generation in Waiting: The Unfulfilled Promise of Young People in the Middle East* (Washington: Brookings Institution Press, 2009); For a recent update, see Nader Kabbani, "Youth Employment in the Middle East and North Africa: Revisiting and Reframing the Challenge," Brookings Doha Center, Policy Briefing, February 2019, www.brookings.edu/research/youth-employment-in-the-middle-east-and-north-africa-revisiting-and-reframing-the-challenge/.

8. For a detailed empirical assessment of corruption in business-government relations, see Ishac Diwan, Adeel Malik, and Izak Atiyas, *Crony Capitalism in the Middle East: Business and Politics from Liberalization to the Arab Spring* (Oxford University Press, 2019). Survey results from a post-2011 assessment can be found at European Bank for Reconstruction and Development (EBRD), European Investment Bank (EIB), and World Bank Group, "What's Holding Back the Private Sector in MENA? Lessons from the Enterprise Survey," 2016, http://documents.worldbank.org/curated/en/170531469775655994/pdf/107174-WP-PUBLIC-7-22-2016-MENAESBookWEB.pdf.

9. See, for example, Hana Brixi, Ellen Marie Lust, and Michael Woolcock, "Trust, Voice, and Incentives: Learning from Local Success Stories in Service Delivery in the Middle East and North Africa," World Bank, 2015, https://openknow

ledge.worldbank.org/handle/10986/21607; Program on Governance and Local Development University of Gothenburg, "Governance in Service Delivery in the Middle East and North Africa," Background Paper for World Development Report, 2017, http://pubdocs.worldbank.org/en/765671485539747061/WDR17-BP-Governance -in-Service-Delivery.pdf.

10. Shanta Devarajan and Lili Mottaghi, "The Economics of Post-Conflict Reconstruction in Middle East and North Africa," The World Bank, Middle East and North Africa Economic Monitor, 2017, http://documents.worldbank.org/cura ted/en/235401491413228678/pdf/114057-REPLACEMENT-PUBLIC-4-17-10-am -Online-MEM-SPRING-2017-FINAL.pdf.

11. According to IMF data, the fiscal break-even point varies by country, ranging from US$39.90 per barrel for Qatar to US$76.10 for Saudi Arabia to US$157.20 for Algeria. See IMF, "Breakeven Oil Prices," https://data.imf.org/regular.aspx?key= 60214246.

12. United Nations Department of Economic and Social Affairs, "2018 UN E-Government Survey," 2018, www.un.org/development/desa/publications/2018-un -e-government-survey.html.

13. See GSMA, "The Mobile Economy Middle East and North Africa 2019," 2019, www.gsma.com/mobileeconomy/mena/.

14. See, for example, Sergio Pinto and Carol Graham, "Men Without Work: A Global Well-Being and Ill-Being Comparison," IZA World of Labor, 2019, p. 464, https://wol.iza.org/articles/men-without-work-a-global-well-being-and-ill-being -comparison/long.

15. See Adel Abdellatif and Ellen Hsu, "Grappling with a crisis like no other: the fragility of Arab countries in the face of COVID-19," Medium, March 31, 2019, https://medium.com/@UNDPArabic/grappling-with-a-crisis-like-no-other-the -fragility-of-arab-countries-in-the-face-of-covid-19-581c8b017f59.

16. See, for example, the assessment reports on the socioeconomic impact of the COVID-19 pandemic on economies and communities that have been completed by the United Nations Development Programme for Jordan, Lebanon, Tunisia, Sudan, and Yemen (www.undp.org/content/undp/en/home/covid-19-pandemic-response/ socio-economic-impact-of-covid-19.html).

17. For a recent examination of the challenges facing education in the region, including governance issues in the sector, see Safaa El Tayeb El-Kogali and Caroline Krafft, "Expectations and Aspirations: A New Framework for Education in the Middle East and North Africa," World Bank, 2020, https://openknowledge.world bank.org/handle/10986/30618.

18. There are also significant economic and resource disparities between regions and within cities in most countries that require concerted attention in the future. See "Convergence: Five Critical Steps toward Integrating Lagging and Leading Areas in the Middle East and North Africa," World Bank, 2020, https://openknow ledge.worldbank.org/handle/10986/33187.

19. See, for example, Rami G. Khouri, "How Poverty and Inequality are Dev- astating the Middle East," Carnegie Corporation of New York, 2019, www.car negie.org/topics/topic-articles/arab-region-transitions/why-mass-poverty-so-danger

ous-middle-east/; Khalid Abu-Ismail and others, "Multidimensional Poverty Index for Middle Income Countries: Findings from Jordan, Iraq, and Morocco," United Nations Economic and Social Commission for Western Africa (ESCWA), 2015, www.unescwa.org/publications/multidimensional-poverty-index-jordan-iraq-morocco; Facundo Alvaredo, Lydia Assouad, and Thomas Piketty, "Measuring Inequality in the Middle East 1990–2016: The World's Most Unequal Region?" *The Review of Income and Wealth*, Volume 65, issue 4, 685–711.

20. How the public sector organizes to respond to increasingly complex policy challenges is a subject of growing debate among academics and practitioners. See Mark Robinson, "From Old Public Administration to the New Public Service: Implications for Public Sector Reform in Developing Countries," UNDP Global Center for Public Sector Excellence, 2015, www.undp.org/content/dam/undp/library/capacity-development/English/Singapore%20Centre/PS-Reform_Paper.pdf.

21. For an extended exposition of these issues in the context of public sector reform efforts in the advanced economies, see Christopher Pollitt and Geert Bouckaert, *Public Management Reform: A Comparative Analysis: New Public Management, Governance, and the Neo-Weberian State*, 3rd edition (Oxford University, 2011).

22. This case method often competes and at times complements experimental and statistical methods. See Sanjeev Khagram and Craig W. Thomas, "Toward a Platinum Standard for Evidence-Based Assessment by 2020," *Public Administration Review* 20, issue 1 (December 2010), pp. S100–S106.

23. A number of other cases address MENA topics and themes but typically from the vantage point of addressing a particular issue or challenge in American foreign policy.

24. OECD, "Progress in Public Management in the Middle East and North Africa," Case Studies on Policy Reform, 2010, www.oecd.org/mena/governance/48634338.pdf.

25. Mehran Kamrava, *Inside the Arab State* (Oxford University Press, 2018); Joseph Bahout and others, "Arab Horizons: Pitfalls and Pathways to Renewal," Carnegie Endowment for International Peace, 2018, https://carnegieendowment.org/files/ArabHorizons_report_final.pdf; and The Atlantic Council, "Politics, Governance, and State-Society Relations," A Working Group Report of the Middle East Strategy Task Force, 2016, www.brookings.edu/wp-content/uploads/2016/11/cmep_201611_mest_paper_final.pdf.

PART I

REFORMS TO CORE INSTITUTIONS AND PROCESSES

TWO

At the Apex

Reforming Cabinet Structures in Jordan

FATEMA ALHASHEMI
TONY GOLDNER

THE HIGHEST OFFICIALS of the government of the Hashemite Kingdom of Jordan are meeting in a cabinet session, the apex government decision-making body in the country. The topic of discussion is: Should chicken slaughterhouses be relocated from the vicinity of Amman, and if so, how? Hundreds of small, antiquated chicken slaughterhouses lie in and around the capital. They pose health and environmental hazards for nearby residential neighborhoods. What should be done with them? The prime minister and his ministers are asked to make a decision, yet they are provided with little information on the extent of the economic or social cost of moving or shutting down the slaughterhouses. After three separate cabinet discussions, no clear decision is made.

Jordan is hardly unique in experiencing problems with its apex mechanisms for policy coordination. Many countries struggle to ensure that the issues that come before cabinets have been properly vetted and that senior decisionmakers have time to focus on the important questions without being bogged down in administration. Yet, as a small country in a volatile region, the challenges confronting Jordan are particularly acute. The country has had to grapple with the geopolitical implications of the ongoing Israeli-Palestinian dispute; external social and economic shocks from conflicts in Iraq and Syria; a heavy dependence on oil imports; austerity measures such as elimination of food subsidies; and the ongoing need for job creation. Having to take up valuable time in three cabinet sessions on the relocation of chickens provoked one former minister to remark, "The cabinet should not have been wasting one minute of its time on this!"[1]

This example, and many others, highlight the recurring challenge of upgrading policy formulation and decision support mechanisms. Senior officials had little time to focus on the policy decisions affecting their nation's future and were, instead, burdened by a never-ending flow of decisions on minor administrative matters. The requisite institutional infrastructures that would provide high quality technical advice were not fully developed. There was no recognized and systematic process for decisionmaking and no procedures for following up on implementation.

This chapter explores efforts to reform cabinet decisionmaking since the mid-2000s. We first examine the political context of reform in Jordan. Next, we detail the institutional challenges of the public sector and outline the steps toward reform. Finally, we assess the impact of the reform efforts and glean lessons from Jordan's experience.

In 2003, a reform team was charged with improving the system of cabinet decisionmaking. The minister heading these reforms at the time, Fawaz Zu'bi, was a capable and dynamic manager in both the public and private sectors. He went forward applying his motto, "It is important to ensure that the brain is working well, because if the brain is working well then the body will function as it needs to."[2] But reform had its share of challenges, such as institutional weaknesses, internal power politics, and broader political opposition. Would Zu'bi and his team succeed?

Cabinet in Crisis

Under Jordan's constitution, authority and power is vested heavily in the king in his roles as commander-in-chief of the armed forces, head of state, and chief executive. The king appoints and dismisses the prime minister and the government. The cabinet is constitutionally responsible for public policies of the state, yet in practice political and decisionmaking power on key issues is heavily concentrated around the monarchy. This includes the Royal Court, advisers close to the king, the armed forces, and the security establishment.[3] In recent history, the involvement of the Royal Court in shaping policy beyond these areas has oscillated between active engagement and a delegation of these responsibilities to the cabinet and the prime minister.

At the core of the challenge facing Jordan's Council of Ministers is time management. Strategic policy development and delivery oversight is structurally "crowded-out" by the crushing compliance burden of administrative decisions, which are required under Jordanian law and regulations to go before the Council of Ministers. A former observer described the scene at one cabinet meeting:

> The secretary of the cabinet had piles of paper in front of him. There was no substantive discussion of the agenda items and no documentation offering analysis. The secretary read out pre-drafted decisions, which were almost all agreed without discussion. The only substantive discussion [in that session] was when an issue was raised about two officials who were going for a conference to North Africa, and the issue at hand was about their stipend of 26 JD [about US$37]. Heated discussion took place about whether 26 JD was a reasonable amount or whether less should be given.[4]

This failing can be attributed to a number of legal, structural, procedural, and capacity constraints.

The first challenge was the sheer number of the administrative decisions that need to be taken. In many OECD countries, the average cabinet will address between 500 and 700 items a year. During 2003, Jordan's prime minister and the Council of Ministers made a total of 22,500 decisions, of which 80 percent were administrative rather than policy in nature.[5] The administrative issues related to the appointment, promotion, and retirement of senior government officials; the formation of official delegations for participation in overseas conferences; land acquisition; and decisions on compensation and payment for overtime work performed by officials, among other concerns. For a variety of reasons, successive prime ministers, cabinets, and parliaments have approved laws that mandate the taking of relatively minor decisions at the level of the Council of Ministers. Furthermore, many of these laws and by-laws called for administrative decisions to be made by the prime minister or the Council of Ministers on a case-by-case basis rather than through the routine application of guidelines.[6]

The second challenge was the legacy structure of the committee system perpetuated by successive governments. Despite the dramatic growth in the volume of administrative decisions that needed to be made as Jordan's population grew and its social and economic systems became more complex through the 1990s and early 2000s, there was little innovation in cabinet decisionmaking processes and capabilities.

Prior to the reforms launched in the mid-2000s, there were no permanent, sector-based subcommittees to oversee the implementation of policies that spanned the mandates of more than one ministry. The Council of Ministers was supported by two permanent interministerial committees—the Development Committee and the Legal Committee. The first was a clearinghouse for all economic and financial policy proposals, and the second was responsible for the analysis and development of laws and by-laws submitted before the Council of Ministers for approval. While specific issues were handled by ad hoc committees, these committees (with some exceptions) tended to meet infrequently. They were subject to very low turnout, had weak secretariat support, and often would not arrive at decisions.[7] Issues under their respective mandates would have to wait for cabinet meetings for final decisions. The committee reporting lines to the cabinet were often weak or unclear, leaving the cabinet answerable for their results but unable to control the quality or timeliness of their outputs.

Third, the secretariat functions supporting cabinet decisionmaking activities were designed, like a mailroom, to provide a processing function. They did not perform the type of independent advisory functions that the Council of Ministers increasingly needed to deal with the compliance burden efficiently and concurrently have the time and brainpower to make strategic policy decisions and oversee implementation activities.

A major shortcoming was the absence of policy advisory support, including functional or technical specialists who could provide analytical services and frame policy options for consideration. This sort of policy capacity did not exist in line ministries. While some senior officials were involved in policymaking, most often the secretary generals (the top civil service position within Jordanian ministries, equivalent to the British permanent secretary post) in line departments were perceived as administrators. As a result, the default means of advancing policy development was to look outside the ministries and the Cabinet Secretariat and to turn to a proliferation of committees that performed quasi-policy functions.

While two units under the cabinet secretary were mandated to manage administrative affairs, they did not provide any forward planning of Council of Ministers business. Consequently, the urgent often crowded out the important on weekly cabinet agendas. There was a lack of interministerial coordination before issues arrived at the cabinet room, along with insufficient follow-up and reporting back to the cabinet on the implementation of previous decisions.

There was no standard template for policy submissions to the Council of Ministers that would enable the secretariat to control the quality of analysis and recommendations brought before the cabinet.[8] One internal review of business over a ten-month period revealed that of 684 decisions that came to that office only seven (less than 1 percent) were related to policy matters. The others were predominantly administrative or information related.

With a crowded and often unstructured agenda, coupled with written advice that often lacked detailed analysis and policy options, it is not surprising that ministers at that time reported feeling overwhelmed and poorly equipped to discharge their collective decisionmaking responsibilities. It was not uncommon for agenda items to be submitted a few minutes before a cabinet meeting was about to begin or simply be introduced during the meeting itself. Many decisions were, therefore, made without substantive discussion, and ministers were often presented with simple yes/no options. With respect to changes in legislative and regulatory language, ministers were frequently presented with a "before" and "after" text with little accompanying commentary or analysis.

By the mid-2000s, reform to Jordan's central decisionmaking activities had to tackle a number of serious questions. How could the burden of administrative and compliance-driven activities be reduced? How could adequate technical support be strengthened to foster better policy decisions and thereby reduce reliance on ad hoc committees and councils? How could procedures be improved to provide a higher level of quality control and consistency in the decisionmaking process? How could coordination with line ministries be improved and, over the longer term, policy capacity in line ministries be developed?

Cabinet Decisionmaking Reform: The Beginning

In October 2003, Minister Zu'bi was tasked to lead the public sector reform agenda as Minister of Administrative Development in the government of Prime Minister Faisal al-Fayez. In his view, the Ministry of Administrative Development was weak, and its young staff were not empowered to move forward with the reform program. But the UK Department for International Development (DFID) was supportive of this reform program and of Zu'bi, encouraging him to move forward with it. At the same time, the political environment for reform was favorable.

With support from DFID, a £3 million public sector reform project was initiated and contracted to PricewaterhouseCoopers (PWC). Though diagnostic work had been undertaken and some drafts for public sector reform developed, the reform work had been progressing slowly. In December 2003, after the new government was formed, DFID added a further £1.5 million to the project budget.

The reform team began by reviewing past efforts at reform. Minister Zu'bi explained, "We wanted to develop a fresh view on public sector reform, [but realized that it was important to look] at past experiences and see what lessons could be learned, and importantly to see how we could move forward."[9] An international consultant intimately involved in these efforts recounted a key lesson they drew from this exercise: "Reforms in the absence of genuine 'buy-in' would not achieve results."[10] All the key stakeholders had to be on board with reforms to implement them effectively.

As a result, a high profile interministerial committee for public sector reform was established. The idea was to appoint champions who would lead the reform program. The team of ministers was made responsible for leading specific components of the public sector reform program. Systematic secretariat arrangements were established to support the committee. Over three months, twenty-two meetings were held.

One weakness of this institutional arrangement was the fact that their decisions had no binding power, as the committee was outside the prime ministry and not a permanent committee attached to the cabinet. Attempts were made to transform the committee into a permanent committee of the prime ministry, but they were ultimately unsuccessful in the face of opposition from senior staff in that office. Speaking of the general public sector environment in which reform had to proceed, a consultant involved in these efforts noted: "If someone is brought on board, someone else will question why this new person is involved in the work and not him or her. If someone is left out of an initiative, they will resist it." This theme would be repeated at multiple junctures downstream.

These challenges did not stop the committee from carrying out its mandate. They examined the overall machinery of government, identifying a number of problems at the intersection of cabinet policymaking, human resource policy, civil service law, and financial management. While the reform team adopted a comprehensive vision, the head of the committee, Zu'bi, explained that policymaking in cabinet was "at the heart of the issue."

Members of the committee went to several countries to try to understand different cabinet models to identify the specific changes that could best improve the Jordanian system. In parallel, a comprehensive performance diagnostic was commissioned focusing on the Cabinet Secretariat and the functioning of the prime ministry. To overcome both the language barrier and sensitivities about divulging information about prime ministry functions to international consultants, a local Jordanian consulting firm, Al Jidara, was hired as a subcontractor to PWC.

The reform team's efforts culminated in the identification of three priorities for cabinet reform:

1. *Review the legal framework to reduce the administrative burdens* on the prime minister, the Council of Ministers, and individual ministers.

2. *Enhance the capacity of the Council of Ministers* by streamlining administrative processes, strengthening the Cabinet Secretariat, establishing permanent, sector-based ministerial subcommittees, and restructuring the prime ministry (see box 2-1).

3. *Strengthen policy capacity within ministries* by enhancing the policy development skills of senior civil servants and improving human resources management policies and procedures.

Reform Plans Are Approved

These efforts bore fruit in the latter part of 2004. Recommendations were presented to the king and the prime minister, who signaled approval of the plan. To formalize and elevate the reform plans, a special White Paper was commissioned. In October 2004, a comprehensive public sector reform agenda, the "White Paper for Public Sector Reform," was presented and approved by the government. All three priorities for reform of cabinet policy decisionmaking were spelled out in the White Paper. Three key institutional changes were also recommended to oversee the implementation of the public sector reform agenda:

- Establish a public sector administration and development directorate in place of the existing line ministry on administrative development. Concomitantly, create the post of Minister of State for Public Sector Development, reporting to the deputy prime minister to oversee this unit.

- Establish a government performance evaluation department inside the prime ministry. The Minister of Cabinet Affairs and Government was to be mandated to oversee this unit as well as units related to the secretariat, political development, and government communications.

- Transform the interministerial steering committee on public sector reform into a permanent public administration cabinet subcommittee.

Minister Zu'bi explained the significance of this institutional arrangement: "The one big achievement I managed to bring about was to raise the profile of the Minister of Administrative Development from being one of the line ministers to effectively being third highest in the hierarchy after the prime minister and the Minister of State for Cabinet Affairs." This arrangement originated from the rationale that any minister mandated to reform government needed to be granted the necessary authority over other line ministries. However, in practice, it was not as straightforward as that, as power within Jordan's political culture is traditionally derived from multiple sources, including seniority, experience in government, and relationship with the king, among other factors.

The cabinet approved this new structure and, in October 2004 following a cabinet reshuffle, Minister Zu'bi left his post and the public sector. In preparation for his departure and to ensure that the efforts and momentum of the past would not be lost, the reform team drafted a detailed public sector reform work program. Their hope was that the incoming minister and cabinet would be guided by this document and be committed to the goals and targets put forth in the White Paper.

Moving Forward, or Not

Among other changes, the cabinet reshuffle of October 24, 2004, ushered in the arrival of Marwan Muasher as deputy prime minister and Minister of State for Prime Ministry Affairs and Government Performance. Muasher had been Minister of Foreign Affairs in the previous government, and he was now made responsible for the overall reform agenda and government performance.

Following the approval of the White Paper, Al Jidara began following up on PWC's analysis and recommendations by mapping out the structure, mandate, and functioning of the different units in the prime ministry. It began developing a cabinet procedures manual, as well as preparing the job descriptions, recruitment criteria, and recruitment process for the government performance department (GPD) that was to be established in the prime ministry.

Concurrent with his efforts to oversee the upgrading of the prime ministry, Muasher also oversaw the development of the National Agenda during this period, of which the planned public sector reforms were one component. The National Agenda was a major initiative to provide a long-term vision for Jordan that encompassed a variety of political, economic, and social reforms. It specified broad strategies to serve as a guide for orienting government policies. It also laid out several key performance indicators to help evaluate government policies, actions, and institutions. The GPD was mandated to oversee the development of these indicators.

Starting in 2005, the concept of creating small policy and institutional development units emerged from the GPD mandate. These units were to be part of a new infrastructure to support policy decisionmaking. The concept envisioned a unit within each line ministry to undertake monitoring and evaluation functions of the ministry and all institutions under its authority. This analysis was to be used for policy formulation and identifying internal weaknesses. These periodic reports were also to be submitted to the GPD, which was to produce higher-level sectorial analytical reports that could be forwarded to the prime ministry and cabinet. The GPD, Ministry of Planning and International Cooperation (MoPIC), and Ministry of Public Sector Development (MoPSD) began cooperating to take this concept further.

Yet challenges to the reform process quickly emerged. Most notably, components of the institutional architecture envisioned for the reforms did not materialize. The public sector development unit, in particular, was short-lived within the prime ministry. Explanations differ for its relatively short existence. One was that the newly appointed Minister of State for Public Sector Development did not agree with this institutional arrangement, which would compromise his autonomy. Others noted that the institutional arrangement itself was not well organized in terms of reporting relationships, budgetary allocations, and staffing needs. The new minister focused his early efforts on building the directorate outside the prime ministry, thereby contradicting the original intent of having public sector reform as a center-of-government function.

Many internal and external observers have identified the frequent change of ministers as among the most detrimental factors in implementing reforms. Each new minister who came in did not feel bound by the

BOX 2-1. Recommendations to Enhance Capacity of Cabinet

Shorten the decisionmaking process in the prime ministry. The protocols for cabinet paperwork were deemed to be slow and cumbersome, with all documents first going to the secretary general of the prime ministry and then between various departments. Such a process meant that the secretary general was overburdened, and the process was slow. Line ministries and other public institutions could not predict when issues would be presented to the cabinet and when decisions would be sent back. A new mechanism was to be developed that would better organize the flow of correspondence to the cabinet secretary, secretary general, and other administrative units.

Introduce a cabinet procedures manual. To address inefficiencies stemming from ad hoc processes in place and insufficient quality control, recommendations were made to develop a comprehensive cabinet procedure manual. This manual was to provide step-by-step guidance on the process through which line ministries were to submit policy items to the prime ministry, templates to be used, timelines to be followed, work flow within the prime ministry before submission of items for cabinet discussions, necessary documentation and dissemination, and follow-up on implementation. This manual was finalized in 2006.

Establish permanent interministerial committees. To augment the efficacy of the cabinet decisionmaking process, recommendations were made to establish four to six permanent interministerial committees. These permanent committees would be mandated to take a cross-sectorial view on policy issues. Each committee was to be staffed with a secretary who was well-informed on the issues before discussion, who would document all minutes, and who would share the recommendations with the cabinet secretary.

Strengthen the cabinet secretariat. The administrative support units under the cabinet secretariat were weak and had no capacity for policy analysis. Recommendations were made to build capacity and to establish a team of policy specialists. The proposal entailed establishing a specific unit staffed with five to six sector specialists who would provide independent technical advice on policy issues and undertake quality control of the process. These specialists would be mandated to make recommendations on policy proposals, be available in cabinet meetings to provide technical advice, communicate with line ministries and departments, and act as secretaries to the permanent interministerial committees.

Restructure the prime ministry. The prime ministry itself required significant reorganization based on a functional approach. Having seventeen individual directorates in the prime ministry presented managerial and administrative challenges. The White Paper of 2004 noted that "there is potential for overlap between directorates in terms of responsibilities for quality control of policy submissions to the prime minister and the Council of Ministers; and for delays as documents are transmitted from one unit to another." Diagnostic work was undertaken over the next two years to develop recommendations for restructuring and streamlining the relationship between the secretary general and the cabinet secretary.

strategies and decisions of their predecessors. This problem is further exacerbated by the lack of political parties within Jordan, which eliminates
the discipline that a party platform can impose on individual ministers. As
a result, civil servants and consultants involved in public sector reform efforts repeatedly found themselves dedicating substantial time to the task of
reeducating new ministers in the hope of keeping reform momentum on
track. Conversely, when new ministers proposed reforms that senior civil
servants did not support, they became accustomed to stalling on the basis
that ministers would not remain in office for long.

While progress was made on some aspects of the government's broader
public sector reform agenda, efforts to strengthen the cabinet decisionmaking processes and restructure the prime ministry encountered direct
resistance. Muasher was a strong advocate of the reforms in the White
Paper, but other senior members in the prime ministry did not agree with
some proposals. Opponents argued that there was no need for a separate
technical unit for evaluation. They were concerned that this unit would
replicate work by the line ministries and second-guess their recommendations. There were conflicting views on where such a unit should be located.
Some senior voices from the prime ministry argued for its placement under
the manager of the prime minister's office (PMO). There was a perceived
need to build the capacity of the office with a team of specialists who could
advise on political, economic, and financial issues. The consultants proposed that it should be located under the Cabinet Secretariat, with the
rationale that the unit could provide support to all cabinet members as well
as the prime minister.

A former consultant noted that "everyone had incentives to oppose."
There were some groups who resisted the proposal because it restricted
their direct interface with the prime minister; others who realized that this
unit would have given more power to one division relative to their own;
others who felt threatened when they realized these proposals would imply
different staffing needs; and yet another group may have agreed with the
proposals but did not want to be seen challenging other senior stakeholders.

Proposals to establish more permanent committees were perceived as
too restrictive, since according to existing procedures, the prime minister appointed ad hoc interministerial committees as he deemed necessary.
Work on the cabinet procedures manual proceeded at a slow pace due to
a combination of meticulousness from some senior officials at the prime
ministry and difficulties in arriving at a consensus on key issues.

In April 2005, a new government, headed by Adnan Badran, was sworn into office. The new prime minister, a liberal academic, filled his cabinet with Western-educated technocrats and private sector reformers. The government quickly came under attack from parliament on a variety of fronts, including "neglecting the country's southern regions in appointments."[11] In July 2005, Prime Minister Badran was forced to reshuffle his cabinet.[12]

The Minister of State for Public Sector Development in Prime Minister Badran's government continued to work with the team of consultants on the prime ministry and cabinet decisionmaking reforms, but little progress was made. He faced several challenges along the way, including continued internal opposition to the reforms from high-ranking officials within the prime ministry.

During this period, DFID decided to reorient its funding toward other priorities. The World Bank agreed to step in and provided a loan of US$15 million as part of a public sector capacity building project in June 2005. The loan met with immediate resistance by some in the new government who objected to having a sizeable share of the borrowed money go toward paying foreign consultants. As a result, the project was significantly reduced and eventually cancelled without any disbursements being made.

A former minister of state for public sector development attributes blame directly to the World Bank for not ensuring the continuation of the loan. In his view, stronger support from the World Bank and conditional assistance based on progress of public sector reforms would have provided reformers with the leverage they needed to counter domestic political opposition.

With the end of DFID funding looming, and wavering World Bank support, by mid-2005 financial support for the program itself became an issue. The contract of PWC/Al Jidara ended in mid-2005. In late September 2005, the UK Foreign Office decided to step in and finance ongoing work on the public sector reform through the Global Opportunity Fund. Al Jidara was awarded the contract to continue to engage a few of the key consultants and to continue the work that had begun under the PWC contract, specifically in the areas of human resource development, streamlining, service delivery, and reforms related to cabinet decision support and the prime ministry.

Broader Political Forces Exacerbate Challenges

A former minister of public sector development believed the absence of political will for reform was not a reflection of an ideological conflict with public sector reforms per se but rather a question of whether such reforms were really considered a priority. In his view, generating necessary support for these sorts of reforms was difficult because they are inherently intangible and their benefits are difficult to quantify. Senior officials, caught up with day-to-day challenges, tended to sideline or neglect such longer-term reforms. These problems were exacerbated by the rapid turnover in governments.[13] Another former minister of state for public sector development believed that, in spite of all the rhetoric, there was no serious political will for reform on the part of several prime ministers.[14]

While the degree of political commitment may be difficult to judge, it is clear that reformers confronted some very real political challenges. The National Agenda included proposed changes in Jordan's electoral law, raising critical issues—particularly those regarding the full enfranchisement of the electorate of Palestinian origin, as well as the potential political role of the Muslim Brotherhood. Such reforms were resisted also by Jordan's traditional "East Bank" constituencies, including those living in predominantly rural communities who dominate the public workforce and are in positions of influence in the bureaucracy and parliament.[15] The bureaucracy in Jordan has historically played an important role in maintaining political stability, and government employment is used as a reward for continued support and allegiance.[16] Any reforms are perceived to threaten not only the well-entrenched bureaucratic elites but also a much wider support base.

While the proposed cabinet reforms did not threaten these fundamental interests, they may have suffered from collateral damage. Former ministers involved in cabinet decisionmaking reforms explained that the opposition did not delineate between the different components of the public sector reform. Rather, the opposition's strategy was to characterize the overall public sector reform process as a liquidation of public institutions and to dismiss reforms as a "liberal agenda."[17]

Even the National Agenda process led by the deputy prime minister suffered. The "old guard" comprised of "a collection of individuals associated with the public sector—government officials, ex-officials, army officers, and long serving bureaucrats"[18] as well as "a handful of businessmen" launched attacks against the Royal Committee charged with developing the National Agenda framework. In Muasher's view, these groups "opposed any widening of the decision-making process" inherent in the National Agenda initiative. He argued that there were no countervailing forces to match the traditional elite, due to lack of unity, organization, and communication with the public about the benefits of reform.[19]

The absence of strong political will to counter this resistance was compounded by the fact that the government leadership was not subject to any accountability vis-à-vis reform progress. According to a former minister, the mandates were not well-defined and there was no performance-based evaluation mechanism. Moreover, the quick turnover in government acted as a disincentive to embark on longer-term reform measures. Parliament was not seen as a strong proponent of these reforms. In Jordan, parliament tends to be dominated by groups supportive of the status quo and traditional interests.[20] In the absence of a broad-based constituency within parliament that would support their agenda, the reformers themselves did not really engage parliament in the reform process.[21]

By late 2005, the momentum for reform had come to a near standstill. Then, on the evening of November 9, a series of bombings targeting three luxury hotels rocked Amman. Al-Qaida claimed responsibility for these attacks, in which sixty people were killed and more than 100 injured. In the following days, tens of thousands of Jordanians took to the streets in protest.

Responding to the new security threat, the king appointed another government within weeks. Marouf al-Bakhit—a former army strategist, ambassador to Turkey and Israel, and perceived security hawk—was appointed prime minister. Conservative loyalists were appointed in the upper house of parliament.[22] Muasher left his post to embark on a new assignment as the minister of the royal court. Reforms would take a back seat to considerations of security and political stability.

Reform Plans See the Light of Day?

In 2006, the MoPSD was established in place of the former Directorate of Public Sector Development—a decision that essentially reversed one of the main accomplishments achieved under Zu'bi's leadership. The reform team at the prime ministry was instructed to work through MoPSD since it was responsible for the reform file. A counterpart to MoPSD was assigned responsibility to oversee the reform work on the cabinet and prime ministry. By August 2006, new restructuring plans were approved by al-Bakhit.

These plans built on the past PWC/Al Jidara work, but with some modifications. Officially, the Minister of Public Sector Development has to sign off on the document, but delays ensued.

In November 2006, there was yet another government reshuffle. Al-Bakhit remained in office, but the composition of the cabinet changed. Muhyieddeen Touq returned to government, this time as Minister of State for Prime Ministry Affairs. Having left in the mid-1990s, he was surprised to see that the prime ministry was facing many of the same old problems and that the structure of the office was outdated.

Plans for restructuring, along with a comprehensive cabinet procedures manual developed by Al Jidara, were presented to Touq in his early days in office. He was supportive of their recommendations and immediately briefed the prime minister. An ad hoc team, consisting of Touq, the Minister of State for Legal Affairs, the Minister of Public Sector Development, and the Secretary General to the Prime Minister, was tasked with reviewing the recommendations. They agreed to a restructuring plan that better distributed the workload within the prime ministry. The committee also recognized the importance of professional technical analysis, and thus proposed the creation of a policy analysis and decision support unit with technical specialists.

In August 2007, the government approved both proposals. Within one week, the cabinet procedures manual was distributed to all ministries. Touq and others tasked to move forward with the reform started the process of identifying individuals to manage and staff the units under the proposed restructuring.

Just as this process was underway, the government resigned, and the reform efforts were once again interrupted. A new government headed by Prime Minister Nader al-Dahabi took office in November 2007. During the Dahabi government, the new policy analysis unit reporting to the PMO was assembled and began providing research and support to the prime minister on domestic and international issues. The scope of this team's resources did not allow it to provide detailed policy support on all policy proposals going before the cabinet, nor were the new process disciplines in the procedures manual fully implemented.

A Renewed Push: The Rifai Government Reforms of 2009–2011

In December 2009, the Dahabi government was replaced by a government headed by Samir Al-Rifai. As a former long-standing senior official at the Royal Hashemite Court, Al-Rifai was a close confident of His Majesty King Abdullah and the first prime minister from the king's generation. His mandate emphasized a need to accelerate economic and social reforms with a stronger focus on transparency and accountability. The first act of the new government was to introduce a ministerial code of conduct, which provided for the disclosure of financial assets and business interests among other ethical requirements.

The government also began work immediately on a one-year government program for 2010. The government program, the first of its kind in the Jordanian context, was formulated around seven thematic goals and included specific projects and key performance indicators. Akin to policy manifestos developed by political parties in OECD democracies, these seven thematic goals were intended to be the foundation for policy development and implementation. The plan was presented to King Abdullah at a special cabinet session and published online within 100 days of the swearing-in of the Al-Rifai government.

In parallel with setting policy priorities and oversight at the cabinet level, Al-Rifai and a small team of officials and external advisers also set about another reform program within the prime ministry. Within the early months of the new government, a rapid-cycle diagnosis of the weaknesses and constraints in the cabinet decision support system was commissioned and involved one-on-one interviews with most members of the cabinet and a number of senior officials across government.

As had been identified as early as 2003, the prime ministry was overwhelmingly focused on administrative tasks and the formal movement of official documents and compliance-driven correspondence between the prime minister and the ministries. While the physical movement of paperwork was relatively efficient, the process of reviewing and making decisions was not. A bureaucratic culture of "reverse delegation"—pushing minor decisions up rather than down—was entrenched.

Despite the intent of earlier reform efforts, the advisory support provided to either the prime minister or the cabinet did not bring sufficient value-added. While the new policy analysis team established under the previous Dahabi administration was now providing some support to the prime minister, they were neither resourced nor empowered to review complex policy proposals going to the full Council of Ministers. Consequently, proposals would be put before the cabinet with little, if any, "whole of government" assessment of their potential implications.

Compounding this lack of policy analysis support, almost all ministers identified significant capability gaps in the decision support system within their ministry. Most important, they lacked dedicated policy specialists and legal advisers to drive the development of policy options. These advisory roles, where they existed, were typically donor-funded secondments to a ministry and, therefore, subject to the vagaries and timelines of external parties. Skilled policy analysts, often trained and funded by the donor community in Jordan, were also frequently attracted away to higher-paying jobs within the GCC.

With these insights in mind, Prime Minister Rifai launched several initiatives to upgrade policy analysis and advisory support. This effort began with support for the prime minister himself. Historically, the prime minister had been supported by an office director focused on scheduling and coordination; a small number of advisers; and administrative, protocol, and security personnel. Rifai upgraded the office director role to a chief of staff position to be occupied by an experienced senior civil servant with substantive policy experience.

Headed by the chief of staff, the new PMO structure included small teams specialized in key policy domains. The policy analysis unit established under the previous Dahabi government was the nucleus of this expanded and more structured policy advisory function. Training in policy analysis and development skills and new templates for the presentation of policy papers were institutionalized with the support of external consultants.

This new team at the PMO inevitably had some teething problems. Not surprisingly, it was perceived by some ministers as potentially complicating their access to the prime minister. Nevertheless, with the passage of time and positive collaborative experiences between ministers and PMO advisers, this dynamic changed. Most ministers came to see the PMO policy team as facilitating their agenda rather than competing for influence. In many respects, it provided the analytic capacity that ministers lacked from their own staff.

The media and communications function at the prime ministry—effectively the government's official communications apparatus—was significantly under-resourced and physically isolated. It was relocated back to the prime ministry building, and a dedicated program of training and capability building was undertaken. The head of the unit doubled as the prime minister's media and communications adviser as well as official government spokesperson. New strategic communications tools and forward planning of government announcements were institutionalized. Given the weaknesses in communications support capacity across the ministries, the unit was designed as a shared service platform supporting all ministers.

The third value-adding advisory function added to the prime ministry was a dedicated prime minister's delivery unit (PMDU). Originally based on the "deliverology" approach pioneered by the Blair government in Britain, the unit was quickly pulled by ministers in the direction of a more conventional monitoring and evaluation function. This team moved quickly to collect data and prepare progress reports on projects across government. Data on over 2,000 individual government initiatives was also made publicly available through a dedicated website linking projects to the 2010 Annual Program. At the time, this was an unprecedented level of transparency at a project level, not just in Jordan but internationally. Despite early push-back from officials across the government about the workload created from additional data requests and the enhanced accountability, these reports were quickly relied on by ministers, cabinet subcommittees, and officials for understanding project status and roadblocks.

Fourth, a new, multidisciplinary unit for the development and delivery of infrastructure mega-projects was also installed at the prime ministry. This unit was born out of frustration at the lack of "joined up" planning and implementation of the Kingdom's major infrastructure projects. Modeled on similar units found in the center of government entities and ministries of finance around the world, the unit reported to the newly created position of Minister of State for Mega Projects.

In addition to this multipronged approach to boost the advisory capacity of the prime ministry, a number of administrative reforms, attempted by previous governments, were relaunched to improve the efficiency of the Cabinet Secretariat in managing the agenda setting function and the flow of paperwork across government. Building on the analysis and recommendations from 2007 as well as international best practice procedures, a new cabinet handbook was formulated and approved by the cabinet. It mandated the presentation of policy options with supporting evidence (including cost estimates and implementation risks) rather than yes/no choices. It also mandated format requirements and deadlines for the submission of papers by ministries and circulation times to ensure that ministers had enough time to read and prepare for cabinet meetings.

To better quarantine the administrative burden on the cabinet and create more time and space for genuine policy discussion, Prime Minister Rifai also convened two cabinet sessions per week. One was dedicated to administrative and compliance-driven decisionmaking; the other to debate on strategic policy priorities and ideas brought forward by ministers.

Despite this bifurcation of cabinet business, urgent administrative business continued to consume the time and attention of ministers. To drive further discipline and coordination of cabinet business, the prime minister created a new position of Minister of State for Cabinet Affairs in July 2010 as part of a cabinet reshuffle. The former minister for planning and international cooperation was appointed to the position with a mandate to support the prime minister with the forward planning of cabinet business and the appropriate triaging of administrative decisionmaking into cabinet subcommittees.

By September 2010, most changes had been completed, and the focus turned to bedding down the new practices. Prime Minister Rifai's determination to transform the capabilities of the prime ministry was met with the same internal and external resistance witnessed during previous reform efforts. It was amplified by the expansion of social media, which created a new platform for reform opponents to quickly spread misinformation.

At the same time, there were many supporters of the transformation program at the prime ministry, including experienced ministers who had served in previous governments and, by late 2010, could see clear improvements. Many younger staff, who were engaged in the transformation program, were also supportive, seeing these efforts as an investment in their own capabilities and in the decision support system. Ultimately, Prime Minister Rifai's push to address the weaknesses in central decision support was born out of the realization, early in his tenure, that inadequate capacity in the prime ministry was itself a major barrier to broader economic and social reform.

The lack of broader economic and social reform boiled over at the end of 2010 and in early 2011 into what became known as the Arab Spring. Those events brought the Rifai government's term in office to an end in February 2011, despite passing its budget and winning a record vote of confidence only weeks earlier. As before, this change in government disrupted progress to reform the prime ministry.

Marouf Al-Bakhit, who had served as prime minister between 2005 and 2007, was reappointed. He faced a very different context this time. His first priority was security and a renewed focus on political reform in response to the Arab Spring movement. Between February 2011 and October 2012, Jordan saw the rapid succession of three prime ministers until the appointment of Abdullah Ensour, who served a full four-year term.

Achievements and Ongoing Challenges

What was ultimately achieved in the reform of Jordan's policy institutions and processes? If reforms are to be judged by forward-looking plans, procedural manuals, cabinet approvals, and new organizational charts, these reforms yielded achievements. If they are to be judged by concrete changes in the "way business is done," the story is far less encouraging.

One achievement was the development of the National Agenda, which in principle served as a strategic framework to guide policy decisions for the decade to 2015. This initiative was followed by the Jordan 2025 national strategy. With these overarching strategic frameworks in place, MoPIC developed medium-term executive programs to guide international development assistance programming and coordination with government priorities. The introduction of these long-term and medium-term planning frameworks marked a small but important step in introducing a more programmatic approach to government and institutionalizing key performance indicators. The programs highlighted and tracked key goals, policies, and initiatives aimed at improving government performance and published them online.[23]

By the time the second National Evaluation Program (NEP) was launched in 2011, over 500 employees received training aimed at supporting policy mechanisms, such as strategic planning methodologies and performance monitoring and evaluation.[24] But the effectiveness of this training remained questionable, and progress on developing and institutionalizing key performance indicators remained superficial and ad hoc.[25]

A second achievement is related to reductions in the administrative burdens. Efforts to delegate administrative decisionmaking led to the amendment of eighteen laws and six bylaws. By 2013, some additional laws were tackled, including the civil service statute.[26] Staff at the PMO and a number of former ministers noted that these reforms have had a concrete and significant impact on the administrative burdens of the cabinet.

Some committees and subcommittees were also tasked with reviewing submissions before they were passed to the prime ministry. Those committees took the time to evaluate submissions before they reached the cabinet for approval, technically reducing the amount of time spent by the cabinet on each policy matter. However, no permanent and systematic arrangements were developed to ensure that future legislation would not require unnecessary referral of administrative decisions to the prime minister and ministers.[27]

There remains significant scope to further reduce these burdens. Additional amendments to laws and bylaws were proposed, but resistance was encountered from parliament and, on occasion, the ministers themselves. Proposed amendments to laws relating to citizenship, bonuses to government employees, and the travel of senior government officials did not receive parliamentary approval. The first matter was perceived to be too politically sensitive. Parliament also believed that the cabinet would be more likely to ensure proper use of funds than lower levels in the bureaucracy.

Interestingly, some ministers resisted efforts to reduce administrative burdens. One government sought to modify civil service bylaws to decentralize the power of the cabinet, the prime minister, and ministers over personnel issues and transfer them to the level of the secretary general. But some ministers formed a coalition to keep the power structure intact. Control over personnel issues was seen as a form of power and influence that they were unwilling to let go. This reform effort was later revisited, and a new system of delegating powers to the secretary general was adopted by the Council of Ministers by 2014. To enhance coordination between line ministries, an annual Government Leaders Forum was also started by the Ensour government between upper level management, including secretaries general and other agency heads, to exchange experiences and practices across the public sector. However, this new system has been utilized at the discretion of each minister, and the relationship between ministers and his or her secretary general depends largely on the willingness of ministers to delegate their own powers.[28]

The infrastructure to support the cabinet continues to remain underdeveloped. Units mandated to provide technical support became part of the new organizational structure of the prime ministry. As of 2018, the units are not "fully operational" according to the secretary general of the prime minister, as they were not staffed with qualified personnel. In practice, the cabinet procedures manual was not being fully utilized. Additional interministerial committees were established, but they faced challenges. The Public Sector Reform Committee, for example, was established at the prime ministry but met infrequently. This is indicative of a more general problem whereby ministers burdened by administrative issues of their own ministry were not able to fully assume their responsibilities in the interministerial committees.

Another achievement was the development of a comprehensive cabinet procedures manual. In addition to providing guidelines and timelines for cabinet decisionmaking, the manual stipulated that all requests for cabinet-level decisions were to be accompanied by policy and strategic analysis reports. This was followed in 2013 by more formalized guidance regulating codes of conduct and ethics for public jobs. This manual could have strengthened the cabinet and the policy analysis units at line ministries but implementation was limited.

Some progress was made toward establishing policy and institutional development units. Line ministries established, staffed, and operationalized special units that reported directly to the prime ministry and MoPIC. Following the initial collaboration between MoPIC, GPD, and MoPSD, disagreements emerged about staffing and the scope of work. The function of monitoring and assessing the impact of policies continued to be ad hoc, and no systematic method was adopted on when such assessments are meant to be conducted and submitted.[29]

Ultimately, Jordan's Vision 2025, launched in 2015, echoed many of the issues identified in the White Paper from a decade before.[30] The cabinet continued to be burdened by minor administrative decisions, and routine procedures were still sent up the chain of command instead of being resolved by middle management. The Council of Ministers continued to lack some key functioning supportive bodies. There was no systematic process for submission of policy items to the cabinet; there was insufficient technical analytical support for policy decisionmaking; and follow-up on implementation was weak.

Understanding Policy Reform in Jordan

Reflecting on Jordan's experience, responsibility for this disappointing outcome could be laid upon many shoulders. The most obvious obstacle to an effective institutional development agenda is the continuous reshuffle of cabinet and ministers, which created sharp breaks in continuity and disincentives for reforms. Between 1999 and 2018, no fewer than twenty-six ministers managed the public sector development portfolio. The average life span of a government was between eight and nine months.

Each incoming government and minister did not feel obliged to move forward with decisions made by the last government. This, in turn, discouraged civil servants from taking initiatives seriously because they expected their ministers to be in power for only a short duration. The departure of

Zu'bi—at the critical juncture after the preparation of the reform agenda but before implementation was firmly entrenched—may have had a particularly pernicious impact.

The institutional apparatus to manage reforms was also not vested with the necessary authority. The reform function was ultimately not institutionalized as a center of government function but, rather, lay outside the prime ministry in a line ministry. Though initial reformers directly attempted to address this issue in their proposed institutional design, a combination of power politics and limitations in design led to failure. Particularly in the context of frequent government reshuffling, there was a need for an overarching council or institution located in the prime ministry to oversee reform until its completion.

The international consulting firm brought on board to advise the public sector maintained a working model that constrained a sustained advocacy effort by its senior specialists. Its model—in line with models typically used by those agencies—was such that junior staff were maintained long-term "in country" for the "nuts and bolts," while the specialized senior consultants were "flown in and out" for short periods of time, sometimes with extended gaps between trips. Junior staff had insufficient practical experience and were unable to garner the confidence of their public sector clients, while the senior consultants who had the requisite background were not in a position to maintain ongoing high-level dialogue with senior bureaucrats. Reform momentum was compromised in part because of this arrangement.

Some domestic reformers felt there were a number of weaknesses in the way donors and international organizations approached public sector reforms, which included failing to truly understand the depth of the challenges Jordan was facing and adopting a superficial approach to reforms; the limited value of recommendations; discontinuous or piecemeal engagement, which gave opposition groups time to overpower the process; insufficient use of donor leverage to support reformers; and ineffective relationships established with counterparts.

Despite the engagement of high-level political champions, senior bureaucrats were not always informed or included in the reform efforts. As a result, many of these officials did not feel ownership of the reform plans. This was particularly problematic in a context in which officials whose power or positions may have been directly threatened by reforms were nevertheless expected to implement them. Moreover, internal power politics created resistance by senior public officials and disincentives for implementation. In the absence of strong political leadership to overcome such frictions, they were allowed to fester and undermine the broader reform effort.

Opponents to reform were well-placed in the major state institutions and were able to generate significant opposition. While cabinet decisionmaking reforms per se may not have been perceived as a threat, these reforms were nevertheless part and parcel of a wider public sector reform program and had to proceed in an environment that was unfavorable to reform. The National Agenda raised broader fears of marginalization and loss of influence among core supporters of the Hashemite monarchy. A long-standing informal "contract" between the state apparatus and its trans-Jordanian support base was threatened by the broader public sector reform program.

These dynamics were exacerbated by a deteriorating international environment and domestic tragedy that brought security considerations to the forefront. In fact, the shift toward prioritizing political stability was exacerbated both in 2006 and following the 2010–2011 Arab uprisings. While the protests in Jordan did not escalate to the kinds of large-scale, anti-regime protests that occurred in places like Egypt and Tunisia, they were enough to propel the government into action. The constitution was amended, parliament was dismissed, and the government set aside US$500 million for public salary increases and food subsidies.[31] Three prime ministers were introduced within a period of eighteen months. Instead of focusing on behind-the-scenes reforms, like restructuring the cabinet, the focus shifted even more heavily toward national security, as crises escalated in neighboring Syria and Iraq, and the Islamic State (IS) emerged as a new challenge on the global security agenda.

Against these forces, the reform proponents were unable to mount a cohesive counterattack. They failed to develop a strong public relations campaign to educate citizens and parliamentarians on the public sector reform program. In fact, the very nature of public sector reform—whose costs are felt in the near term whereas benefits accrue downstream—made it difficult for them to garner the necessary support.

Reflecting upon this experience, some who participated in the reform effort have argued that the overall public sector reform process suffered from lack of political will and absence of accountability mechanisms. While there were highly motivated individual proponents of reform, they did not have the necessary institutional backup or the sustained support of the top leadership to see these reforms through. Moreover, those ministers and senior officials who did not meet their commitments under the reform plans were not held accountable.

Conclusion

The Hashemite Kingdom deserves credit for addressing such an important set of public sector reforms. In a region where many policies are decided behind closed doors among limited numbers of advisers, Jordan recognized the importance of more effective, transparent, and formalized policy structures that improve coordination and ensure high quality technical analysis. These reforms were carefully thought through and advanced by some of the most capable ministers in government in a country that is widely acknowledged to have one of the best-performing public sectors in the region. Several leading bilateral and multilateral donors provided extensive technical inputs in support of this effort.

Yet in spite of these efforts, reforms did not take root and transform the operations of the cabinet and the PMO as anticipated. Significant strides were made in the initial period, at a time when public sector reform became an imperative in the context of the wider economic reforms. Incremental changes were made to improve existing systems and procedures. But the objective of broader and more systematic reform captured in the White Paper was not realized, and reform momentum was ultimately thwarted by a host of complications both within and outside of government.

In the end, several important questions are left unresolved. Are reforms in cabinet systems possible when they touch on politically charged issues at the core of government decisionmaking? Would Jordan's reforms have survived in an environment with less frequent changes in government or in an environment where the "political economy" of reform was different? Was the timing simply unfortunate, in that promising reforms were set aside as key decisionmakers diverted their attention to a deteriorating security or economic environment? Did donors fail to ensure continued support for cabinet reform? Could these reforms have been implemented in a way that garnered more support and neutralized opponents? Did they receive adequate political support from the highest levels of government? Or are such reforms too dependent on a few talented individuals whose departure from government meant that they were bound to fail?

Reasonable observers can and do differ as to how such questions should be answered. However, what is clear is that the nature of these answers will have important implications within Jordan and the broader Middle East and North Africa region.

Notes

The authors would like to express their gratitude to Nithya Nagarajan for her excellent and extensive inputs into earlier versions of this case.

1. Interview with former Jordanian minister, November 2008, Amman, Jordan.

2. Interview with Fawaz Zu'bi, former Minister of Information and Communications Technology, May 2018, Amman, Jordan.

3. "The Constitution of the Hashemite Kingdom of Jordan," January 1, 1952, www.unodc.org/tldb/pdf/ Jordan_const_1952.pdf.

4. Cabinet meetings were divided into two sessions: one that is attended by the prime minister and one that is not. This description presumably pertained to the former. Former ministers characterized the portion of the meetings attended by the prime minister as very orderly.

5. Government of Jordan, "Better Government, Delivering Better Results: Policies and Programs for Public Sector Reform 2004–2009," White Paper X/04 (internal document), October 2004.

6. Government of Jordan, "Better Government, Delivering Better Results."

7. In 2004, the list of ad hoc committees included: Extension of Service Committee; the Regional Conflict Economic Impact Committee; Passports Law Committee; Anti-Corruption Committee; Assistance Funds Committee; Public Sector Reform Committee; Prime Ministry Legal & Administrative Procedures Committee; and the Prime Minister's Visits to Governorates Committee.

8. Government of Jordan, "Better Government, Delivering Better Results."

9. Interview with Zu'bi, May 2018.

10. Interview with international consultant, November 2018.

11. Shadi Hamid, "Democracy at a Dead End in Jordan," Carnegie Endowment for International Peace, Arab Reform Bulletin, May 2005, http://carnegieendowment .org/2005/05/11/arab-reform-bulletin-may-2005/7ku. For another reference to this issue, also see Curtis Ryan, "Reform Retreats Amid Jordan's Political Storms," Middle East Research and Information Project, June 10, 2005, www.merip.org/ mero/mero061005.

12. Hamid, "Democracy at a Dead End."

13. Salem Khazaleh, interview with Nithya Nagarajan, November 2008, Amman.

14. Tayseer Smadi, interview with Nithya Nagarajan, November 2008, Amman.

15. Khazaleh, interview.

16. Julia Choucair, "Illusive Reform: Jordan's Stubborn Stability," Carnegie Endowment for International Peace Middle East Series, no. 76, December 2006, http://carnegieendowment.org/files/cp76_choucair_final.pdf.

17. Smadi, interview.

18. Quotations from Marwan Muasher, *The Arab Center: The Promise of Moderation* (Yale University Press, 2008).

19. Ibid.

20. For historical overview, see Glenn E. Robinson, "Defensive Democratization in Jordan," *International Journal of Middle East Studies* 30, no. 3 (August 1998), pp.

387–410. Election laws were one of the themes discussed in the National Agenda document, which noted "The Election Law should achieve . . . election of a politically representative parliament." See Ministry of Planning and International Cooperation, "National Agenda: The Jordan We Strive For 2006–2015," Government of Jordan, 2005, p. 14, http://inform.gov.jo/Portals/0/Report%20PDFs/0 .%20General/2006-2015%20National%20Agenda.pdf.

21. H. E. Hala Lattouf (Minister of Social Development and former secretary general in the Ministry of Administrative Development), interview with Nithya Nagarajan, November 2008, Amman.

22. Rana Sabbagh-Gargour, "Jordan: A Balancing Act that Keeps Political Change at Bay," Carnegie Endowment for International Peace, November 2006, http://carnegieendowment.org/files/sabbaghgargour_nov06.pdf.

23. Ministry of Planning and International Cooperation, "Executive Program 2007–2009," Government of Jordan, p. 80, www.mop.gov.jo/EchoBusV3.0/SystemAssets/pdf/Executive%20Program%202007-2009en.pdf.

24. Ministry of Planning and International Cooperation, "Executive Development Program 2011–2013," Government of Jordan, pp. 66–80.

25. Ibrahim Saif, telephone interview with Fatema Alhashemi, June 7, 2018.

26. "Executive Development Program 2011–2013," Ministry of Planning and International Cooperation, pp. 66–80.

27. Saif, telephone interview.

28. Ibid.

29. Ibid.

30. Ministry of Planning and International Cooperation, "First Section – Jordan Vision 2025," Government of Jordan, p. 39, http://inform.gov.jo/Portals/0/Report%20 PDFs/0.%20General/jo2025part1.pdf; Ministry of Planning and International Cooperation, "Second Section – Jordan Vision 2025," Government of Jordan, p. 77, http://inform.gov.jo/Portals/0/Report%20PDFs/0.%20General/jo2025part2.pdf.

31. Amendments to Articles 53, 55, and 67 of the constitution introduced some major changes to the cabinet, including in terms of its responsibilities toward the House of Representatives. However, none of these changes significantly affected the kinds of administrative reforms addressed in this case.

THREE

Reforms to Public Financial Management in Palestine

ROBERT P. BESCHEL JR.
MARK AHERN

WHEN SALAM FAYYAD BECAME Minister of Finance in June 2002, he faced the twin challenges of leading the Palestinian Authority (PA) out of its economic crisis and establishing trust in the quality of its financial management. The PA was on the verge of a fiscal crisis. The second *intifada* was contributing to a sharp drop in economic activity; unemployment and poverty were rising across the West Bank and Gaza (WBG). Internally, there was political discontent directed against the PA leadership over the failure of the Oslo peace process. The international community had marginalized the president of the PA, Yasser Arafat, and expressed serious reservations over his stewardship of PA resources. The Israeli army had just finished a major military operation inside the West Bank. Meanwhile, political opposition groups and activists, as well as the general public and the international community, were calling for immediate reforms to PA institutions and practices.

Fayyad was well aware of these challenges. He had to introduce public financial system reforms while simultaneously managing a severe crisis. These reforms would signify the start of a transformation in PA governance. Many were counting on him to fail. How was he going to proceed?

Challenges of Building a State: 1993–2002

POLITICAL DEVELOPMENTS

The 1993 Oslo Accords envisaged a five-year transition period that would lead to the establishment of a sovereign Palestinian state alongside Israel. The accords established a framework for negotiations on complex final status issues such as Jerusalem, the right of return of Palestinian refugees, Israeli settlements, and borders. Though there was no Palestinian state delineated in the Oslo Accords, the underlying premise was that the establishment of the PA as an interim body would lead to the development of institutions that could evolve into the fully functioning government of a future Palestinian state.

On the Palestinian side, Yasser Arafat was the driving figure behind the accords. He brought international recognition and legitimacy to the Palestinian cause, and his political career, personal traits, and leadership style strongly shaped the institution-building process of the nascent PA. While the accords were hailed as historic, realities on the ground were far less promising. Both internal and external dynamics provided a challenging context for state building. Internally, Arafat faced opposition among important Palestinian constituencies, including refugees, intellectuals, Islamists, and activists who had struggled from within WBG. Their main concerns related to the ambiguity of the agreements and the control Israel continued to maintain over land, borders, and trade. As subsequent agreements in Cairo and Paris were negotiated, Arafat was perceived to have made some major concessions, which further incensed his opposition.[1]

Economic pressures inside WBG also intensified. The economy was heavily dependent on Israel—for both employment and trade. In addition, Israel collected clearance revenues on behalf of the PA that constituted nearly two-thirds of total PA revenues. The Oslo framework gave Israel control over external trade, and the economic arrangements detailed in the Paris Protocol allowed Israel to control a range of the PA's fiscal and economic policy instruments.[2] The political conflict subjected the WBG economy to large fluctuations.

The divergent legacies of the Palestine Liberation Organization (PLO) and civil administration inside WBG also made state building more difficult. PA institutions inherited the physical and administrative infrastructure that had existed under earlier Israeli, Egyptian, and Jordanian regimes, whereas the PA leadership largely originated from the PLO leadership. A significant cadre of PLO officers based in Tunis came back to

WBG as part of the Oslo Accords. These officers became part of the PA bureaucracy, and employing them was seen as a way of partly compensating them for their years of service. By 1996, 85 percent of the civil and security personnel on the PA payroll originated from the civil administration and the PLO.

Furthermore, the PA was not yet a government with power over resources and borders, nor was there a sovereign Palestinian state. As the conflict on the ground continued, tension remained between revolutionary ideology and a focus on democratic state-building. Some groups believed that reforms and national liberation went hand in hand, while others believed that having a well-functioning state or PA would lead, eventually, to full sovereignty.

In the face of such powerful dynamics, Arafat's response was to move toward the centralization of authority and the personalization of power.[3] Political opposition was co-opted into the PA bureaucracy, and patronage methods were used to buy political loyalties. He expanded his official leadership position to various public bodies. The PA leadership exploited the ambiguities in the Oslo interim agreements to secure power for the executive over other branches of government, including the Palestinian Legislative Council (PLC). The core leadership did not want to be subject to PLC oversight and, as such, ignored legislation that would have strengthened accountability.[4]

STATE OF PUBLIC FINANCIAL MANAGEMENT

Public financial management (PFM) suffered from major problems, including nontransparent revenue management, weak budgeting practices, and ineffective expenditure management. The lack of institutional know-how as well as underlying structural and political dynamics were important factors contributing to this situation.

The Oslo framework had created certain preconditions where rent-seeking activity could flourish. The PA was keen to promote economic development and private sector growth, yet incentive packages offered to various companies, particularly for large-scale infrastructure projects, yielded limited success due to the unstable political and economic environment. To attract investors, the PA granted monopoly concessions in telecommunications and electricity as a way of guaranteeing returns. It also went into partnership through complex holding companies with private investors in several businesses, including hotels, casinos, cigarette traders, and flour millers. The PA also developed public sector monopolies for key strategic commodities, such as petroleum and cement. Terms of the Paris Economic Protocol and on-the-ground procedures for clearance of goods essentially gave Israel a monopoly position in the supply of petroleum and cement to the Palestinian market. In this context, the creation of counterpart Palestinian import monopolies allowed the PA to capture some of the rents that would have otherwise accrued to Israel.[5]

Powerful political figures in the PA and PLO establishment exploited the opportunities that were created from this situation. Ties were forged between senior leaders of the PA, the PLO, and some private sector or quasi-government organizations to advance business interests. Members of the security apparatus provided services to these leaders in exchange for fees or revenues that were not channeled through the public budget.[6] The PLC, which undertook an extensive corruption investigation in 1997, also found that some public contracts were awarded based on connections to political figures. The blurring of boundaries between the public good and private interests further created disincentives for transparency and accountability.[7]

Beyond personal material benefits, the PA and PLO leaders were also compelled to leverage financial resources for their political survival. The loss of financial support after the first Gulf War created additional pressures to find resources. Part of the revenues of PA monopolies and investments contributed to this end. Off-budget contingency funds were also used to buy internal political loyalties. A degree of opacity was useful in generating and disseminating finances for these political purposes.

Negotiations with Israel further incentivized the PA to engage in off-budget commercial activities. Ghassan Khatib, former Minister of Planning and Labor, explains: "Arafat was convinced that financial support [by donors] was used for political reasons and to extract concessions. The more flexibility he had outside the budget or not known in specific detail by the donor, the more he could do to resist pressure by Israel on donors."[8] In a context where Israel controlled nearly 60 percent of the PA's annual revenues and the PA was dependent on donor financing for virtually its entire capital budget, its leadership feared their financial vulnerability would be used as a weapon.

These factors—combined with a lack of institutional and state-building experience—resulted in a PFM system characterized by three fundamental weaknesses:

No System for Revenue Consolidation and Management. PA revenues were not consolidated under one account, nor were they controlled by the Ministry of Finance (MOF). Most notably, petroleum, tobacco, and alcohol excises were channeled to outside accounts. Petroleum taxes were transferred directly to a special account held in an Israeli bank, which was controlled by President Arafat and his economic adviser Mohammad Rachid. The IMF estimates that a net of US$591 million of excise tax revenues was diverted from the MOF between 1995 and 2000.[9] Revenues of line ministries were not managed in one central account. Rather, those ministries generating revenues maintained their own accounts instead of transferring the amounts to the Treasury. Line ministries would spend from these accounts at their discretion, even beyond their budgetary allocations. As a result, the Treasury had control over neither revenues nor expenditures.

In addition, PA commercial activities were mismanaged. The PA acquired shares in several commercial enterprises, which were placed under a holding company called the Palestinian Commercial Services Company (PCSC). Following a public inquiry in 1997, the PLC found that the government's partial or full ownership of several companies was not monitored by the General Audit Institute, nor were their revenues included in the government's budget. The absence of balance sheets or published annual reports meant that no concrete information was available on the profits generated from 1995 to 2000. Moreover, the inquiry showed undisclosed commercial dealings between public officials and private sector actors in which the former gave the latter exclusive privileges and contracts. In a 2003 International Money Fund (IMF) study, PA commercial assets were estimated at US$633 million. Conservative estimates suggest that approximately US$300 million in profits was diverted outside the budget between 1995 and 2000.[10]

Weak Budgetary Processes. For several years immediately after the Oslo Accords, budget development suffered from major technical weaknesses. There was poor coordination between donors and the PA, which resulted in superficial integration of public investment expenditures into the budget. The Ministry of Planning and the MOF were cosignatories to all development projects financed by donors, but these two entities had limited engagement in project selection. Donors often engaged directly with line ministries, PA institutions, and local government bodies, and there was no centralized agency monitoring all projects. The projects were not evaluated in the context of a broader macroeconomic framework and failed to account for future recurrent costs and debt servicing capacity. As a result, the PA budget did not reflect donor-financed public investment.

After repeated requests from the PLC, donor countries, the World Bank, and the IMF, the PA agreed to submit a budget in 1996. But the budget preparation process had many weaknesses; budget proposals were not integrated into any comprehensive framework. It was not possible to hold serious cabinet-level discussions on various fiscal policy issues or their medium-term implications. Moreover, no regular financial statements were released to the public or to the PLC. As a result, there was no proper oversight or broad-based consultations in the budget process.

Inadequate Systems for Expenditure Management and Control. President Arafat retained huge personal discretion over spending, and the Minister of Finance had only partial control. There were multiple spending centers in WBG. Treasury checks were issued and transfers made without approval of the minister. Line ministries routinely overspent their budgets, and systems for internal audit and payment control were very weak. Security personnel were paid in cash instead of bank transfers, which opened the system to significant abuse.

Inadequate management and payroll controls also contributed to uncontrolled hiring in the civil service and security apparatus, which in turn led to an unsustainable wage bill. By 1999, the PA's wage bill accounted for 15 percent of GDP and 55 percent of current expenditures; by 2002, it had increased to 70 percent of current expenditures. This resulted in insufficient resources for nonwage expenditure, along with unpaid bills and debts to the private sector. The main problem was that the General Personnel Council, which was responsible for all recruitment, was outside the control of the MOF. As a result, hiring was undertaken without any regard to the budget.

The lack of adequate systems for cash management, combined with high levels of discretionary spending, led to significant debts, preferential payments to suppliers, and opportunities for corruption. By March 2000, debts reached US$370 million, mainly in the form of unpaid bills to suppliers. Nevertheless, the MOF continued to issue checks even without adequate resources to cover them. When suppliers went to cash their Treasury-issued checks, the commercial banks had the discretion to decide which checks would be cleared. There were concerns that bank officials as well as some MOF officials were receiving bribes for these transactions.[11]

Another significant problem was the lack of any credible external audit institution. The General Audit Institute was established in 1995, but it lacked both the necessary independence and the capacity to perform its functions. It reported to the president, who had the power to exempt any public institution from audit. Effectively, in the World Bank's judgment, the General Audit Institute "had no discernible effect on public accountability."[12]

THE REFORM MOVEMENT

The reform of PA institutions and operations had strong domestic support from the outset, including from members of the PLC, technocrats, various political parties, NGO leaders, academics, and the international community.

The first major reform initiative followed a report published by the PA comptroller general, Jarrar Al-Qudwa, in 1997. The report, based on an extensive audit of PA financial activities, highlighted serious violations and operational inefficiencies. It concluded that two-thirds of the PA budget had been either mismanaged or illicitly spent. The PLC demanded that all accused persons be brought to trial and that a new technocratic cabinet be established. Reformers in the PLC wanted public revenues to be reported and information on licensing to be made available to the public. Arafat established a presidential commission that further expanded on Al-Qudwa's report and called for a meeting with key PLC members and political leaders. He argued that without yet having achieved national liberation, it was not the appropriate time to pursue these issues.[13] Ultimately, no action was taken.

At the same time, multilateral and bilateral development agencies in the Palestinian territories had pushed for more transparency in PA finances. Several attempts were made in the mid-1990s to consolidate all revenue streams under the control of the MOF, such as in the Tripartite Action Plan agreed upon by the PA, Israel, and the donors in April 1995. This was followed by a commitment by the MOF in the first quarterly report to the Ad Hoc Liaison Committee (AHLC), in which the PA committed to consolidating all accounts in a single Treasury account by August 1996.

Yet, for a variety of reasons, both the PA and the donors backed away from implementing these agreements. While donors and foreign governments were calling for PFM reforms in the 1990s, many were also under pressure to provide funding to the PA and, in practice, were willing to accommodate the existing regime.[14] A consistently high premium was also placed by donors and foreign governments on security—in particular requiring the PA to uphold its security commitments toward Israel at the expense of reform and even democracy.

Reaching near crisis proportions in 1999, the mismanagement of public finance threatened to create a major dispute between the donor community and the PA. Demands from the PLC to put the budget in order and consistent encouragement from the World Bank finally led PA Finance Minister Muhammad Zuhdi Nashashibi to agree that all PA revenues would go to the Treasury; he also agreed to the liquidation of public sector firms. The latter never occurred.

Moreover, in 1999, IMF Resident Representative Salam Fayyad initiated a major reform program—the Economic Policy Framework (EPF)—with President Arafat. The first wave of reforms was undertaken in 2000, following a severe crisis in tax administration, revenue management, and expenditure control. The two major achievements of the EPF were the consolidation of petroleum, tobacco, and alcohol excise revenues with other tax revenues and the auditing of the PCSC. The commitments to transfer payroll control to the MOF and ending the diversion of profits from PA commercial enterprises were not addressed at this time.

Implementing Reforms: 2002–2005

ORIGINS OF THE REFORMS

It was at the most unexpected moment—during the "darkest days" of the second *intifada* in spring 2002—that President Arafat called for reforms in several areas, including public finance. This can be attributed to two key dynamics: first, Arafat and the PA leadership were weakened by the PA's poor performance and the failure of the peace process to generate dividends; and second, the economy fell into recession in 2000 as closures led to a decline in internal economic activity, with total employment falling by 32 percent from the third quarter of 2000 to the third quarter of 2002.[15]

Poverty levels also increased significantly. Before the start of the second *intifada*, 21 percent of the population was estimated to be living below the poverty line of US$2.10 per day. That increased to 60 percent by December 2002.[16] In addition, the PA struggled with its fiscal situation. The diversion of excise taxes and commercial enterprise revenues from the public budget, and an uncontrolled wage bill, resulted in significant cash deficits. In January 2001, Israel suspended the transfer of clearance tax revenues collected on behalf of the PA, which represented nearly two-thirds of PA revenues. The Arab League donations to the PA also fell by half.

In addition, political opposition was growing. By the late 1990s, Arafat was beginning to face internal challenges from within his own Fatah party. Underlying these issues was the allegation that the Palestinian leadership had failed to deliver an agreement on final status issues. With the second *intifada*, the balance of power began to shift from the old guard toward younger activists. Opposition groups gained power through popular legitimacy, and Palestinians became increasingly opposed to the PA's method of rule and felt the need for reform. These calls for reform were not focused on strictly technical matters relating to administration. Rather, it was a broader call to establish more accountable leadership and institutions that could lead the national movement.[17]

In April 2002, Israel launched Operation Defensive Shield, a large-scale military operation in which major cities of the West Bank were reoccupied by Israeli forces. The Israeli Army seized the president's compound in Ramallah, with Arafat inside, in an effort to isolate him diplomatically and physically. In the wake of the military operation, the Palestinian public realized that the PA was not able to defend Palestinian national interests. As a result, domestic calls for reform erupted. By April-May 2002, demand for change came from the Fatah Revolutionary Council, the Fatah Central Committee, the PLC, and some senior advisers of Arafat. On May 16, 2002, the PLC met with Arafat and his cabinet to propose sweeping reforms, starting with the appointment of a new government in forty-five days and organizing elections within six months.

Simultaneously, the PA leadership and President Arafat were facing political marginalization from the international community. Arafat's standing within the American administration was low. On June 24, 2002, President Bush called for "a new and different Palestinian leadership" and "entirely new political and economic institutions," stating they were prerequisites for moving forward with the peace process. Other members of the international community also called for comprehensive reforms, including the Quartet (the European Union, Russian Federation, United Nations, and the United States).

INSTITUTIONAL FRAMEWORK

On June 9, 2002, President Arafat appointed a new cabinet that included a new Minister of Finance, Salam Fayyad. In the initial days, the reform agenda moved quickly. By June 12, an interministerial reform committee was formed to oversee the reform program in public security, public finance, the justice system, and the electoral system. On June 16, a "100-day plan" was approved by the PLC, and, on June 23, 2002, the PA issued the "100-Day Plan of the Palestinian Government." In January 2003, the Reform Coordination and Support Unit was set up as the secretariat to the Ministerial Reform Committee (MRC).

In support of the PA reform agenda, the international community established the International Task Force on Palestinian Reform in 2002 to help develop a comprehensive action plan. The task force, consisting of representatives of the Quartet, World Bank, IMF, Japan, and Norway, was the international counterpart to the MRC. It was tasked with monitoring the reform process and guiding the international community to support the reform agenda. Reform subgroups were established to coordinate reforms and help mobilize donor support.

The establishment of this international task force was considered a positive step. Donors were criticized for not taking a coordinated and comprehensive approach in WBG in the years after Oslo, and the working groups were an attempt to learn from past mistakes. The benchmarks developed by the task force were also an important step toward holding the PA accountable. However, views vary on the effectiveness of the relationship between the MRC and the international task force. Concerns were raised about the level of coordination; the relationship between the donor community and the PA; and the level of independence given to the PA.[18]

In late June 2003, newly appointed Prime Minister Mahmoud Abbas widened the base of those involved in the reform program. He established the National Reform Committee (NRC), consisting of some twenty-five members of the PLC, academics, civil society leaders, and businessmen. The NRC was to develop general strategy and submit recommendations to the MRC. The MRC was to implement reforms, provide oversight, and report back to the cabinet. However, the mechanics between the MRC and NRC were not so clear in practice. Problems emerged when members of the NRC wanted to expand its role. Political resistance to reform, even from some of the top leadership, adversely affected the operations and effectiveness of these committees.[19] By 2005, several members of the NRC resigned, and the committee eventually stopped meeting.

PUBLIC FINANCIAL MANAGEMENT REFORMS

While Fayyad was a key figure in championing the PFM reforms, President Arafat's role remained significant. Though Arafat was under great pressure to devolve executive power, he continued to wield significant political clout. Progress in all areas, including PFM reform, required his consent. Fayyad was brought in for his technocratic background and for the credibility he enjoyed with the donors and international community; however, he did not enjoy a broad political mandate or strong backing from the PA establishment.

This context strongly influenced the way Fayyad approached reforms. His fundamental strategy was to adopt a technical approach, focusing on concepts and structures required for a sound PFM system. He avoided direct confrontation to the extent possible and adopted a more conciliatory approach. He did not focus on weeding out corrupt individuals or directly challenging the integrity of existing PFM bureaucrats. Rather, he positioned his reform efforts as part of the state-building process. In so doing, he attempted to garner public support for even the most technical of reforms.

Fayyad was different from past PA leaders. He had neither been a political activist in the PLO or the territories, nor was he attached to any of the leading political parties. Born in the West Bank, he was educated in Jordan, Lebanon, and the United States. He served as the IMF's representative in WBG from 1995 to 2001. As a technocrat with intimate knowledge of the PA's finances, he had developed a reputation for professionalism and a no-nonsense style of getting the job done.

A DIFFICULT CONTEXT

Fayyad's abilities were tested from the outset. He had to manage a grave fiscal crisis while trying to move forward with major reforms. Since late 2000, Israel had withheld monthly clearance revenue transfers that belonged to the PA. The IMF estimated that, by the end of 2002, a total of US$500 million had accumulated.[20] This lack of critical funds led to a growing budget deficit. By mid-2002, the PA was operating on forced credit from the private sector, which was suffering from a severe drop in demand brought on by Israeli closures and was struggling to service its own bank loans. As a result, suppliers started to service the PA only against cash, and the PA was unable to finance its budgetary appropriations and monthly salary payments for public sector workers.

Concomitantly, there were overarching internal political challenges. Arafat and other PA leaders were perceived to be moving very slowly with reform. This led the PLC to undertake a no-confidence motion in September 2002, which prompted the cabinet to resign preemptively. Fayyad was reinstated as finance minister in the new cabinet, and in March 2003, Abbas was appointed as prime minister. However, strong tensions between the PM and President Arafat ultimately forced Abbas to resign in September 2003, and the government of Abu Ala (Ahmed Qureia) replaced it.

A PRAGMATIC STRATEGY

Fayyad had to negotiate his way through this highly politicized environment. He explained some core principles of his strategy:

- *Focus on the structural.* Fayyad wanted to tackle the structural aspects of the PFM system instead of focusing on corruption directly. He explained: "When you get into a situation like this, people are usually looking at the 'sexier' aspects of managing the public finance question—corruption, who took what, when and how—but not this structural aspect. I was really preoccupied with that."[21]

- *Know the priorities.* Fayyad began with revenue and expenditure management. He observed: "There are elements without which you cannot have a well-functioning public finance system. Conceptually, unless you have central treasury operations, unless you have consolidation of your revenues, and unless you are executing expenditures within a budgetary framework, you do not have much of a public finance system to speak of."[22]

- *Be opportunistic.* At the same time, Fayyad adopted a flexible view, recognizing that he could not *a priori* determine the sequencing of reforms or have control over the entire process. He explained: "You are working within a system of deeply entrenched habits—not good ones—so you basically have one of two choices. Either to come in and say, 'this is what I want to do. Either it's done, or I'm out,' which is what everyone was expecting, or maybe even banking on. Or, you could be opportunistic: do what you can, as soon as you can do it, wherever you can do it. I chose the latter way."[23]

- *Generate credibility from the start.* Fayyad wanted to generate confidence in the reform agenda by taking specific, quick steps that would signal intent. He explained: "I have learned about the need to move fast and make an impression. It gets more difficult with time, not easier. You need to use your success as a stepping-stone. Success breeds success."[24]

Fayyad decided to begin by "stopping the hemorrhage." The starting point was the consolidation of PA accounts.

CONSOLIDATING PA ACCOUNTS

Two key issues pertaining to the consolidation of PA accounts were the need for a strong central treasury and the creation of the Palestinian Investment Fund (PIF).

Central Treasury. A basic prerequisite of a solid public finance system is a central treasury that controls all public finance operations, whether on the revenue or the expenditure side. Hence, the starting point for Fayyad was to ensure that all revenues came into the Central Treasury account. While reforms in 1999 had led to some consolidation of revenue streams, the PA still had multiple accounts where revenues were being deposited. A number of money-making ministries that collected revenues retained these funds and did not transfer them to central accounts. In the absence of a proper accounting framework, the scope for impropriety was significant.

The banking system played an important role. Fayyad issued a circular through the Palestinian Monetary Authority, instructing all banks that all government accounts had to be fed into one central account. Any checks issued directly by line ministries had to be blocked. Hence, the banks were legally obligated to ensure that funds were transferred to the central account. Following this move, Fayyad issued a "For Your Information" to all the relevant ministries about the change, arguing that this indirect approach was the most efficient one. Instead of tackling the problem "at the source" (that is, with ministries, who may have had incentives to challenge and disobey the change), he employed an administrative mechanism to achieve the result.[25]

This move also sent a very important signal about the role of the MOF. In contrast to the previous system, the MOF would exercise oversight over all PA finances. Fayyad recalls: "Everybody knew that if they wanted something they had to come to the MOF—that was really basic. When I issued that directive, money started to come in, and that's when they realized there was a central source of funding, and then we started to pay them out of the treasury. They started to get used to it."

The Palestinian Investment Fund. Another major reform centered on the creation of the PIF. The handling of PA assets had been a particular source of contention for those concerned about corruption. As early as 2000, a Higher Investment Council was formed and mandated to set up the PIF.[26] However, this objective was not realized. Those involved in these commercial activities were well connected, powerful personalities in the PA bureaucracy and security establishment. The potential for opposition was significant, and such reforms needed to be handled diplomatically.

Within the first months of his appointment, Fayyad moved forward on this issue, adopting a conciliatory approach. He emphasized the forward-looking objective of building institutions and proper systems instead of an investigative approach of identifying sources of corruption. Within two months of Fayyad's appointment, the Articles of Associations of the PIF were drafted, and the organization was formally established in October 2002. A board of directors was appointed with the Minister of Finance as ex-officio chair. New bylaws ensured that it was illegal for the PA to be engaged in commercial activities outside the PIF or to have income diverted from the Treasury.

Sensitive to past concerns about the management of these assets, Fayyad and the new board engaged two external institutions. Standard and Poor's undertook a full valuation of PA assets and the Democracy Council in the United States conducted a transparency assessment. Fayyad recalls: "So the consolidation process began, going to this company and that company, finding out how much the PA owns, what is it valued at and record it. We did this, very impressively, and all the while not being seen as threatening to the regime or the system at all."[27] The valuation of assets as of January 1, 2003, amounted to US$633 million, including sixty-seven commercial entities and liquid assets.[28] By January 2003, the work was complete.

EXPENDITURE CONTROL

Another major problem related to the issuance of Treasury checks, as the PA was issuing checks without sufficient funds. Thus, Fayyad began by undertaking "simple administrative steps" to improve the system. He explained his approach:

I gathered people who were involved in the check writing process. I told each of them to continue what they do. There were no changes, except for the person who sends the check to the bank. I instructed him to put the check in his drawer, and advised him that at the end of every day, he would be instructed on the total value of the checks that could be sent to the banks depending on the availability of funds in the Treasury. The check had to be accompanied with a note specifying beneficiary name, check number, etc.[29]

By implementing this method, Fayyad aimed to bring the check issuing process under the full control of the MOF and remove the discretionary power that was previously in the hands of commercial banks. In so doing, he also reduced the scope for rent seeking in the disbursement process. This process was not without its challenges. Some senior officials within the MOF bureaucracy had an incentive to maintain the prior system and could intervene in the work of lower ranking staff. To deal with this problem, Fayyad issued a statement to the press that the MOF would never again issue a bad check, and senior officers were strictly prohibited from interfering in the designated check-issuance process.

This example is illustrative of how Fayyad tried to tackle internal opposition within the bureaucracy. He was working in an environment in which a heavily politicized staff enjoyed civil service protections. He was also trying to introduce a new professional culture in which adherence to institutional principles and agendas took precedence over personal and political loyalties. The internal opposition could not be dismissed easily, as many of those resisting his proposed changes also had significant political clout within Fatah.

Soon after he came to his job, he promised his employees that he would not fire any of them and would give each an opportunity to demonstrate their commitment to the reforms underway. If staff were unwilling to comply, he simply redirected work away from them. In doing so, he reduced their power in the day-to-day operations of the ministry while allowing them to physically stay in their post. He considered this the most politically feasible way of "cleaning the system."

Fayyad also tried to maximize political support. He wanted to bring credibility to the system by honoring checks and reducing PA debts despite the lack of liquidity. He explained:

Since we were in a tight liquidity situation, I thought what we should do is pay people who had smaller debts. This covered a much wider segment of people and targeted the less-fortunate segment of society. That also gave the program public support. There is nothing of reform in a structural sense about this. This is a question of decision-making, to better take stock of where you are and how best to manage the situation. So I decided, let's really spend most of the money on people who were owed small amounts.[30]

BUDGET AND FINANCIAL DISCLOSURE

Significant reforms were made in the budget process. The IMF's 2003 assessment identified major improvements in several areas. The first was in the comprehensiveness of the budget, which now included macroeconomic parameters, comparisons to actual performance in 2001 and 2002, PIF profits, employment data, limitations on civil service hiring, and public investment expenditures. Another improvement enhanced transparency by posting the budget speech and budget data on the MOF website, along with monthly data on budget execution. Other reforms included eliminating the significant discretionary funds allocated to the president's office and introducing a budget law that banned the MOF from borrowing from the central bank.[31]

For Fayyad, these reforms were not merely a process to improve the technical tools of public financial management; they were fundamental to promote the concept of accountability. Of the 2003 budget, he recollected:

Here is something that people do not eat or drink. Information you publish makes little difference to someone on a hand-to-mouth type of existence. Whether you publish information or not, they cannot read it or eat it. But my political sense is that it made a difference. It mattered to people—partly because we made it so. We said, "It's your money, you really need to know what happened to it."[32]

He also tried to generate domestic political support for reforms by linking them to the broader struggle to create a viable Palestinian state. He explained: "This was about a project for national liberation and building towards statehood, so linking what you do to that broader goal, which is something of value and importance to everyone, was always important. So now we really have a key building block of the public finance system."[33]

While the extent to which this resonated among ordinary Palestinians is debatable, Fayyad was attempting to address a very sensitive issue for ordinary households: the PA's mismanagement of public finances.

The improved financial disclosure fostered significant enthusiasm and good will among donors. It addressed a fundamental concern that had long troubled the international community. According to Fayyad, after President Bush commented about the PA's move to publish their budget online, "people started to think of finance as really something on the mend in Palestine, both internationally and domestically."[34] This reputation gave Fayyad the necessary leverage to generate external political support, which ultimately translated into much needed financial inflows.

As noted earlier, Israel's withholding of Palestinian clearance revenues since December 2000 had been one of the major contributors to the PA's dire fiscal situation in mid-2002. The credible progress of reform generated significant support in the American administration, which subsequently encouraged Israel to release revenues. Israel heeded this push and started the regular release of monthly clearance revenues from early 2003.[35]

THE PETROLEUM COMMISSION

As the reform program gained credibility, Fayyad began taking on some of the more contentious issues. The Petroleum Commission (PC) had been the monopoly supplier of petroleum products in WBG since 1996. Managed as a stand-alone entity outside the jurisdiction of any PA monitoring institution, its profits were directed outside the budget. The PC was known to exercise its monopoly power and engage in a number of uncompetitive practices, including differential pricing, product alteration, authoritative licensing policies for distributors (that is, gas stations), and imposing some form of partnership on gas stations as a precondition to licensing. Their pricing policy, which attempted to maximize profits, also created incentives for cross-border smuggling and unofficial sales of petroleum products. This resulted in lost revenues and excise taxes for the PA.[36]

Fayyad recognized that these reforms would be difficult. But he took on the challenge precisely because of the significant revenues it was generating and the potential positive impacts of these reforms on people's daily lives. As a first step, Fayyad notified the head of the PC that all monthly profits had to be transferred to the MOF. In the first month, the PC transferred US$5 million to the MOF. The next month, similarly, US$5 million was transferred to the Treasury. Fayyad became suspicious—why was exactly the same amount transferred from one month to the next? He realized there was no possibility of fixing the system unless he took serious action. He ordered all PC accounts to be transferred to the MOF and froze their accounts in the spring of 2003.[37] The PC was then brought under the full control of the MOF in June 2003, followed by a change in management and governance structure and a full audit of its financial transactions.

By bringing the PC into the MOF, Fayyad transformed its incentives from profit maximization for the commission to revenue maximization for the state. As a result, one of the first steps he took after the take-over was to change the PC's pricing regime. He eliminated the monopolistic pricing structure. Product prices were reduced by decreasing the profit margin as well as by renegotiating prices with the Israeli supplier. The objective was to regain the market share lost from smuggling and unofficial sales, and the strategy proved successful. Within a month, official sales increased dramatically and were accompanied by proportional increases in VAT and excise taxes, thereby increasing Treasury revenues. Fayyad views this as one of his greatest successes: "Here is a very good example where reform meant something concrete: people started to pay much less for oil, relative to before."[38]

PAYROLL AND PROCUREMENT IN THE SECURITY FORCES

The payment and procurement methods in the security services were among the most contentious practices that required reform. According to Dr. Jihad Al Wazir, "Arafat viewed money and security as two critical things to his authority. A system of allegiance based on personalized relations was created. Arafat did not want intervention in this, because he considered this as interference in his domain."[39]

Payroll. Recognizing that cash-based payments to security personnel opened the system up to significant corruption, Fayyad pursued a reform that would institute direct bank transfers. But President Arafat and other security sector leaders were not willing to cooperate. He held a meeting with the security chiefs in Gaza. Two of them had already allied themselves with Fayyad, but the others refused to submit employee bank details, stating that it would jeopardize the security of their personnel.

Fayyad then appealed to the PLC to push this reform through, and provided the names of all the security officials who were unwilling to comply. For the security sector workers, in fact, direct bank transfers represented an advantage, as it ensured timely salary payment and allowed them to qualify for bank loans. When the security officials continued to oppose this reform, Fayyad decided to publicly announce the elimination of the "*intifada* tax" on all PA employees if the security chiefs agreed to the necessary reforms. But this announcement was unfortunately timed; a political battle was brewing between Arafat and Prime Minister Abbas, and so the push for reform had to temporarily take a back seat.[40] By the end of August 2003, four security organizations belonging to the Interior Ministry had accepted this scheme. The forces under the president's control did not agree.

Lobbying directly with President Arafat was required. Fayyad and other reformers emphasized to Arafat that the current cash-based system allowed corrupt officials to benefit and worked against the interests of lower ranking security sector personnel. This lobbying, together with pressure from the donors, ultimately led to success in 2004. The donor community established the Public Reform Trust Fund in 2004, as a budget support mechanism to the PA, but such support was made conditional on reforms and meeting certain benchmarks.[41] Among them was the full implementation of the 2004 budget law, which stipulated that salary payments of all security personnel were to be directly deposited into bank accounts. Using this provision as leverage, the MOF finally succeeded in February 2004 in getting the president's approval that all salaries of the National Security Forces (under the president's control) had to be paid through bank transfers.[42]

Procurement. Supply to the security forces was monopolized by one agency, and there were significant concerns about impropriety. The committee responsible for security sector procurement was brought under the oversight of a centralized procurement agency at the MOF, and procurement was opened to a bidding process. Fayyad gradually bankrupted the monopoly until it ceased operation.

While significant scope remains for further improvements in procurement, these reforms were a step in the right direction. They also reflect Fayyad's overall reform strategy captured in Jihad al Wazir's words, as one of a "gradual, systematic approach, [that] got the job done." Al Wazir elaborates that though Fayyad was a technocrat, "[he] learned very quickly how to be a politician. Knowing where to push, where to back off . . . By avoiding the dramatics, being consistent . . . By seeking consensus whether internationally or locally. It is a testament to his political skills."[43]

INSTITUTIONAL REORGANIZATION

To achieve fundamental public finance reform, Fayyad decided to centralize MOF operations under his oversight. This significantly improved financial responsibility, and by 2004, institutional reform of the MOF itself came on the agenda. Dr. Jihad al Wazir, the son of a prominent Fatah political figure, was brought on board as the deputy finance minister to manage the reform.

Al Wazir worked on strengthening the organizational structure of the MOF and its internal processes. The MOF was reorganized into two basic centers: revenue and treasury. Departments were classified within these centers to improve coordination. New departments were also created, such as the General Directorate of Accounts (which collected the data of all departments), a quality assurance department, and a department of assets (which registered all public assets). Internal processes for daily operations were also improved, such as those related to the processing of payments. Front offices were established and procedural reforms put in place. Some staff, dubbed "angels," were designated to ensure that the new procedures were being followed.[44]

The End Game: Late 2005 and 2006

While Fayyad advanced the PFM reform agenda further than many had dared hope, by 2005 a host of dynamics began slowing this progress. The broader political and economic situation was deteriorating. With the 2006 PLC elections looming, the Fatah leadership was becoming desperate. They began resorting to a series of populist measures to shore up support among core Palestinian constituencies. Fayyad correctly recognized that such measures were fiscally unsustainable and risked alienating the donor community, yet he was increasingly unable to convince his colleagues within the government of the looming fiscal dangers.

Reforms to contain the public sector wage bill were among the most challenging. In the six years since the start of the second *intifada*, total public sector employment grew by nearly 70 percent. Following wage increases in 2003, the PA agreed in 2004 to a wage bill containment plan (WBCP) for the 2004–2006 period. Adherence to the WBCP was established as a benchmark for disbursements from the World Bank-administered Public Finance Reform Trust Fund. Other steps were taken, including moving payroll management from the General Personnel Council (GPC) to the MOF; passing a resolution through the cabinet to enforce public sector retirement at age sixty; and changing the criteria for pensions.

However, powerful dynamics got in the way. Demographic pressures, combined with a sharp reduction in work permits in Israel and the private sector's limited capacity to absorb new entrants into the labor market, put pressure on the PA to provide employment for the 40,000 workers entering the labor force annually. With the severe economic downturn following the second *intifada*, pressures on the public sector to serve as a buffer against job losses intensified. Moreover, movement restrictions between cities and villages of the West Bank led to labor market inefficiencies, as it created the need for multiple health centers, schools, and public offices at the local level.

Also, in election mode, labor unions demanded salary increases with the threat of strikes. In the end, the government capitulated and approved major salary increases. As a result, in 2005, average wages increased by 13 percent for civil sector personnel, adding to the 20 percent increase they had already received in 2003 with the implementation of the civil service law. Average wages increased by 28 percent for security sector personnel, and around 3,666 employees were added to the civil service in 2005 alone.[45]

Control over the security sector was much more difficult. The success of wage bill containment was directly contingent on broader reforms to restructure the security services, but this did not substantially move forward. The independent task force monitoring the progress of reforms concluded that an initial flurry of measures did not lead to a sustained reform process. Despite severe budgetary restraints and the threat of penalties from the international donor community, the PA expanded police recruitment throughout 2005.

The hiring and wage hikes placed the PA in clear violation of its agreement with donors. According to World Bank estimates, the total wage bill surpassed US$1 billion in 2005, up from US$870 million in 2004. By the end of 2005, the wage bill represented nearly 23 percent of the WBG annual GDP and 82 percent of gross government revenues.[46] The PA was becoming dangerously dependent on external sources of finance for not only its investment budget but its recurrent expenditures as well. Donor disbursements through the World Bank Trust Fund were suspended.

In December 2005, Fayyad ran for the 2006 parliamentary elections under the party he cofounded, called the Third Way, which received 2.4 percent of the vote. The election resulted in Hamas forming a new government.

ONGOING CHALLENGES

While the reforms championed by Fayyad (and subsequently by al Wazir) from 2002 to 2006 were largely successful, they did not do enough to strengthen public oversight and to better link the development budget to national priorities.

Public Oversight of PA Finances. The 2002–2005 reforms achieved major strides in terms of establishing an internal audit division, posting internal financial controllers in line ministries, and promoting finance and budget transparency. But more work was necessary to strengthen external audit, to enhance parliament's role in financial oversight, and to combat corruption.

- *External audit.* An effective and fully operational external audit institution that could maintain oversight over government financial activity was not established. While a General Audit Institution was created in 1995, it lacked independence and capacity. The auditor was politically connected to Arafat and well entrenched in his position.[47] In 2004, the PLC passed law No. 15, creating a new external audit institution, the Financial and Administrative Control Bureau. Unfortunately, the new law lacked a champion, so implementation proceeded slowly. The Minister of Finance believed that development of this institution was the responsibility of the PLC, the president, or the prime minister's office rather than the MOF, given its position as an auditor.[48]

- *Parliament's oversight role.* The PLC Committee on Budget and Financial Affairs had important roles in budget development, budget execution, and follow-up. It could review the draft budget law; propose reductions in expenditure; recommend approval or rejection of the law to the PLC; question the government on financial plans and fiscal stability; discuss and approve proposed budget amendments; and undertake oversight of budget implementation. But the PLC was not able to adequately undertake and sustain these functions, despite attempts made in the 2002–2005 reforms to improve PLC engagement in these processes. Reforms did not succeed due to a combination of internal political dynamics within the PA, weak technical capacity on the part of the PLC itself, and the highly volatile revenue environment. By 2006, a variety of factors, including uncertainty surrounding domestic revenue flows and lack of capacity due to a major civil servant strike, rendered the passing of the budget impossible.

- *Combating corruption.* While the 2002–2005 reforms reduced the scope for corrupt practices, dedicated institutions and mechanisms to investigate and penalize corruption were not developed. Existing bodies involved in corruption issues, such as the public prosecution or Office of the Commissioner for Illicit Gains, were restricted due to limited mandates and resources.

Linking Resource Allocation to National Priorities. Another core area that did not witness marked improvement was integrating budgeting with policymaking and planning—an acute challenge given the volatility of PA revenues and the high levels of donor financing. However, among the positive developments was the inclusion of nearly US$212 million of capital expenditures financed by donors in the 2003 budget. The integration was possible only to the extent that it captured donor finances that were deposited in subaccounts within the Central Treasury account. In November 2005, the cabinet went a step further and approved a plan to implement an integrated budgeting framework at a time when the G8 had pledged to provide financial support. Its objectives were to develop a planning and budgeting process that integrated existing development planning processes with recurrent budgeting processes.

A Ministry of Planning (MOP) analysis in 2005 identified numerous challenges in this area. These included: the institutionalized separation of planning and budgeting; the absence of a policy framework at the national level; weak cabinet and PLC engagement with medium-term development policy and planning; organizational rivalries within the government and between the public and private sectors; and incompatibility between the accounting systems used by some government ministries and those of the MOF. In addition, the analysis identified that a plethora of bilateral donor assistance created incentives to adopt a "project-driven approach to development as opposed to a policy and outcome-driven approach." Donors themselves often contributed to an uncoordinated approach by interfacing directly with line ministries and other governmental institutions instead of ensuring sufficient MOF and MOP engagement. As a result, comprehensive information on the total level of donor-financed capital expenditures was not available.

Conclusion

Following the Hamas victory in January 2006, the international community boycotted the newly elected government. Donor finance stopped for a period, as did the transfer of clearance revenues by Israel. External donor finance was eventually redirected to pass through the Office of the President directly to employees, beneficiaries, or suppliers, reversing years of work to build up the MOF's capacity to manage PA finances.

Sixteen months later, in the wake of the split between Hamas in Gaza and Fatah in the West Bank, Fayyad was appointed as both the prime minister and finance minister of the emergency government established in the West Bank. Fayyad subsequently focused on several ongoing PFM reforms. In the West Bank, he reestablished the Central Treasury account and ensured that all finances would be channeled to this account. The MOF also reestablished monthly reporting and monitoring of PA revenues and expenditures and recreated financial statements for 2006. Another major task was to address the operational challenges resulting from the Gaza–West Bank split.

In 2007, he developed the Palestinian Reform and Development Plan (PRDP). This three-year initiative set a broad, reformist agenda for the West Bank. It focused on improving the institutional capacities of the Palestinian National Authority (PNA); rebuilding health and education systems; economic and private sector development; infrastructure investment; and shifting fiscal priorities. This first PRDP attributed the need for a "restart" of reforms on "the unstable political environment," indicating that "the embargo on international assistance in 2006 and early 2007 contributed to the reversal of progress that had been made in reforming the PNA."[49]

Donor support was critical in this period. The budget deficit in 2008 had swelled to 28 percent of GDP, but this was manageable thanks to increased donor flows. But these levels of donor support were unsustainable, and the delicate interplay between a declining budget deficit and declining budget support has been a dominant feature of fiscal management ever since.

Along with the PRDP, a new role of Accountant General was created at the MOF, tasked with supervising the Treasury's key functions. Steps were also taken to address the lack of financial statements. In 2009, an initial set of statements was prepared based on International Public-Sector Accounting Standards (IPSAS), which were not suitable for an audit opinion. Because of disruptions during the Hamas period, these were the first accounts presented since 2003. Over subsequent years, the quality of these accounts improved, and the State Audit Office provided a qualified opinion on the accounts in 2011.

The PRDP was renewed in April 2011. However, Fayyad—the reformist champion—was replaced as finance minister in May 2012 by Nabil Kassis, who stayed in the post until his resignation in March 2013. Upon his resignation, Kassis cited his inability to tackle the burgeoning public deficit as his reason for leaving. The 2013 budget deficit had declined dramatically, to 14 percent of GDP, but with donor support also declining, further action was needed. However, politicians and labor unions objected to austerity measures. Ultimately, Fayyad resigned as prime minister in the summer of 2013, and the Finance portfolio was assigned to Shukri Bishara.

Bishara prioritized and made progress addressing the fiscal challenge, and the fiscal deficit declined to less than 8 percent in 2017. However, with a simultaneous reduction in donor support, the fiscal position remained precarious. Given the priority placed on fiscal management and the departure from the MOF of key members of Fayyad's reform team, progress on public finance reform has been limited. Although a challenging political environment has diminished the appetite for significant reform within the MOF in recent years, further strengthening of financial management is needed, particularly in linking budgeting to planning and in establishing accurate and timely accounting and fiscal reporting.

Although their implementation often encountered fierce resistance, many within WBG have argued that Fayyad's reforms did not go far enough. Hamas attacked him for leaving them with an empty treasury and an excess of public debt when they entered office in 2006. While incomplete, the PFM reforms undertaken between 2002 and 2005 have shown themselves to be among the most successful and enduring reforms in WBG. They also rank among the decade's most far-reaching PFM reforms in the broader Middle East and North Africa region. It is all the more impressive that they took place against a backdrop of acute conflict, instability, and political and economic crisis.

Notes

The authors would like to express their gratitude to Nithya Nagarajan for her excellent and extensive inputs into earlier versions of this case.

1. Said K. Aburish, *Arafat: From Defender to Dictator* (New York: Bloomsbury Publishing, 2004).

2. Ibrahim Abu-Lughod, "Public Administration and Civil Service Reform in Palestine: Drivers of Change," Discussion Draft, Institute of International Studies, Birzeit University, May 2007.

3. Menachem Klein, "By Conviction, Not by Infliction: The Internal Debate Over Reforming the Palestinian Authority," *Middle East Journal* 57, no. 2 (Spring 2003).

4. Nathan J. Brown, "The Palestinian Reform Agenda," Peaceworks 48, United States Institute of Peace, December 2002.

5. Mushtaq H. Khan et al., *State Formation in Palestine: Viability and Governance During a Social Transformation* (London: Routledge, 2004).

6. Abu-Lughod, "Public Administration and Civil Service Reform in Palestine."

7. For more examples, see Mushtaq Khan et al., *State Formation in Palestine*, chap. 4.

8. Interview with Ghassan Khatib, May, June 2008.

9. IMF, "West Bank and Gaza: Economic Performance and Reform under Conflict Conditions," Washington, DC, September 2003.

10. IMF, "West Bank and Gaza."

11. Interview with Prime Minister Salam Fayyad, November 2007.

12. World Bank, "West Bank and Gaza Public Expenditure Review: From Crisis to Greater Fiscal Independence," Washington, DC, 2007.

13. Interview with Azmi Shuaybi, December 2007.

14. Independent Task Force on Strengthening Palestinian Public Institutions, "Reforming the Palestinian Authority Concluding Report," 2006.

15. IMF, "West Bank and Gaza," p. 34.

16. World Bank, "Twenty-Seven Months – Intifada, Closures, and Palestinian Economic Crisis: An Assessment," Washington DC, 2003.

17. International Crisis Group, "The Meanings of Palestinian Reform," Amman/Washington, November 12, 2002.

18. Interview with Ghassan Khatib, May and June 2008.

19. Independent Task Force Report on Strengthening Palestinian Public Institutions, "Reforming the Palestinian Authority: An Update," 2004, pp. 8–9.

20. IMF, "West Bank and Gaza," p. 71.

21. Transcript of Rami Khouri interview with Prime Minister Salam Fayyad, October 2008.

22. Ibid.

23. Ibid.

24. Interview with Prime Minister Salam Fayyad, November 2007.

25. Ibid.

26. Interview with Waleed Najab, former board member of PCSC and former chief operating officer and CEO at PIF, June 2008.

27. Interview with Prime Minister Salam Fayyad, November 2007.

28. IMF, "West Bank and Gaza."

29. Interview with Prime Minister Salam Fayyad, November 2007.

30. Transcript of Rami Khouri interview with Prime Minister Salam Fayyad, October 2008.

31. Interview with Dr. Jihad al Wazir, June 2008.

32. Transcript of Rami Khouri interview with Prime Minister Salam Fayyad, October 2008.

33. Ibid.

34. Ibid.

35. IMF, "West Bank and Gaza," pp. 72, 91.

36. IMF, "West Bank and Gaza."

37. Interview with Prime Minister Fayyad, November 2007.

38. Transcript of Rami Khouri interview with Prime Minister Salam Fayyad, October 2008.

39. Interview with Dr. Jihad al Wazir, June 2008.

40. This paragraph and the previous two were drawn from James Bennet, "The Radical Bean Counter," *New York Times*, May 25, 2003.

41. IMF, "West Bank and Gaza."

42. Independent Task Force Report on Strengthening Palestinian Public Institutions, "Reforming the Palestinian Authority: An Update," 2004.

43. Interview with Dr. Jihad al Wazir, June 2008.

44. Ibid.

45. World Bank, "West Bank and Gaza Public Expenditure Review," chap. 2.

46. Ibid.

47. Interview with Karim Nashashibi, June 2008.

48. Interview with Claus Pram Astrup, June 2008.

49. Palestinian Reform and Development Plan (PRDP), "Building a Palestinian State: Towards Peace and Prosperity," Executive Summary, December 17, 2007, www.un.org/unispal/document/auto-insert-206297/.

FOUR

Downsizing the Public Sector

Morocco's Voluntary Retirement Program

KHALID EL MASSNAOUI

MHAMED BIYGAUTANE

SIMILAR TO OTHER MIDDLE East and North Africa (MENA) countries, where the public sector is a primary "source of employment for a relatively large portion of the population," the Moroccan government faced significant fiscal constraints in early 2000 due to rising wage bills.[1] In 2005, its wage bill consumed around 11.2 percent of GDP. Morocco's civil service was not particularly large by global and regional standards, either in terms of absolute numbers or as a proportion of the labor force, but a series of competitive pay increases between different cadres exacerbated expenses. Given the financial pressures Morocco was facing, it was necessary to look for a solution to this unsustainable phenomenon.

Against this backdrop, the government of Morocco, with assistance from the World Bank, launched a comprehensive Public Administration Reform Program (PARP) initiative in 2003. The PARP aimed to improve budgeting efficiency and human resource management while reducing the burden of the wage bill on the budget. The voluntary retirement program was an essential element in placing the wage bill on a sustainable fiscal trajectory. Morocco implemented its VRP in two completely different cycles.

The first program was designed in 2003 and implemented in 2004. However, due to numerous shortfalls in its design and administration, it failed to achieve its targeted reduction of 20,000 employees by 2005.

The Moroccan government quickly learned from its past mistakes and immediately launched a second program, called *Intilaka* (literally meaning "the start"), in reference to a new beginning in the careers of retired employees envisioned under the new scheme. The second VRP had the short-term goal of streamlining the civil service and containing the wage bill at fiscally sustainable levels. More than 50,500 civil servants applied to the program (10 percent of the central government civil service) and 38,600 became beneficiaries (7.6 percent of civil servants). Thus, the program succeeded in achieving immediate fiscal gains by reducing the number of civil servants. Nevertheless, it was not successful in achieving the decrease in the wage bill's weight on national GDP or the retention of top talent.

This chapter reviews the performance of Morocco's VRP. After describing how the Moroccan government's attempts to contain the wage bill gave birth to the VRP, it details how the first and second VRPs were implemented. It then discusses the strengths and weaknesses in the design and implementation of each program and analyzes the financial and fiscal gains of the second VRP as well as its economic achievements.

Government's Evolving Role in the Labor Market

Since the 1980s, the Moroccan government has implemented numerous policies regulating public sector hiring. A restrictive employment strategy and incentives for early retirement became the two most important public sector staffing policies. Recruitment slowed down in the mid-1990s in an attempt to consolidate restructuring efforts in state-owned enterprises (SOEs) and to contain the central government's rising wage bill. Furthermore, in the context of the liberalization and privatization policies launched in the early 1990s, SOEs implemented early retirement schemes to complement the restrictive recruitment policies. These initiatives resulted in the early retirement of some 25,000 employees over the 1994–2005 period, which represented 17 percent of total SOE employment.

Recruitment was curbed by the interdiction of low-ranked personnel whose activities were progressively contracted out. Also, all vacant positions resulting from normal personnel attrition were canceled out. The adoption of a no-net recruitment policy ensured that the new hires did not exceed normal attrition, thereby stabilizing the overall number of public employees. As positions became vacant through attrition and were canceled, new recruitment took place only where there were urgent needs—typically in social sectors such as education, health, and, to a lesser extent, security.

The new changes resulted in the government playing a reduced role in the labor market, with the proportion of public sector workers to the general labor force shrinking steadily over roughly fifteen years. With 800,000 civil employees in 2004, the size of the public sector relative to the labor force in Morocco was smaller than that of any other country in the MENA region. In 2004, it accounted for 14.2 percent of the urban labor force as compared with 17.6 percent in 1990. However, despite measures taken from 2002 to 2004 to contain the central government's civil personnel, it remained an important employer in the public sector, with a share of more than 59 percent of total employees.

But the Moroccan public sector paid wages that were more than twice those in the private sector. They were three times the minimum wage and six times GDP per capita. The purchasing power of public wages averaged a 3.4 percent annual increase over the period from 1990 to 2004, while real GDP per capita increased by only 0.3 percent a year. These differences reflected the many rounds of wage revaluation—born of social dialogue agreements negotiated with trade unions and employer associations—that had taken place in the public sector during the previous decade.

The high wage bill-to-GDP ratio could be explained by the high wages paid to senior staff who benefited from outdated statutes governing recruitment, pay, and promotion. Civil servants still relied mostly on seniority for promotions and wage increases rather than skills or productivity gains. As a result, trade unions used loopholes in the system to their advantage to obtain increases that went beyond maintaining the purchasing power of wages. The nominal average wage increased by 5.5 percent annually over the period from 1990 to 2004, while inflation stood at 3.2 percent, denoting an increase of real wages by 2.3 percent annually.

The First Voluntary Retirement Program

In 2003, the government of Morocco approached the World Bank with a request for quick loan disbursement to support the implementation of its reform program. The loan would address the key constraints impacting the effectiveness of public service delivery, support key goals of private sector development and poverty reduction, and ensure macroeconomic stability by controlling the wage bill. In response, the Public Administration Reform Loan I (PARL) programmatic development loan was approved by the World Bank in 2004. A series of subsequent loans followed, as PARL II was approved in 2006 to build on the public administration reform framework initiated by the government in 2003,[2] and PARL III and IV were approved in 2011.[3]

A key component of the PARL operations was the consolidation and control of payroll. Measures were identified under this component to keep the wage bill under control, reducing it in the interim. They included an early retirement mechanism, along with yearly quantitative restraints on recruitment and promotion aimed at avoiding the bottlenecks experienced under the current extremely restrictive system. The establishment of a voluntary retirement mechanism was studied by the Ministry of Finance (MOF) on the assumption that 20,000 to 60,000 staff would participate in the program.

The VRP was one of the most important components of the PARL process. The VRP was the central element in helping to retrench and streamline the civil service and control the wage bill. The initiative originally aimed at reducing the central government by 35,000 civil servants over a period of three to four years, of which 5,000 would retire in 2004 and 15,000 would retire in the following year. However, only 696 civil servants retired under the original scheme—well below the anticipated level of 20,000 employees expected to exit by 2005.

The failure of the first VRP operation can be attributed to several factors: an unattractive incentive package; a limited targeted population; the taxation of severance payments; and an ineffective information campaign. The pension benefit parameters were those of the existing pension regulations, which provided the equivalent of 2 percent of annual gross salary for each year of service to the early retiree. Overall, few civil servants opted to retire early under those provisions, which were viewed as insufficient. The severance payment, calculated at one month's gross salary for each year of service, was not enough to compensate for the low pension.

The package was made even less attractive by the decision to limit the eligible population to those in the lower salary ranks (Grades 1 to 9) who met the seniority requirement for pension benefits. This translated into relatively low net severance benefits, a ceiling of thirty months on severance payments benefiting Grades 6 to 9, and the imposition of income taxes on such payments. Finally, the information campaign was timid at best. It was limited to a brochure explaining the eligibility criteria and financial package, along with a posting of the related decree and the ministerial orders. This limited communication effort meant that most public sector employees were unaware of the program's existence.

Another factor that led to the failure of the first VRP was a lack of co-operation among the main actors in the government. The MOF and the Ministry of Modernization of the Public Sector (MPSM) were known to disagree on the sequencing of the various components of the reform. The latter was of the view that it was important to first implement a staffing strategy and redeploy civil servants on the basis of the renewed role of the state. This directed efforts at de-concentration, performance management, and decentralizing distribution of the civil service distribution away from the Rabat and Casablanca regions.

The MOF was concerned about addressing urgent fiscal challenges, most notably putting the budget deficit on a sustainable path by containing expenditures, of which the wage bill was the principal component. This led to the prime minister's decision to implement the first VRP without due regard to the resistance of the MPSM. Furthermore, during the design phase, the MOF carried out the preparatory work internally, without adequate consultation with major stakeholders.

Learning from VRP I; Re-Investing in VRP II

After the failure of the first VRP, the government acknowledged the importance of strong organization, coordination, and supervision in any endeavor of such size and importance. The prime minister proposed a "technical" reshuffle in June 2004 to focus on the ongoing major reforms, including the PARP and VRP. One of the main objectives was to provide strong political support for the new initiative. A new MPSM minister, Mohamed Boussaid, was appointed with a clear mandate to advance civil service reform, especially the VRP. Minister Boussaid was already known as an effective leader from supervising earlier reforms, including the restructuring of public agencies and SOEs. The mistakes from the first VRP were studied carefully and translated into various institutional, legal, and administrative mechanisms that were put in place prior to the launch of the second VRP.

Roles of the Main Actors. The prime minister stood as the head of the operation in his capacity as the president of the Strategic Committee of Administrative Reforms.[4] He provided guidance and instructions to ensure a streamlined and efficient VRP process. The MPSM was in charge of the Secretariat of the Strategic Committee of Administrative Reforms, the central commission, and the central committee. These were the main actors charged with the responsibility of monitoring the overall implementation of the VRP operations. The MPSM also regularly organized meetings between the various parties and partners in the process and served as the central repository of information, which permitted regular preparation of statistics on the progress of implementation. This was possible because the MPSM received application copies, requests, and lists of successful applicants on a daily basis. The MPSM continued to carry out communication activities throughout the process, reaching out to television and radio programs and holding press conferences. Other bodies involved in the process included:

- A budget department in the MOF, which ensured that follow-ups on all issues had a financial impact.

- A state expenditures authority (SEA), tasked with ensuring the conformity and legality of requests submitted and approved by the ministries.

- A principal paymaster office (PPO) that issued severance payment orders for the beneficiaries.

- The Pension Fund (PF), which processed the documents of authorized applicants, prepared their retirements, and paid the pensions.

Coordinating and Supervisory Mechanisms for the Second VRP. There were three coordinating and/or supervisory bodies in charge of monitoring the voluntary retirement process:

1. The central commission, which was made up of representatives from the MPSM, MOF, and Ministry of Privatization and met once a week to solve problems arising from the implementation process and prepare reports for the prime minister.

2. The PPO.

3. The PF, whose representatives monitored and assessed the various stages of the process and facilitated coordination with the concerned administrations.

Within each ministerial department, cells were created to coordinate information, communication, and monitoring. The cell members benefited from training programs specific to this operation. Hence, their effectiveness remained high despite pressures from the influx of applications to their units. A central voluntary retirement cell was set up by the MPSM for the overall coordination of the process. This unit significantly facilitated coordination among the responsible ministries and accelerated the processing time of the applications.

A prime ministerial order was issued to clarify the VRP decree's provisions and to give guidance to ensure efficiency of implementation. The PMO defined the main steps of the VRP's process and underlined their milestones. To be eligible, applications were to be submitted over the established six-month period. In addition to submitting the original application form to their departments, the candidates sent copies to the MPSM for information and monitoring purposes, either through postal mail, fax, or email.

A precise timeframe for each phase was defined so that only a maximum of thirty days would be needed for successful applications to go through the entire process from initial submission to the SEA visa. After receiving an application, the ministerial departments had to then decide within fifteen days whether to authorize the candidate for early retirement. In most departments, it was the responsibility of the director to decide on the application. If the response was positive, then forms validating work tenure and the voluntary retirement decision had to be prepared within the same period. The proposed removal date of the applicant from the personnel list had to coincide with the end of the month in which the application was formulated without exceeding the June 30, 2005, deadline.

The PF and SEA had fifteen days to process the application and obtain clearances from their respective departments. At this stage, the main task of the PF was to assess whether the applicant had the right to a pension, and then validate their work tenure before sending the documents to the SEA. All this had to be accomplished within ten days. In turn, the SEA had only five days to process the application, decide whether or not to grant a visa, and then forward the application to the ministerial departments. The ministerial departments had to then resend the approved applicant forms immediately to the PF, which determined the pension amounts and issued payment orders.

To ensure the credibility of the VRP operation and prevent any hesitation among potential candidates, the payment process for both compensation and pension was streamlined. Hence, the PPO had to process the payment of severance compensation by the end of the month following that in which the applicant's documents were received. For its part, the PF had to start paying pensions by the end of the month. Otherwise, payments were to be made by no later than the end of the subsequent month. Beneficiaries without the right to pension would collect their employee contributions from the PF by the end of the month following that in which the documents were received.

Accompanying Support and Retraining Measures. In the spirit of the Intilaka program, the government aimed to help VRP beneficiaries in financing and starting their own small businesses. Two conventions were signed with the Banking Federation and the Ministry of Industry and Commerce. The first convention committed several large banks to consider financing under streamlined processes and favorable conditions for projects developed by the beneficiaries. The second convention with the Ministry of Industry and Commerce established a partnership framework to support the beneficiaries to create their projects. Toward this end, the Ministry of Industry and Commerce, together with the participation of regional centers for investment, organized training workshops for VRP beneficiaries. Those workshops focused on practical details related to business startup, including preparing feasibility studies, planning finances, and processing documents and loan requests. A website was also dedicated to the operation, which contained the information necessary to implement an investment project.

The Communication Campaign. The communication campaign played a pivotal role in the success of the second VRP. At the outset, a broad communication campaign was executed by a specialized agency established specifically for this purpose. The campaign consisted mostly of inserts published in the printed press and commercials diffused throughout audiovisual media. Officials organized press conferences to explain the VRP's objectives and the nature of the compensation packages, with particular emphasis upon how the program pushed for a new "start" in the private sector. Messages stressed the values of entrepreneurship and the rewards successful retirees would gain by launching investment projects. The communications effort characterized the Intilaka program as an opportunity to be seized by those privileged with the opportunity to retire.

In addition, a toll-free telephone line was available for candidates seeking additional information and explanations, and two dedicated websites were set up to support this operation. These sites included a simulation model that allowed potential candidates to calculate the financial compensation they were entitled to, along with answers to frequently asked questions (FAQs). The sites also allowed visitors to download forms, informational material, and regulations concerning the VRP. Within the framework of the communication campaign, a two-day training program was developed for 100 civil servants selected to be part of the ministerial cells in charge of information and communication. Since they were to be on the front lines of the process and had the role of advising the VRP applicants, participants were briefed on all phases of the VRP.

Legal Provisions Underpinning the Second VRP. The existing civil service pension regulations provided the legal basis for early retirement, but their provisions did not establish an appropriate incentive package in a large downsizing operation. Regulations were not set up for downsizing purposes in the first place. Rather, civil servants were allowed to retire under exceptional circumstances, such as instances of critical illness, family constraints, or firing with pension rights. A candidate for early retirement could benefit from immediate pension allowances if the minimum work tenure had been met, namely twenty-one years of service for men and fifteen for women. In the event the work tenure had not been met, the retiree was entitled to recover the total amount of his or her contributions to the PF.

The regulations surrounding the first VRP program deterred early retirement. On the one hand, evaluation of early retirement pension benefits was based on 2 percent of permanent gross salary for each year of service instead of 2.5 percent. This provision translated into a relatively large loss, amounting to 25 percent of yearly pension for early retirees. On the other hand, regulations put a ceiling on the total number of civil servants retiring early during a given year. The quota system authorized a maximum of 15 percent of civil servants within each corps to qualify for early retirement. This constraint was put in place to prevent an abrupt and unwanted drain in any category of corps in an effort to shield the pension system from severe financial shocks stemming from an eventual (although unlikely) early retirement rush. However, even after disincentives surrounding the pension regulations were relaxed, only a small number of civil servants opted for early retirement. To address this, a decree was adopted that provided a mechanism for severance payments—on an exceptional basis—for beneficiaries of the VRP program.

Cross-Ministry Management of the Program. Effective management of the program during its different processing phases was another instrumental factor behind the VRP's success. Considering the importance of the VRP and the expected large number of applications, each ministerial department had to react rapidly and organize itself for the efficient implementation and monitoring of the process. Some ministerial departments tried to introduce additional criteria as a basis for accepting or turning down an application by considering the specificity of their sectors. Most of the departments processed applications as they received them, except in those where potentially severe adverse selection problems raised fears of service disruptions. Generally, applications were examined within the set deadlines, and some departments approved all requests received. In the Departments of Interior, Agriculture, Higher Education, and Transport, acceptance rates were 100 percent, leading to the departure of between 14 to 22 percent of their workforce.

Departures of such magnitude did result in some service disruptions. Ministries tried to be parsimonious in authorizing retirement to avoid disruptions in service delivery. This was the case in primary and secondary education and health. In the Ministry of Education, it was impossible to let teachers leave during the middle of the school year, knowing there would be no feasible prospect for redeployment within such a short amount of time. Thus, the Ministry of Education did not process the applications until the end of the school year (July). At the Ministry of Health, it was relatively easy to accept applications for early retirement from medical staff in large cities, while more selectivity was required in rural areas and small towns.

Evaluation of the Second VRP

Why Was the Second VRP More Successful than the First? The Intilaka program benefited from a new incentive package and a more appropriate target population formulated in light of lessons learned from the failure of the first VRP. To enhance the attractiveness of the second VRP and ensure maximum participation, new exceptional provisions were implemented to improve severance amounts and extend the eligible population to include all civil servants (see table 4-1). Pension benefits were aligned with those that applied to normal age retirement—the equivalent of 2.5 percent of gross salary for each year of service, to be paid after reaching legal retirement age. Until retirement age was reached, the existing pension regulations for early retirement would apply—a pension equivalent to 2 percent of gross salary for each year of service.

TABLE 4-1. Comparison of the First and Second VRP Operations

	First VRP (2004)	Second VRP (2005)
Targeted Population	■ Civil servants of the central government, Grades 1 to 9 ■ Work tenure required to receive pension benefits: 21 years for men and 15 years for women ■ Exemption of civil servants that would retire for age limit reasons by the end of 2004	■ All civil servants of the central government ■ Work tenure required to receive pension benefits not a constraint ■ Exemption of civil servants that would retire for age limit reasons by the end of 2005
Pension Benefits	■ Two percent of gross salary for each year of service ■ Immediate benefit upon early retirement	■ Until the normal retirement age, 2 percent of gross salary for each year of service ■ After the age of normal retirement, 2.5 percent of gross salary for each year of service ■ If not entitled to pension, collection of employee's contribution to pension schemes
Severance Amount	■ One month for each year of service ■ A ceiling of 30 months for retirees belonging to Grades 6 to 9 ■ Total amount not to exceed 50 percent of total salary the retiree would have earned until age limit retirement if staying	■ 1.5 months for each year of service ■ A ceiling of 36 months for retirees belonging to Grades 6 and above ■ Total amount not to exceed 50 percent of total salary the retiree would have earned until age limit retirement if staying
Income Taxes on Severance Payments	Applicable	Exempt
Application Period	January 1 to May 31, 2004	January 1 to June 30, 2005

Civil servants retiring before completing the minimum work tenure that would allow them to benefit from their pension could recover their employee contributions to the PF. Severance benefits were raised by a half point to 1.5 months' salary for each year of service with an increased ceiling of thirty-six months for servants in Grades 6 and above. For all grades, however, the severance payment was not to exceed 50 percent of the total salary the beneficiary would have earned until the normal retirement age. The financial package was made more attractive for higher grade civil servants by exempting the severance payments from income taxes since, at 44 percent, the marginal tax rate was high. Unlike the first VRP experience, the quota was set at 100 percent within each corps, significantly relaxing the 15 percent constraint under the existing regulations.

A Qualitative Assessment. The technical implementation of the second VRP was undoubtedly a success.[5] At the beginning, the government encouraged all departments to speed up the processing of the first requests and settlement of payments to enhance the credibility of the process through a demonstration effect. In this regard, the government carried out communication campaigns centered on the severance payments made to the first eligible applicants. In addition, the first batch of retirees received their pensions in just a few weeks following their retirement. The government paid most of the pensions within a timeframe of four months, on average. In doing so, the personnel of the PF demonstrated impressive organization and high levels of productivity. The performance of the PF was particularly noteworthy given the large influx of pension documents from 38,600 retirees, roughly six times the number processed in any previous given year.

Many stakeholders perceived the discretion granted to managers to approve or reject an application under the "necessity of service" criterion as a weakness in the program's implementation. The implicit vision behind the VRP was to retain the most productive and skilled civil servants while offering those less skilled a way out. However, many applicants in the higher salary grades saw the generous compensation offered in the context of the VRP as an opportunity and opted out. The remaining mid-level civil servants anticipated an increased workload resulting from the retirement of their superiors and interpreted the VRP decision process as unfair. They perceived the process as penalizing good personnel who had given a lot to the administration while rewarding those who were less productive by offering them generous compensation. In the absence of any transparent and objective criteria, managers were left on their own to make judgment calls about who should stay and who should go. In most cases, applicant preference and determination to retire prevailed over the opinions of managers.

Fiscal Savings and Losses from VRP II

The second VRP was an immediate success in terms of securing important financial and fiscal gains for the government's budget, at least in the following five years before the wage bill started climbing again. Fiscal savings were earned in the following three expenditure categories: the wage bill, contributions to the PF, and contributions to the health insurance funds (National Fund for Social Protection [CNOPS] and other small sectorial funds).

The published results showed that the average gross salary of the retirees was about MAD 123.4 thousand per year (US$14,700), and that the total salary distributed to the 38,600 retirees was about MAD 4.8 billion (US$571.4 million), or 1 percent of GDP in 2005. The budget was expected to continue to save this amount on the wage bill from 2006 forward, assuming no substantial rehiring would take place. However, the Budget Law of 2006 created approximately 5,000 additional public positions over and beyond the number freed up by normal attrition. The impact of these hiring decisions on the budget was modest, estimated at less than 0.1 percent of GDP. Subsequent budget laws, however, provided between 8,000 and 10,000 more positions than the number of those retiring. These new recruits were hired to fill gaps in the social sectors, such as education and health, especially in rural areas. The security sector also benefited from these hires. As a result, over time, the central government rebounded to its pre-VRP size.

The employer contribution rate for the PF benefiting civil servants was 9 percent of the gross salary. This rate was increased to 10 percent of gross salary starting from 2006, following the decision to raise employer and employee contributions to the PF by 1 percentage point each year between 2004 and 2006. The savings for 2005 were then calculated at MAD 192.4 million (US$22.9 million), or 0.04 percent of GDP, and MAD 475.1 million thereafter (US$56.6 million), or 0.1 percent of GDP. Nevertheless, as figure 4-1 shows, the government wage bill witnessed a slow but steady decline from 2005 to 2008, but then began an upward climb to reach 11.40 percent of GDP in 2012. Although the wage bill began to decline again in 2013 to reach 10.30 percent in 2016, it is evident that the VRP program did not effectively stabilize the wage bill consumption of GDP as expected.

FIGURE 4-1. Government Spending on Wage Bill as Percentage of GDP

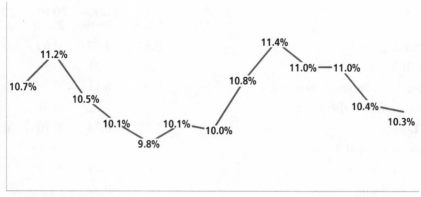

Source: Ministry of Finance (2017).

The three fiscal losses related to the VRP were: one-off severance payments, foregone personal taxes on salaries of the retirees, and foregone revenues through loss of retirees' additional payments to the PF. Table 4-2 provides estimates of these losses. The total severance payments amounted to MAD 10.5 billion (US$1.25 billion), or some 2.3 percent of GDP in 2005. The average ranged from MAD 40.8 thousand for the lowest salary grade personnel to more than MAD 576.7 thousand for the highest salary grade, a ratio of 1 to 14 (approximately US$4,900 to US$68,700). More than one-third of the total severance payments benefited the three highest among the twelve existing salary grades. The lower grades (Grades 1 to 6) benefited from only 6.5 percent of the total severance amount. This indicates that the incentive package was far less attractive to employees at the lower end of the salary scale, which explains in part the small number of retirees from this group.

The budget also lost the personal income taxes it collected on retiree wages. However, it collected new personal income taxes on the pensions the retirees received from the PF. The difference between those two amounts represented a net yearly loss for the budget of about 0.15 percent of GDP. The PF incurred additional outlays resulting from the VRP that progressively faded after thirty years as retirees reached the retirement age of sixty to sixty-five. The results showed that total nominal additional pension funds would amount to 3.9 percent of GDP for 2005. The present

TABLE 4-2. Summary of Estimated Savings and Losses (as Percentage of GDP)

	2005	2006–2009	2010–2020	2021–2036
Gross Savings	0.52	1.07	0.69	0.32
Wage bill	0.47	0.93	0.58	0.25
Employer's contribution to pension fund	0.04	0.13	0.09	0.06
Contribution to health insurance	0.01	0.02	0.01	0.01
Gross Losses	2.37	0.54	0.10	0.02
Severance payment	2.30			
Personal income tax, net	0.07	0.05	0.03	0.01
Pension fund support		0.39		
Wage for rehiring		0.10	0.07	0.01
Net Savings (+)	–1.85	0.54	0.58	0.30
Memo				
Employees rehired (beyond normal retirement)		5,600	5,100	1,100

Source: Ministry of Finance (2004–2006).

value—calculated based on a discounted rate of 5 percent—would correspond to 1.6 percent of GDP. The authorities indicated that the budget would support the PF by paying a lump sum amount in four installments of MAD 2 billion each (US$238 million) starting in 2006.

Failure to Achieve Savings through the Second VRP. In the medium- and longer-terms, the expected net savings for the budget from the VRP, unfortunately, did not materialize, casting doubt on whether the program had any actual impact on helping the Moroccan government "rightsize" its public administration. In 2005, the fiscal deficit was 5.2 percent of GDP, which mainly reflected one-off severance payments from the VRP involving 38,600 civil servants. The one-off net impact of severance payments was equivalent to 2.3 percent of GDP (or 1.9 percent of GDP in net terms, when including wage savings from staff retired by mid-year, and equivalent to 0.4 percent of GDP). Because of additional contributions to the PF, it took five years for the budget to recover the initial net outlays made in 2005, which amounted to 1.85 percent of GDP. Such savings do not, however, consider the gains in efficiency and effectiveness due to the program.

The hard reality is that the net savings estimated by the economists who structured the VRP had not been achieved as of 2019. It was expected that the net savings would average 0.54 percent of GDP in 2006–2009, 0.58 of GDP in 2010–2020, and 0.3 percent of GDP in 2021–2036 (table 4-2). In contrast, it seems that gross losses have increased considerably, corresponding with an increased wage bill as a percentage of GDP from 2010 to 2012. The MOF reported that, during the period from 2007 to 2017, the number of public servants in the central government rose from 525,049 to 570,165, resulting in an overall increase of 8.59 percent. In the period between 2007 and 2017, a total of 219,237 budget posts were created, translating into 19,931 new budget posts per year.

More important, the Audit Court published a report in October 2017 indicating that the VRP had failed to reduce the cost of the wage bill.[6] It stated that, between 2008 and 2016, the total payroll increased from MAD 75.4 billion to 120 billion (US$7.97 billion to US$12.68 billion), an annual increase of 5.3 percent compared to a GDP annual growth rate of 3.92. Furthermore, the report showed that the total number of public sector employees (including central government employees) increased from 800,000 in 2014 to 860,253 in 2016. In contrast to the projections in table 4-2, the Audit Court's report warned that the weight of the payroll as a percentage of GDP would increase from 2018 until 2021 before declining again. The report implies that such projected outcomes are largely due to the fact that several steps were not undertaken following the VRP, despite plans to do so. For instance, the government did not implement rigorous workforce planning strategies, nor did it overhaul the Welfare Office. Therefore, the project was successful only in achieving "a one-off measure of lightening of the workforce, thus losing its ambition to be part of the long-term measures aiming at establishing the bases of modern management of human resources."[7]

Economic Gains from VRP II

It is essential to assess the full economic impact of the VRP, especially given the large financial transfers made in the form of severance payments under the program. These payments amounted to more than 2.3 percent of GDP, an amount equivalent to half the annual investment budget of the central government. However, a general assessment of the economic impact of the VRP on the Moroccan economy reveals mixed results. While most of the retirees in the program decided to invest their severance payments in creating their own businesses or in real estate projects, they were among the most talented senior public servants within Moroccan public service. Their departure left several government departments in the hands of less talented and less qualified employees, which undoubtedly affected the effectiveness of their operations.

Two unpublished studies, one undertaken by the MPSM and another conducted jointly with KPMG International Cooperative, provide important insights concerning the use of the severance payments and subsequent investment, production, and employment decisions undertaken by VRP beneficiaries.[8] The first study relied on an online survey taken by 7,750 beneficiaries of the program, who collectively constituted 20 percent of the total beneficiaries. The survey asked specific questions regarding the plans of those beneficiaries and the nature of their intended investments. Results indicated that 59 percent of respondents intended to invest their money in private sector projects. Around 46 percent of respondents wanted to invest in establishing businesses in private education. The appeal of investing in private schools is likely due to their tax-exempt status. Another 21 percent of the participants indicated they wanted to invest in various commercial activities.

The MPSM conducted another online survey in which the public sector employees taking part in the program were asked to indicate both the main reasons for their early retirement and in what sectors they wanted to invest their severance payment. Around 1,985 employees took the survey.[9] One-third of respondents (31 percent) indicated their intention to open a private business as the main driver behind applying for this early retirement scheme. Roughly 24 percent of respondents stated they no longer wished to work in the public sector, and 18 percent considered health issues as a barrier to continuing their work for the government. When asked how they were going to use the severance payment they would receive from the retirement scheme, 41 percent considered investment in personal projects and 18 percent prioritized paying outstanding loans. Around 11 percent intended to utilize the money to build a family house.

Although not conclusive, these studies suggest that the overall returns to the Moroccan economy were positive. In a plurality of cases, the retirees' movement to entrepreneurial and private sector activities was likely to have offset their loss in the public service. They were expected to contribute to job creation, as well as to the consumption of goods and materials necessary for constructing houses or businesses. They were also expected to pay taxes and service fees for their newly established businesses.

Candidate Selection for the Program

Overall, the results show that most of the retirees were high-ranking civil servants between the ages of fifty and fifty-five who belonged to Grades 10 and higher. They accounted for more than 53.5 percent of the retirees, while medium (Grades 5 to 9) and lower (Grades 1 to 4) levels represented only 38.5 and 8 percent, respectively. As the public sector workforce is concentrated in the middle grades, the profile of retirees does not match that of the broader public sector. The expected re-profiling of civil servants away from low grade jobs toward managerial and technical jobs in higher grades was only partially fulfilled.

In the end, 38,600 civil servants were authorized to retire out of some 50,500 applicants, which reflected an average acceptance rate of 76.3 percent. Acceptance rates ranged from 50 percent to 100 percent within different departments. Most social ministerial departments were careful in allowing applicants to participate in the program. This was the case in the Departments of Justice (50 percent), Primary and Secondary Education (58 percent), and Health (68 percent). In contrast, other important departments accepted all applications, including the Departments of Agriculture (99 percent), Interior (100 percent), and Higher Education (100 percent).

Most VRP beneficiaries were playing a central role in conducting and supervising managerial, technical, and teaching activities. The departure of such personnel had a negative effect on the functioning of civil administration and service delivery in some key departments, such as education, agriculture, housing, and, to a lesser extent, health. The loss of such skilled personnel was the result of adverse selection, as there was no framework in place that could identify redundant or productive employees. This observation begs the question of whether the departure of high-level staff weakened the supervisory capacity of Morocco's public administration.

In fact, the departure of some of the most skilled staff left a significant void in the public sector that remains difficult to fill. Just under 54 percent of retirees belonged to Grade 10 of the public service and were among the most senior employees, with decades of accumulated expertise in their fields. Although the results varied across departments, it is interesting to note that many supervisors did not use the mechanisms at their disposal to prevent the departure of talented staff, choosing not to "penalize" high performers. While it was hoped that, in the medium term, this lacuna would be offset by a younger and more efficient staff supported by focused training, the hard reality is that no sufficient planning had been conducted prior to laying off these cadres.

In terms of sectoral distribution, almost half of the high-ranked personnel (13,000) were school teachers (primary and secondary). In view of the difficulties in carrying out efficient reallocation processes to fill existing gaps and meet new needs in terms of human resources, mainly in rural areas, the impact of this relatively high number of teacher retirements on the education sector translated into some discrepancies in service delivery, particularly in rural areas and small towns. Teachers in those areas found the VRP program to be a "lifesaver" to rescue them from the harsh working conditions they were enduring and, therefore, they opted out, leaving the chances of re-filling their positions dim.

The VRP also identified a large number of civil servants who were missing or otherwise unaccounted for, whose respective administrations had lost track of them due to lack of adequate management and monitoring systems. The education department in particular has now eliminated 40 percent of its redundant positions. Some of these "ghost workers" were civil servants seconded to other departments, whose records became blurred over time. Others included civil servants with long-term illnesses who left office but continued to receive their salaries. Loose monitoring systems had allowed them to "disappear" without notice, usually to undertake private activities. Many such civil servants rushed to benefit from the VRP, fearing they would be forced to join their respective departments to replace those who had already taken advantage of the program. It could be argued that the departure of such "ghost staff" helped improve the quality and productivity of the remaining staff.

It is possible that more serious consultations with stakeholders at the outset, especially with trade unions, would have allowed the VRP to avoid some of its shortcomings. For example, consultations could have provided objective and transparent selection criteria to accept or turn down applications. Another weakness was related to the lack of communication downstream. The government carried out an upstream communication strategy in a professional manner. However, communication efforts faded away as soon as the operation was closed. The lack of accurate information about the VRP outcomes fueled rumors and speculation about the real objectives of the operation and its actual impact, leading some to believe that the VRP operation was overly expensive and would result in an administration emptied of its best staff. Others believed the government was going to take harsh measures against incompetent staff the VRP could not "get rid of," or that another VRP operation was being prepared to cull any remaining redundancies.

What Did the Second VRP Fail to Achieve? A decade after its implementation, it is clear that the VRP failed to achieve several targets, including the two core objectives: to accrue financial savings through a systematically reduced wage bill as a percentage of GDP and the retention of the most skilled employees. However, it is important to emphasize that, beyond the immediate program, any assessment of the VRP cannot be disentangled from the broader structural challenges within Morocco's public administration—issues such as poorly targeted recruitment, overstaffing, unbalanced geographic concentration, lifelong tenure, ineffective training, seniority-based wage increases, and subjective performance evaluations.

In the context of the PARP, the VRP program helped advance a major reevaluation and improvement of management methods, pressing ministries and departments to reexamine their organization and resource management. By making the VRP one of the cornerstones of administrative reform, the Moroccan government committed itself to reforming a number of other important aspects of human resource management (HRM), ranging from recruitment and training to performance evaluation and monitoring.

The unbalanced distribution of staff in regional administrations and among various departments resulted in localized overstaffing, which generated chronic redundancies and underemployment. The VRP did not significantly improve the geographic distribution of the workforce, which remained biased in favor of the two most privileged regions (Casablanca and Rabat) at the expense of the other fourteen regions.

The most critical shortcoming of the second VRP program was adverse selection. The government lost some of its most talented and experienced employees because the retirement program did not target specific jobs or grades. This is especially the case in higher education, where 100 percent of applicants were successful. Even in 2018, many informants stressed the severe shortage the VRP program caused at Moroccan universities. Some of the most competent professors left the higher education system and joined private schools, leaving a considerable gap that still has not been adequately filled.

Moreover, the departure of civil servants who were very much in demand was not accompanied by personnel redeployment and training to ensure the uninterrupted delivery of services. Most were temporary and minor but surfaced in some important sectors, such as education, health, housing, and agriculture. The implicit objective of reducing the number of redundant and unproductive staff fell short of expectations. In some small ministerial departments, the VRP facilitated the departure of such personnel. However, their share with respect to total redundancies was small, and only the education department could boast of having reduced redundancies by some 40 percent.

The VRP failed to shrink the share of personnel in the lowest pay grades (1 to 4), who represent about 20 percent of civil servants. The government had stopped recruitment in this category many years earlier and started outsourcing the services they performed, aiming to gradually reduce their relative numbers. No more than 3 percent of this category retired. Had the government designed compensation geared toward lower-paid personnel, this problem could have been avoided.

Unfortunately, to the extent that underemployment and overstaffing do exist, most observers believe them to be concentrated at the bottom and middle ranks of the civil service salary structure. Since the majority of applicants did not belong to these categories, this objective was not fulfilled in its entirety. The VRP did not succeed in giving the underemployed or low-ranking personnel (Grades 1 to 8) sufficient financial incentives to leave. The linear design of the incentive package mostly favored senior civil servants whose salaries were high enough to benefit from generous compensation. This encouraged high-ranking employees to quit and lower-ranking ones to remain.

The reallocation of redundant employees and their intended transfer to higher value-added activities in the private sector was meant to improve productivity within both the agencies they left as well as Morocco's broader economy. With assistance from various international organizations, the government subsequently embarked on an endeavor to restructure its human resource management practices, including traditional methods of recruiting employees, and to adopt a more strategic approach to performance assessment. Unfortunately, the sequencing would have been more effective if this effort had been implemented before the conclusion of the VRP program, not after.

Conclusion

Morocco's experience in downsizing its public sector can serve as both an inspiration and a cautionary tale for other MENA countries suffering from acute overstaffing and fiscally unsustainable wage bills. Morocco is somewhat unique in the way senior officials quickly learned from the mistakes of the first program in 2004, making critical adjustments before launching the second round in 2005. The greatest shortfall of the second VRP was that it could not produce substantial and progressive fiscal gains through wage bill savings.

This chapter raises a number of important questions. First, why did the program design overlook the global experiences that warn against the pitfalls of adverse selection? Why did the program fail to maintain the reduced wage bill? What are the overall economic outcomes, and were the VRP candidates successful in their entrepreneurial activities? What strategies should the Moroccan government officials and World Bank advisers have designed differently to avoid the shortcomings of the VRP? Answering these questions will require a rigorous reexamination of the VRP program, and can potentially guide other countries in their design, implementing, and monitoring of similar initiatives.

Looking forward, future VRP efforts will be more effective when they are not one-off exercises but, rather, part of the routine and ongoing processes that continuously renew the government workforce. It would be sound to consider the rationalization policy of the workforce in yearly budget laws and to implement and revise those policies throughout the public sector on a continuous basis. In this manner, workforce rationing would become a permanent concern. This would require managing human resources through a systemic approach—integrating the management of jobs, workforces, skills, mobility, training, and remuneration.

Notes

1. World Bank, "Unlocking the Employment Potential in the Middle East and North Africa: Toward a New Social Contract," World Bank Publications 15011, Washington, DC, 2004.

2. The World Bank provided the government of Morocco with advice, training, and knowledge transfer as required in the areas of budgetary management, civil service reform, and wage bill containment.

3. World Bank, "Morocco—Third and Fourth Public Administration Reform Loan Projects," December 22, 2011, http://documents.worldbank.org/curated/en/

661781474566109555/Morocco-Third-and-Fourth-Public-Administration-Reform
-Loan-Projects.

4. The Strategic Committee of Administrative Reforms was set up in the context of the broader public administration reform.

5. The bulk of this assessment is based on information drawn from various government documents and informal interviews with government actors and other protagonists conducted in the context of this case study. It also relies on data from internal reports prepared by the MPSM in Morocco to assess the effectiveness and shortfalls of the two VRPs.

6. The Audit Court, "The Civil Service System: Summary Report," Kingdom of Morocco, October 2017, www.courdescomptes.ma/upload/MoDUle_20/File_20_526.pdf.

7. Ibid., p. 9.

8. These studies are not published, and we had access to the data used by MPSM to assess the program for internal evaluation purposes.

9. We relied on the data gathered for the purposes of this study.

FIVE

Strengthening Meritocracy in Human Resource Management in Lebanon

SIMONIDA SUBOTIC

ADELE BARZELAY

WHEN SHE DECIDED TO return to Lebanon, bringing along a doctorate in organizational psychology from Canada, Charlotte Karam was eager to participate in her country's recovery. Giving up an opportunity for a successful career abroad, Charlotte came to Lebanon hoping to put her skills to work in the reform and revitalization of Lebanon's public sector. As such, Charlotte was an ideal candidate for the Lebanese government. She was young, talented, educated, and energetic, with a guiding belief in Lebanon's potential to transform itself into a stable, modern, and prosperous democracy. Furthermore, she shared an understanding with many Lebanese expatriates that an emphasis on professionalism and merit was essential in lifting the country's public institutions out of the mediocrity induced by a system of nepotism and patronage. Charlotte was hired in late 2008 by Minister of State for Administrative Development (OMSAR) Ibrahim Shamseddine to help design a better procedure for screening and selecting candidates for senior civil service positions. The procedure was part of a broader reform effort to infuse the highest posts of public administration with meritocracy and skill. Her belief in such potential had initially taken Charlotte back home. Now, disillusioned with the reform's limited progress and wary of the government's interest in her skills and expertise, she is hoping to build a career in academia and the private sector.[1]

In many respects, Lebanon provides a unique window into the challenge of instilling meritocracy within the public sector—a challenge that confronts governments throughout the Middle East and North Africa region and beyond. On the positive side, Lebanon has a large diaspora and a history of entrepreneurship. Many Lebanese are familiar with cutting edge managerial and administrative practices in OECD countries and elsewhere, and their experience in the private sector has underscored the importance of talent and performance. Yet, traditional norms and practices also loom large, particularly within the public sector. As is true in many MENA countries, one of the most important of these is *wasta*, which is Arabic for "connections." A traditional form of association initially based on tribal affiliations, *wasta* today takes the form of familial, confessional, or political ties. Such ties in MENA not only define the private lives of individuals but also extend to the professional sphere and determine the prospects of employment or university admission.[2] Prevalent in public employment, *wasta*-based recruitment has left many public sector institutions riddled with corruption, nepotism, and cronyism, which, in turn, has contributed to poor public service delivery across MENA.

Although *wasta* is commonly blamed for the lack of talent and performance within many Arab public sectors, calls for its abolition have met with strong resistance. In Lebanon, the twin dynamics of the push for a more modern, performance-oriented, meritocratic civil service and the legacy of a more traditional public sector dominated by patronage and *wasta* were particularly pronounced. With powerful forces aligning along both dimensions and a legacy of meritocratic reform efforts stretching back for decades, Lebanon would serve as an important test case for the broader prospects for implementing human resource management reforms throughout the MENA region.

In the early 1990s, ravaged by fifteen years of civil war, Lebanese public institutions were in dire need of reform. Almost twenty years later, while moderate progress was evident, Lebanon's public administration remained filled with tenured, unskilled staff selected based on a quota system corresponding to confessional delineations and partisanship rather than professional qualifications and merit. In 2009, a large number of civil service positions were vacant. Due to both the post-war hiring freeze and the lack of standardized hiring procedures, approximately 50 percent of all civil service positions remained empty.[3] The deficiencies were most severe in the highest ranks of the public administration, which included such positions as director generals of urban planning and social affairs. As a result, public service delivery was highly impeded.

In 2009, in the absence of a transparent hiring process, the ministers continued to nominate candidates for the highest level civil service positions based on a system of confessional patronage. Such a procedure was an open-ended, indeterminate process of collective bargaining often resulting in no appointments for months at a time. For instance, at the onset of the June 2009 general elections, after four years of negotiations, an agreement was reached in the Council of Ministers, the executive body in the Lebanese system, to appoint five members to the vacant seats of the Constitutional Council. Established by the Ta'if Agreement at the end of the civil war with the mandate to monitor the constitutionality of the laws and to settle electoral disputes, the council was incapacitated between 2005 and 2009 due to political disagreements over appointments of its vacant seats.[4] To avoid holding yet another parliamentary election without the main electoral dispute mechanism, a deal was struck in such a way that three of the five vacant seats would be appointed by the majority, two by the opposition, and one by the president. The justice minister, Ibrahim Najjar, characterized the appointments as a "gift to the Lebanese people," as he was not fully satisfied with the appointed candidates but still accepted the compromise. The compromise exemplified the contentious nature of public appointments in the Lebanese political system—a system populated by a diverse set of political and confessional interests entrenched in the process of collective bargaining. Furthermore, it also warned of systemic impasse and collapse of public service delivery in the absence of civil service recruitment reform.

The interest in a more transparent civil service recruitment process had been gaining ground. In 2005, fundamental reforms were introduced in the recruitment of Grade One positions, the highest positions in the service. For the first time, such positions were opened up and made available to all Lebanese.[5] The main human resource body, the Civil Service Board (CSB), received hundreds of applications from applicants both within the country and abroad. The hiring process under the 2005 draft law was anonymous and, instead of confessionalism, screened applications based solely on qualifications and merit. However, with the 2006 war with Israel and the government boycott by Hezbollah, the procedure was seen as a threat to political interests and was discontinued after only seven senior positions were filled.

One of those seven was Kamal Shehadi, who was appointed head of the Telecommunications Regulatory Authority (TRA). While he deemed the process fair and transparent, Shehadi claims it lacked professionalism; his credentials were never checked and no personality test was used. Moreover, the appointment process took almost a year, during which Shehadi was never contacted or notified of being shortlisted.[6] He claims the only pull toward civil service and away from an undoubtedly more lucrative career in the private sector was his devotion to public service and his close relationship with Prime Minister Fouad Siniora. However, discouraged by public sector recruitment practices, not many applicants followed Shehadi's footsteps.

In February 2009, the Office of the Minister of State for Administrative Reform (OMSAR) introduced an implementation bill building on the 2005 draft law and outlining an even more sophisticated recruitment process. Charlotte Karam developed a proposal that included a team of organizational psychologists to oversee the process, a carefully tailored structured interview, and a psychometric assessment tool. However, when put to a vote in front of the Council of Ministers, the proposal was overwhelmingly defeated. Subsequently, project funding was depleted, and Charlotte and OMSAR's 2009 reform work came to an end.

To better understand the contentious nature of the civil service reform and the reasons behind its failure, it is necessary to first explore the Lebanese political organization and the notion of reform within it.

The Politics of Reform in the Lebanese Context

Political Organization. Lebanon is one of the rare cases of representative government in the Middle East. Although a guardian of democratic organization in a region dominated by authoritarian rule, the Lebanese political system has its challenges. The Lebanese system is characterized by confessionalism—a specific type of consociational democracy organized along religious lines. Vestiges of confessionalist organization can be found as far back as 1843; however, the system fully developed after Lebanese independence from France a hundred years later. While the system was always deemed provisional, it operated successfully for about thirty years until it came to a catastrophic collapse in 1975, resulting in a bloody fifteen-year civil war. This war was ended by the Ta'if Agreement in 1991.

Because the threat of a return to conflict is an ever-present fear among many Lebanese, there is a recognized need for greater diffusion of power.

The post-Ta'if confessional configuration mandated a more equal balance between confessional communities across all aspects of government. Today, an equal division between Muslims and Christians is required in government, parliament, and the civil service. Additionally, each of the eighteen officially recognized sectarian communities, the largest of which are the Sunni, Shia, Druze, and Maronites, is proportionally represented within the overall ratio (see table 5-1). Finally, the highest political posts—president, prime minister, and speaker of parliament—are divided among the Maronite, Sunni, and Shia communities respectively, while the rest of the government positions can be freely allocated as long as the Christian-Muslim balance is maintained.

TABLE 5-1. Division of Lebanese
Parliament by Confession

Confession	Seats
Christians	
Maronite	34
Greek Orthodox	14
Greek Catholic	8
Armenian Orthodox	5
Armenian Catholic	1
Protestant	1
Other Christian minorities	1
Subtotal	64
Muslims	
Sunni	27
Shiite	27
Druze	8
Alawite	2
Subtotal	64
TOTAL	128

Source: Carnegie Endowment for International Peace, 2006.

Reform and Its Driving Forces. In Lebanon, confessionalism encapsulates all forms of public life. For any reform to pass, consensus is required among different confessional factions. Confessional affiliation is similar to the notion of party loyalty in Western democracies, but as power sharing is spread across all aspects of public administration, the line between government and opposition is blurred. Contrary to many Western democracies, dynamism and reform can be perceived as threats to the system's survival, as any deviation from the status quo threatens to shift the confessional balance at the expense of other parties involved.[7]

Moreover, many Lebanese feel that the system's confessional characteristics are frequently manipulated to provide cover and justification for what are more accurately calculations based upon favoritism and personal gain. Lebanese politics have witnessed some unusual coalitions in recent years, as political interests have often trumped confessional associations and the latter have been suspended in the search of short-term political gain. The opposite is also true, in that deep religious cleavages are manipulated and exaggerated to allow elites to consolidate their power and influence. In fact, some civil society advocates argue that Lebanon's greatest ills do not emanate from confessionalism but, rather, from its misuse to justify and perpetuate cronyism and nepotism.

The Ta'if Agreement recognized the perils of confessionalism and called for its gradual abolition. The document calls for a national council to be formed to propose ways to do away with confessional representation.[8] However, no tangible progress has been achieved thus far. Such a radical overhaul of the confessionalist system is deemed too unpredictable and threatening for the factional interests. Initiatives such as security, civil service, and electoral law reform have historically faced tremendous opposition from confessional and political interest groups. The civil service reform comes closest to challenging the confessional nature of the Lebanese system and, as such, faces the strongest resistance. Nonetheless, various initiatives toward reform indirectly affecting the confessionalist configuration have taken place over the past twenty years. These reforms were not intended to eliminate the confessional system entirely but, rather, to make the existing structure more transparent and fair.[9]

By 2005, other dynamics were also at work that were raising the profile of reform and improving its prospects. Like many countries in the MENA region, Lebanon enjoyed a growing middle class and a maturing, highly-skilled professional cadre. Although a country of only 4 million people, the Lebanese diaspora is a much larger agglomeration of approximately 12 million people, many of whom are educated abroad with limited exposure to *wasta* and the Lebanese confessional political system.[10] In the aftermath of the civil war in the 1990s, many Lebanese émigrés were encouraged by Prime Minister Rafik Hariri's reconstruction efforts to return home. Many were willing to consider coming back to Lebanon.

These dynamics were given further impetus by the Cedar Revolution, which erupted in February 2005. Driven by popular anger at the assassination of Prime Minister Hariri, widely perceived to have been orchestrated by Syrian intelligence agents, the Cedar Revolution witnessed an outpouring of popular opinion through mass protests that resulted in the ultimate withdrawal of Syrian troops from Lebanon and a reduction in Syria's direct influence over the Lebanese government. It marked a particularly hopeful and idealistic moment within Lebanon's history and politics, and one that captured the imagination of many Lebanese, both at home and abroad. Many young, idealistic professionals were willing to consider a career in public service to help rebuild their country.

The Lebanese Civil Service

A Confessional Legacy. The Lebanese civil service consists of five grades, with Grade One being the highest. As of mid-2009, excluding security personnel and teachers, there were 24,000 official civil service positions.[11] Of those, 10,000 were vacant due to either the post-war hiring freeze or disagreements over confessional appointments. In the highest ranks, there were seventy-eight positions, of which thirty-eight were unfilled. (Examples include members of the board of directors for the Electricity Regulatory Authority or Investment Development Agency, or director general positions in social affairs or urban planning.).[12] Although Article 12 of the Lebanese Constitution states that "every Lebanese has the right to hold public office, no preference being made except on the basis of merit and competence, according to the conditions established by law," many civil service positions are traditionally filled based on confessional legacy. That is, positions are "reserved" for individuals within a particular confession rather than for those most qualified for a given post. As a former OMSAR minister explains, "Sometimes the candidates would be well-qualified and other times, not. If the candidate was not good, the government was stuck with him/her until the person turned 64 years old."[13]

Such a system left the Lebanese civil service filled with largely unqualified and underperforming staff. For instance, at the Ministry of Economy and Trade, few if any lower ranking civil servants held a degree in economics or some other qualification suitable for a position within that ministry.[14] Furthermore, the tenured staff, averaging fifty-six years of age, had an uncompetitive wage (US$500 to US$1,500 per month) and low incentives to perform. Salary cuts or demotions were uncommon, and work days were typically from 8 a.m. to 2 p.m.[15] Finally, the country was going through a demographic transition, and 45 percent of the public labor force was expected to retire by 2020.[16]

A Government of Contractual Labor. To avoid civil service implosion, bypass the hiring freeze, and bring in badly needed talent, the Lebanese government resorted to recruiting contractual labor in all but the highest levels of the civil service. In 2009, the government employed thousands of contractual employees, the highest proportion of which worked for the Ministry of Economy and Trade, the Ministry of Finance, and OMSAR.[17] While many were unskilled day laborers who bloated the lower civil service ranks, some were formally employed by international organizations. Compared to the tenured staff, these contractors were better skilled, more efficient, and willing to work longer hours.[18] Also, their salaries were much higher, which further increased the strain on the public budget. Moreover, contractual workers were selected by individual ministries on an ad hoc basis for periods intended to be brief but frequently spanning years and even decades. Such practices created a parallel public administration of qualified but largely unregulated government employees. Their lines of accountability were not clearly defined, and their hiring and performance measurement processes were only provisional. As a general rule, this contractual labor was lacking in transparency, accountability, and an established organizational culture. As such, it was a functional but a rather poor substitute for an institutionalized and professional public administration.

Impetus for Reform and Its Evolution

Early Attempts at Reform. By 2005, Lebanon had already witnessed a number of noteworthy attempts toward reforming the public sector, although they tended to occur only within a particular set of circumstances. They invariably took place in the aftermath of a major historical event or in the presence of strong central leadership (sometimes both were required). For instance, in the 1960s, a brief civil conflict resulted in the presidency of Fouad Chehab. President Chehab is widely remembered for his impartiality, integrity, and deep devotion to public sector reform.[19] Specifically, Chehab's reform efforts aimed at modernizing the public sector and infusing it with an efficient and qualified public administration. As such, his leadership is credited with the creation of most of Lebanon's modern ministries and agencies. This includes the CSB—the government's apex human resource management agency established in 1959, still operational today.[20]

The creation of the CSB marked a major effort to enshrine meritocratic practices in Lebanon's public administration. The CSB was intended to introduce professionalism and reduce nepotism in human resource management for the public sector. It served as a central recruitment agency for all ministries and, as such, it advertised vacancies, screened candidates, and administered assessment tests. The CSB was also given a powerful standing, as its board had the same powers as line ministries.[21] Nonetheless, in the absence of Chehab's leadership and momentum for reform during the civil war, the CSB lost its mandate and succumbed to divisive political interests, almost leading to its abolition in 1995.[22] In the post-Chehab civil war era, both the CSB and the broader civil service reform effort were stalled until they were revived under the leadership of Prime Minister Hariri in the early 1990s.

The Post-War Era. A graduate of the Beirut Arab University's business administration program and a self-made billionaire, Hariri spent most of his career as a businessman in Saudi Arabia. The conclusion of the civil war in 1990 prompted his return as an investor in Lebanon's post-war reconstruction. However, he quickly migrated into politics and became prime minister in 1993. Devastated by war, public sector reconstruction was high on Hariri's agenda. The public administration was lacking both in staff and infrastructure, unable to deliver even the most basic services. Consequently, international donor organizations, such as the World Bank, launched public administration projects and encouraged the creation of a National Public Sector Development Strategy.[23] As part of this public sector restructuring, Prime Minister Hariri advocated a systemic dismissal of underperforming, under-qualified, or corrupt civil servants. As a result, during his term, approximately 3,700 civil servants were let go, while an additional 3,400 accepted severance packages.[24] To reduce the strain on the public budget and to avoid *wasta*-based hiring, Hariri also proposed the drafting of a new law to allow contractual meritocratic employment for the first three ranks of the Lebanese civil service. Fiercely opposed by unions representing mainly the second and third rank members, the proposal was eventually abandoned.[25] Hariri, instead, introduced a hiring freeze on any new civil service positions apart from the highest ranks. Finally, the prime minister encouraged the creation of eight new ministries, among which the most prominent for public administration reform was OMSAR, which was given a specific mandate to design and implement a public administration restructuring.[26]

OMSAR was mainly preoccupied with increasing the level of skill and expertise among the public servants, reforming the CSB while fighting nepotism and corruption.[27] Although it had strong leadership and committed staff, OMSAR lacked the legal status of a ministry. As such, it had no authority to enforce its recommendations, which were regularly contradicted or overruled by the Council of Ministers. Additionally, OMSAR's staff consisted mainly of technical experts from international organizations or contractual staff who lacked the official status to advocate and implement the reforms they were designing. While it had great potential, OMSAR soon lost its appeal to other ministries with greater political clout. Over the next seven years and throughout Hariri's second term, OMSAR remained unable to pioneer any major reform process until 2005, when the election of a government under the leadership of Prime Minister Siniora reintroduced public administration as part of the reform agenda.

Meritocracy and the Lebanese Civil Service

The Political Environment. A tense political relationship with Syria culminated in the assassination of Prime Minister Hariri in February 2005. Hariri's assassination left the newly formed opposition coalition of Sunni, Christian, and Druze leaders united against Syria's presence in Lebanon. Amid such resistance, the Syrians withdrew, leaving Lebanon at the onset of the 2005 parliamentary elections. Both Hariri's death and Syrian withdrawal proved to be catalysts for reform. Syrian withdrawal intensified international pressures for reform, as its presence, manifested through support for various factions, was often blamed for reform failure. On the other hand, Hariri's death resulted in loss of confidence in the stability of the Lebanese economy by the international donor community. Consequently, the new government needed to provide stability assurance through a reform platform as a guarantee for continued international financial assistance. In this context, the new government, formed by Prime Minister Siniora, pledged to devote its attention to pressing reform areas.

One of the most essential reform initiatives was the electoral law and fiscal policy reform. Addressed through a larger fiscal restructuring program, the civil service reform was perceived as one of the more feasible initiatives for the new government. At the beginning of his term, Prime Minister Siniora, Hariri's adviser and the Minister of Finance during his tenure, was faced with recurring budget deficits emanating, in large part, from public sector expenditures amounting to about 38 percent of the GDP. As a large proportion of the budget was going toward supporting the wages of an underperforming public sector, reforms focused on competitive recruitment of qualified contractual labor had the potential to bring better value. Moreover, apart from fiscal considerations, Siniora also brought with him a legacy of meritocratic recruitment. During his term as the Minister of Finance, he had strengthened the ministry by infusing it with qualified professionals, making it one of the most professional ministries in Lebanon today.[28] Given the broader political circumstances and his technocratic background, Siniora was determined to implement civil service reforms that would advance meritocratic recruitment.

Meritocracy in the Making. In 2005, Siniora contacted the newly appointed OMSAR minister, Jean Ogassapian, and proposed that OMSAR draft a law on meritocratic hiring procedures, as had been initially suggested by Prime Minister Hariri. However, to circumvent the unions that blocked the initiative in 2003, Siniora focused solely on Grade One civil servants— the highest and the least unionized grade—instead of the first three ranks in Lebanon's public administration.[29] As part of the new law, Siniora proposed the formation of an independent committee to evaluate applications and recommend the most suitable candidates for available positions to line ministers. In preparation for the new draft legislation, Ogassapian consulted with prominent leaders in the private sector, academia, and public administration on best practices for transparent recruitment of senior public officials. A team of experts within the Finance Institute was asked to produce a guide on merit-based mechanisms for recruitment in accordance with international standards for human resource management.[30]

By September 2005, the new recruitment law was drafted and passed by the Council of Ministers. The law was then transferred to the Committee on Administration and Justice for amendment. Upon committee approval, it was sent to the Speaker of the House, where it awaited introduction to the floor of the parliament.[31] As the 2005 draft preserved the constitutional jurisdiction of line ministers to nominate candidates for cabinet approval and merely added a nonbinding recommendation on most qualified candidates by an independent committee, OMSAR deemed it constitutional to start implementing the draft law while awaiting a final parliamentary vote. Therefore, together with OMSAR, Prime Minister Siniora started recruiting the relevant experts and forming selection committees. Pending a parliament vote, the new hiring procedures started to take place in November 2005 under an interpretation of the Employment Law, Decree 112 of 1959, in effect at the time.[32]

The 2005 Hiring Process in Detail. The 2005 hiring process was a sophisticated procedure guided by international standards for human resource management. It included a public announcement of available vacancies in the print media and the internet, candidate eligibility criteria, and an electronic application form. The screening process consisted of four phases (see table 5-2 for a full description). In the initial phase, applications were reviewed and their minimum eligibility requirements were checked. This was done anonymously to minimize the risk of applicant names signaling a certain confessional affiliation. Initial screening was followed by a more detailed evaluation criteria based on a point system, which was used to determine a short-list of applicants who would be invited for a personal interview in front of a committee.

The committees were headed by the CSB, as it was the official recruiting body. They also included representatives from OMSAR, the line ministry with the vacant position, and other experts from both the public and the private sector relevant to the position in question.[33] The committees were comprised of some of the most highly qualified business people, academics, and ministers in Lebanon, who were driven by their professional ethics and had little interest in perpetuating a system that relied on nepotism and patronage. Once they interviewed the shortlisted candidates, the committees made a list of the three highest-scoring candidates, which would be submitted to OMSAR and then transferred to line ministers for nomination. It was then the minister's prerogative whether to submit the candidates' names to the Council of Ministers for approval or not.

While religion was not mentioned at any point in the selection process, at the final stage, line ministers could choose to take it into consideration. They could either approve the most qualified candidate irrespective of re-

TABLE 5-2. Mechanism and Phases of Selection of the First Three Candidates for a Vacant Position

Evaluation Phase	Goal	Result
Phase 1: Primary Screening	The first phase aims at screening anonymous applications on the basis of accurate, predefined legal criteria to eliminate ones that do not meet minimum requirements. A chart of primary criteria is used to screen the applications.	A list of accepted applications to be processed during the accurate evaluation phase
Phase 2: Examining Resumes/ Applications	The second phase aims at evaluating accepted anonymous applications in a more in-depth and detailed manner to determine to what extent they meet the required conditions, qualifications, and skills. This evaluation, based on detailed evaluation criteria, generates a short list of applicants who will be invited to a face-to-face interview.	A short list of applicants accepted for the third phase, and applications are rated
Phase 3: Face-to-Face Interview	The third phase aims at interviewing the applicants listed on the short list and studying thoroughly their personality, experience, and skills, which cannot be inferred from applications. This will be done based on defined interview evaluation criteria. A number of questions on various aspects will be asked to give a grade for each criterion.	A table listing face-to-face interview grades of the applicants on the short list and another table with the weaknesses and strengths of each candidate interviewed
Phase 4: Conclusion	The last phase aims at selecting the best three applications by adding the application evaluation grade to the interview evaluation grade, as follows: Final Grade = 40% of the application evaluation grade + 60% of the interview evaluation grade.	A final list (no ranking) with the best three applications (if found)

Source: OMSAR, 2006.

ligious affiliation or reject the committee recommendations if they did not include any representatives from the confession traditionally occupying that position. If there was a member of the desired religious sect among the three candidates and they were one of the most qualified individuals from a larger pool of applicants, at least the process made it more likely that such a candidate would be hired for the position. The system had no method to counter the preferences of individual ministers or the Council of Ministers to choose someone based on their confession or to reject all of the proposed candidates.

Between November 2005 and July 2006, the committee members worked tirelessly to go through the 2,726 applications and recommend at least three individuals for each of the thirty-eight available positions. "The review took a lot of time and hard work, but if the procedure was to be done correctly, it had to follow the appropriate steps," remembers Lamia Moubayed, an expert from the Finance Institute who helped design the guide on recruitment practices and served on twelve evaluation committees.[34] She noted that the enthusiasm for the new procedure was pervasive and the need for professionalism and meritocracy was evident. Positions that had been vacant for years suddenly had hundreds of interested candidates whose trust in the public administration seemed to have been restored.

Nonetheless, at the end of the review process, only seven of the thirty-eight positions were filled according to the committee recommendations. All seven positions, including four committee members and one director general position for the Telecommunications Regulatory Agency and one director general position for the High Commission for Privatization, were new posts without confessional legacies. Moreover, appointment of the director general for privatization was an urgent issue tied to external pressures, namely reform-conditional financial pledges that required quick administrative action.[35] Such an outcome was followed by a great deal of frustration on the part of both applicants and the experts who assisted in the new recruitment practices. In their perception, it was clear evidence that confessionalism trumped meritocracy and professionalism in staffing Lebanon's public administration.

After the initial evaluation and appointment process for these seven positions, the 2005 hiring procedure was discontinued. This decision was due both to political opposition and the changing political circumstances that played out during the summer of 2006. As the application process made no mention of religious affiliation and allowed candidates to apply from anywhere in the world via the internet, it directly challenged the entrenched system of nepotism and patronage. As a result, the confessional and political interest groups converged in their opposition; Parliament Speaker Nabih Berri played an instrumental role in blocking legislation, and the 2005 draft law never made it to the parliament floor. Furthermore, the momentum for reform was lost: The enthusiasm for the new recruitment practices was overwhelmed by a dispiriting war with Israel in July 2006 and an ensuing political stalemate between the Siniora administration and Hezbollah. As a result, civil service reform was abandoned for the next two years.

The 2009 Implementation Law. In September 2008, a decision was made at the Council of Ministers that the OMSAR minister at the time, Ibrahim Shamseddine, should prepare a proposal outlining hiring procedures for senior level civil service positions in line with 2005 reform initiatives. Minister Shamseddine had analyzed the 2005 recruitment procedure and proposed that additional mechanisms, such as the psychometric assessment tool, be included in the process. Moreover, to revive the process that was never voted on by the parliament, Shamseddine proposed that a decree be introduced making the procedure binding while it awaited parliament vote. The initiative received support from Prime Minister Siniora, as a successful reform law would have not only prevented confessional interventions in civil service appointments but also left a legacy of civil service reform for the new government at the onset of the June 2009 general elections.

The Mechanism for the Appointment of Senior Leadership Positions in the Lebanese Government, an implementation law introduced in 2009, outlined the criteria for committee selection, application screening, and the structured interview process reflecting the system briefly put in practice in 2005.[36] A psychometric assessment tool and a team of organizational psychologists, developed by Charlotte Karam, were introduced to serve as an independent advisory body.[37] This initiative was initially supported by the Council of Ministers. However, when put to a vote in front of the council six months later, the proposed legislation was overwhelmingly defeated by a margin of twenty-eight votes against and two in favor. The proposal was then passed on to a ministerial review committee, which significantly diminished the likelihood for its future passage.[38]

The Reform in Retrospect

Both the broader civil service reform agenda and the future of meritocratic selection for senior leadership within Lebanon's public administration are on hold for the foreseeable future. In the eyes of different stakeholders, there are many factors that contributed to the perceived failure of these civil service reforms. The hiring procedures represented a groundbreaking recruitment approach that directly challenged the entrenched system of patronage. As 2005 OMSAR Minister Ogassapian remembers, "They [the political leaders] did not feel it was realistic for someone not to have any prior interaction with the government, [that they] could be at home, send a CV, application, etc. over the internet and have the committee review him/her seriously for a position. That was too radical of a change."[39] However, the successful appointment of seven Grade One civil servants underscored the possibility that qualified external candidates could be placed in the highest posts in public administration. Moreover, while the proposed reform attempted to reduce the sway of the confessional system over recruitment, it did so within the system's constraints and with proposed concessions and alternatives. For instance, Minister Ogassapian proposed that "rotations"—proportional appointments based on religion but not explicitly on the confessional legacy—be brought into the new process. For example, if the most qualified person for a traditionally Shia position was a Maronite, then the Maronite would get that position and, in return, a traditionally-held Maronite position would be given to a Shiite, should one be qualified for it. However, such a proposal did not gain much traction as it threatened positions that were viewed as entitlements by some confessions (for example, the post of Army Commander in Chief is traditionally occupied by a Maronite).

Another critique focuses on how the reforms were implemented, particularly the general lack of support and lobbying for the reform law. While working closely with the Council of Ministers, OMSAR had very little interaction with the members of parliament. In fact, most members were unfamiliar with the proposed procedural reforms, as OMSAR introduced the draft without much public awareness or deliberation. As Ogassapian remembers, "We talked to the cabinet beforehand, and sought their initial approval, but not the parliament. We knew we wouldn't get anywhere with them."[40] Instead, knowing that the procedure had a small chance of being adopted by the parliament, OMSAR tried to minimize the bill's innovative proposals in the hope that their successful implementation would pressure the parliament to take the issue of meritocracy under closer consideration. On the contrary, such a strategy gave the parliament and line ministers enough room to question the procedure and avoid any pressure from civil society to abide by committee recommendations. A campaign of outreach to civil society, NGOs, and international organizations perhaps would have laid the groundwork for the reform's introduction. With enough support and pressure from such groups, line ministers might have been forced to justify their appointment choices, making it more difficult to get away with rejecting committee recommendations.

According to Lamia Moubayed, OMSAR should have been focusing on building stakeholder awareness and support before the introduction of the 2009 implementation bill. Instead, the focus was on improving the technical aspect of the hiring process. "The technicalities of this are irrelevant when the groundwork has not been done to garner the political will for the reform to pass," she stated.[41] Moreover, the 2009 political climate was less receptive to any major reform process. Compared to 2005, the 2009 cabinet was filled with far less enthusiastic ministers whose mandate was characterized by war-induced impasse and a general distrust in the reform potential. As their terms were nearing an end, the ministers had no incentive to uphold a long-term reform platform. In addition, at the onset of the 2009 elections, the country was polarized in its support for either the pro-Western "March 14" or the pro-Syrian "March 8" alliance. As the civil service reform was not significant for either camp, it found little support from the individual ministers or parliament members.[42] In addition, there was little public awareness or pressure about the reform process, which further undermined the incentive for its support. By bringing the draft law in front of the Council of Ministers before the general elections, OMSAR may have misjudged the timing of this reform.

Where Do These Reforms Currently Stand?

At the time of Siniora's first attempt to instill meritocracy in the selection of civil servants in Lebanon in 1996, his reform agenda was sidetracked because promoting infrastructure investment and protecting the confessional balance enshrined in the Ta'if Agreement were deemed to take precedence over human resource management reforms in the aftermath of the civil war. The second impetus, occurring in 2005 under Hariri's leadership with support from Siniora and Mohammad Chatah, was weakened by the prime minister's assassination and the subsequent political cleavage between the March 8 and March 14 groups. This crisis was further exacerbated by the war with Israel in the summer of 2006. With these shocks, the reform agenda again lost importance and was once more viewed as a threat to the stability of the confessional system.

These external dynamics were compounded by inherent weaknesses in Siniora's reform agenda, which were apparent at the conception stage but had not been addressed: chiefly, that these reforms were conducted without a strategic reevaluation of the civil service as a whole and were not designed in a consultative manner. Unfortunately, the lack of a broader and more strategic approach has resulted in certain key institutions for civil service restructuring being ill-equipped to support the reforms adequately, as their structure, mandate, or frameworks are too archaic. For example, the CSB still operates as it did in the 1950s, with the same number of staff and the same recruitment criteria. This is problematic, as the competencies required for the civil service have developed considerably since then.

Since the 2009 reform initiative, there has been no serious attempt to reform the hiring process for civil servants. Even more modest reforms have floundered in the face of intense public sector opposition, such as a 2013 attempt to increase working hours. The reforms of 2005 did retain one modest but important legacy, the maintenance of a selection committee that would screen potential applicants for Grade One positions and provide a short list to the relevant minister. Subsequent partial attempts at reform by successive OMSAR ministers, such as Ibrahim Shamseddine (who served as minister from 2008 to 2009) or Mohammed Fneish (who served as minister from 2011 to 2014), were mostly unsuccessful, leading OMSAR and other entities like the *Institut des Finances Bassil Fuleihan* to turn, instead, to more practical forms of capacity building and training of civil servants while waiting for an eventual new reform process to gain traction.

Areas of Progress and Areas of Struggle

Reforming Grade One Appointments. Michel Aoun's accession to the presidency in October 2016 was viewed by many within the Lebanese cabinet as an opportunity to revisit the mechanism for Grade One appointments and to restore it to its original pre-reform standard of providing ministers with total discretion regarding appointments.[43] This high-level debate on the merits of the new meritocratic approach resulted in the postponement of announcements for several Grade One vacancies despite the nomination of qualified candidates. In addition, it has pressured OMSAR to coordinate with the CSB to expedite the screening of candidates to prove the value of the system to reticent ministers.

Even though the reformed selection process for Grade One positions by means of a selection committee is a successful (albeit time consuming) approach, appointments for these positions are still viewed as inherently political decisions.[44] If the relevant minister does not accept the nomination of the selection committee, he or she can create significant delays between the time candidates are nominated and when the position is formally filled.

These delays, unfortunately, remain prevalent today. Most recently, the committee has appointed qualified candidates to lead the National Authority of Museums (ninety-four applications), the National Library (107 applications), and the National School of Music (thirty-five applications), but no selections have been made. In another high-profile example, the Minister of Information and President of the Republic clashed over who held the prerogative to appoint the head of *TeleLiban*, the national television station, with the result that the effort to fill the position was put on hold. Despite the fact that the minister has the discretion to appoint his chosen candidate, the Minister of Information has chosen to adopt the appointment mechanism that is supported by OMSAR and the CSB.[45]

Instilling a fully meritocratic appointment process for Grade One positions will be impossible as long as ministerial discretion is legally enshrined.[46] That said, political discretion does play a positive role in maintaining the confessional balance and representation within high level government positions in a country where seventeen religions coexist. Within this dynamic, it is essential to ensure that political appointments should not be made to the detriment of selecting qualified candidates, even if they are chosen from a pool hailing from the traditionally appointed sect for the role. This is particularly important in areas that require strong technical expertise, such as agencies regulating food safety, civil aviation, and petroleum.[47]

Reforming the CSB. A consensus exists within Lebanon that the CSB is in serious and urgent need of reform, as its standards and examination procedures are widely viewed as being out of step with current needs. Outdated selection criteria detrimentally affect the CSB's ability to select candidates with relevant qualifications, which affects both the capacity of public entities and the performance of the entire civil service.[48] Some former civil

servants argue that the CSB must be given increased competency and capacity, fearing that as long as administrative appointments are left to the
discretion of the Council of Ministers, HR management in Lebanon will
always be a race to the bottom. In their view, qualified candidates will
inevitably be replaced at the final stages of the recruitment process by ap-
pointees chosen for their confessional or political ties.[49]

Beyond Recruitment to Retention. While this case study has focused heavily on recruitment, the question of how qualified candidates are retained
once appointed is equally important. Even when meritocratically recruited
candidates have been accepted by ministers, their ability to fulfill their
mandate can be limited by political inertia or opposition. Kamal Shehadi,
as head of the TRA (from 2007 to 2010), experienced this issue firsthand,
after successive ministers of telecommunications refused to partially devolve their authority to the TRA and blocked all attempts at regulation
of the industry—in spite of a law passed by parliament. Ultimately, after
battling political elites for three years of his five-year term, he was forced
to resign in protest.

Mitigating Factors and Islands of Progress. Yet islands of limited progress remain. OMSAR has positioned itself as a frontrunner in the reform
agenda, receiving considerable funding from the European Union to help
modernize and manage the CSB and to develop its human resources (HR)
functions. In addition, it has launched an HR project to train employees
from *ENA Liban*, the national school of government, in addition to those
from the CSB. OMSAR is also working closely with four pilot ministries
to develop job descriptions based on competencies, in a bid to increase the
meritocracy of the selection process.[50] Several ministries have established
standalone HR task forces that work with OMSAR directly to implement
these reforms. It is too early to evaluate the full impact of these projects,
but they demonstrate encouraging new trends.

Outside of OMSAR, other entities, such as the *Institut des Finances
Bassil Fuleihan*, while waiting for the next opportunity for systematic
reform, have established programs to train civil servants falling under the
remit of the Ministry of Finance (tax, customs, and land registry) in management, language, and IT skills, to build internal capacity.

Political and Fiscal Constraints. Like many of its regional peers, the civil
service in Lebanon is still viewed as a tool of recruitment for social employ-

ment.[51] The size of the public sector has implications for Lebanon's fiscal balance, as well as for the country's ability to instill a genuine performance culture within its civil service. Research conducted by the Institute of Finance concluded that Lebanon's wage bill has exploded, with aggregate salaries and generous pension packages amounting to 40 percent of public spending. This trajectory is fiscally unsustainable.

In this context, the recent decision by Lebanese President Michel Aoun to increase civil service salaries may compound this unsustainable trend. The merits of this decision have been hotly debated in Lebanon, with some claiming it is likely to increase the incentive to perform and reduce petty corruption and others arguing that the decision was opaque, politically motivated, and missed an opportunity for genuine reform.[52] The law itself claims salary increases will need to be commensurate with performance appraisals, more accurate job descriptions, and increased working hours, though it is unclear whether these conditions have been met either in whole or in part.[53] In all likelihood, the effort to strengthen meritocracy within Lebanon's civil service will remain an ongoing struggle for the indefinite future.

Conclusion

Lebanon's effort to upgrade its recruitment practices for civil servants provides valuable insights into the systemic obstacles surrounding public administration reform in MENA—even in an area that would appear as straightforward and noncontroversial as strengthening talent and meritocracy among senior staff. On both sides of the equation, the dynamics pressing for and against reform were strong. Forces supporting the retention of the status quo include a fragile polity, an entrenched confessional system that provides patronage opportunities for senior officials, and an age-old tradition of doing business through *wasta*. On the other side, the pressures for change include a talented professional class, a numerous and educated diaspora, a clear recognition that Lebanon's traditional recruitment practices were dysfunctional and woefully inadequate for the future, and a dedicated and committed prime minister. The outcome, so far, represents a clear victory for the forces opposing reform.

Like Lebanon, many countries in the MENA region often rely upon a series of temporary fixes or patches to overcome the obstacles to reform to gain access to the talent they need. This is particularly evident in the use of contractual employees to fill critical gaps in areas where it would be difficult to obtain the skills needed from within the civil service. What are the strengths and weaknesses of such an approach? Can contractual labor become a viable, sustainable substitute for an institutionalized public administration? Is this the best approach, given the broader dysfunctions within the public sector and the inherent difficulties surrounding civil service reform? Or is it likely to be a short-term solution with pernicious long-term consequences? While the answers to such questions might differ, the discussion they provoke should serve as a starting point for any future civil service reform initiative.

Notes

The original case was drafted by Simonida Subotic. The conclusion was drafted by Adele Barzelay.

1. Charlotte Karam, interview with author, Washington, DC, July 2009.

2. Jihad Makhoul and Lindsey Harrison, "Intercessory Wasta and Village Development in Lebanon," *Arab Studies Quarterly* 26, no. 3 (Summer 2004), p. 25.

3. Atef Mehri (OMSAR director), telephone interview with Simonida Subotic, Washington, DC, and Beirut, Lebanon, July 2009.

4. "Constitutional Council Complete, Draft Budget Stalled," *Now Lebanon*, May 27, 2009.

5. Lamia Moubayed, telephone interview with Simonida Subotic, Washington, DC, July 2009.

6. Khamal Shehadi, interview with author, Beirut, Lebanon, July 2009.

7. Julia Choucair-Vizoso, "Lebanon: Finding a Path from Deadlock to Democracy," Carnegie Endowment for International Peace, January 5, 2006, p. 6, https://carnegieendowment.org/2006/01/05/lebanon-finding-path-from-deadlock-to-democracy-pub-17844.

8. Ibid., p. 9.

9. Ibid.

10. Estimates on the size of the Lebanese diaspora vary between 10 and 15 million people.

11. Mehri, telephone interview.

12. Ibid.

13. Jean Ogassapian, interview with Simonida Subotic, Beirut, Lebanon, July 2009.

14. Alia Moubayed (former employee at the Ministry of the Economy and Trade and candidate for the Director General of the Ministry of Economy and Trade), interview with Simonida Subotic, Washington, DC, July 2009.

15. Fouad El-Saad, "Strategy for the Reform Development of the Public Administration in Lebanon," Office of the Minister of State for Administrative Reform, September 2001, p. 5; Paul Salem, "Lebanon: Governance Reform and Development," World Bank, Washington, DC, p. 32.

16. "World Bank Country Governance Briefs: Lebanon," World Bank Group, 2009.

17. Lama Oueijan (UNDP contractor at the Ministry of the Economy and Trade), interview with Simonida Subotic, Beirut, Lebanon, July 2009; Mehri, telephone interview.

18. Oueijan, interview.

19. Charles C. Adwan (MENA vice presidency), conversation with Simonida Subotic, Washington, DC, July 2009.

20. Salem, "Lebanon: Governance Reform," p. 21.

21. "Chapter 5: Public Sector Employment," in "Lebanon: Public Expenditure Review," World Bank Publications, 2004, p. 8.

22. Republic of Lebanon Civil Service Board, "The Reforms of the Civil Service in Lebanon," 2005.

23. Fares El-Zein and Holly Sims, "Reforming War's Administrative Rubble in Lebanon," *Public Administration and Development* 24, no. 4 (2004), p. 282.

24. Salem, "Lebanon: Governance Reform," p. 30.

25. Mehri, interview.

26. Salem, "Lebanon: Governance Reform," p. 31.

27. El-Zein and Sims, "Reforming War's Administrative Rubble," p. 282.

28. Moubayed, telephone interview.

29. Mehri, telephone interview.

30. Moubayed, telephone interview.

31. Mehri, telephone interview.

32. Ibid.

33. Mehri, telephone interview.

34. Moubayed, telephone interview.

35. Atef Merhi (OMSAR director), telephone interview with author, Washington, DC, and Beirut, July 2009.

36. OMSAR, "Mechanism for the Appointment of Senior Leadership Positions in the Lebanese Government," 2008.

37. Charlotte Karam, telephone interview with author, Washington, DC, July 2009.

38. Merhi, interview.

39. Ogassapian, interview.

40. Ibid.

41. Moubayed, interview.

42. Adwan, conversation.

43. Government official (CSB), interview with Barzelay.

44. Official at *Institut des Finances*, interview with Barzelay, Beirut, December 2017. The main reason for the time-consuming nature of the exercise is that no competency framework has been devised for many of the positions recruited for, leaving the selection committee to rely on outdated legislative texts for DG (Grade One) positions. This reform lay within the purview of the CSB, but it was not achieved.

45. OMSAR official, telephone interview with Barzelay, Washington, DC, October 2017.

46. Former head of TRA, telephone interview with Barzelay, Washington, DC, November 2017, referring to provisions in the Ta'if Agreement and national bylaws.

47. Former head of TRA.

48. OMSAR official, interview.

49. Former head of TRA, interview.

50. OMSAR official, interview.

51. *Institut des Finances*, interview, Barzelay, Beirut, Lebanon, December 2017.

52. OMSAR official, interview; *Institut des Finances*, interview.

53. OMSAR official, interview.

SIX

From Electronic Government to Smart City

Dubai's Digital Transformation

FADI SALEM
OKAN GERAY

DUBAI E-GOVERNMENT (DEG) WAS launched in 2000 as a government initiative that aimed to deliver innovative government services through digital channels to businesses and society in the city of Dubai. The stated
vision of the DeG was to ease the lives of people and businesses interacting with the government. For more than a decade, the initiative was
part of a larger effort to reinvent the government of Dubai in terms of legislation, regulation, and services by utilizing information and communication technologies (ICT). After large-scale public service transformation
and near-universal societal adoption, the e-government initiative was restructured under "Dubai Smart Government" (DSG) in 2013, with the
objective of expanding its impact on governance. The DeG—later DSG—
is considered the nucleus of "Smart Dubai,"[1] a much larger initiative
launched in 2015 with the objective of transforming the whole city, not just
the government, of Dubai into the "smartest" city in the world, utilizing
data and digital innovations. Under this umbrella, the DeG was restructured into "Smart Dubai Government Establishment," the government-
focused technology arm of Smart Dubai.

Almost two decades since the launch of Dubai's digital transformation journey, public services have been revolutionized in the digital age, with rapid urban evolution taking place. During this period, this transformation has continued to be viewed as a global "best practice," both in digital government and urban digital transformation, offering a model that potentially can be reproduced on the national, regional, and global levels. This chapter describes the evolution of Smart Dubai, from its inception under the DeG initiative through its stages of evolution as a full government department as "Dubai Smart Government," until its current mature stage as part of Smart Dubai, the transformative smart city project creating local and regional impact. It presents the implementation process, challenges encountered, achieved results, policy implications, and future directions. Based on primary data and interviews with key stakeholders, this chapter highlights key challenges and milestones in the digitization of public services and its impact on Dubai's wider societal and urban transformation into a "smart city." The lessons learned and policy responses throughout two decades of digital transformation in Dubai provide valuable policy learning opportunities both on the regional and global levels.

Dubai's Vision and Strategic Development Plans

Dubai, one of seven emirates in the young federation of the United Arab Emirates, has enjoyed strong economic growth for decades, establishing itself as a global economic hub with a sustained record of real GDP growth and "very high" human development. Since the late 1990s, the emirate reinvented and reformed its economic and governance foundations by closely aligning its institutions, governance mechanisms, infrastructure, and economy. The city-state, as it is usually called, managed to find a rapidly growing economic niche and to assert itself as a successful regional developmental model.

In the years 2000 and 2007, respectively, Sheikh Mohammad bin Rashid al-Maktoum, vice president and prime minister of the UAE and, later, ruler of Dubai, launched two strategic development plans, namely Dubai Vision 2010 and Dubai Strategic Plan 2015, both of which aimed to diversify Dubai's economy and to push development forward.[2] One of the key pillars of both of these plans was to position Dubai as a regional hub for logistical and financial services by 2015. Dubai was to become a knowledge-based economy driven mainly by service industries (for example, financial services, tourism, trade, professional services, transportation, and storage).

Service economies revolve around the transactions between government, businesses, and individuals (citizens, residents, and visitors). Therefore, increasing the efficiency and effectiveness of these transactions (for example, government-to-business, business-to-business, government-to-citizen, etc.) became a key objective for Dubai. The city upgraded its infrastructure and public government services to accommodate those new requirements. In return, this propelled the adoption of ICT in the early 2000s, which shifted Dubai's economy from a traditional economy into a globally connected one.

During this period, the DeG was one of the key drivers of this transformation, along with various other government-led ICT-based initiatives (for example, Dubai Internet City, Tejari.com, Dubai Trade, Dubai Media City, Knowledge Village, and Dubai Silicon Oasis). At the time, ICT was viewed by policymakers as a key driver of improving effectiveness and efficiency of services in public services. In 2000, the government announced the establishment of the DeG initiative as the central engine to achieving Dubai's future vision of governance.

The first part of this chapter discusses the origins of the DeG, its achievements, and its challenges a decade after its launch. The second part explores the evolution of electronic services (and DeG as an organization) during a period of almost a decade until today, into the wider digital transformation project (and Smart Dubai Office), including the new challenges and successes, and their policy implications, on Dubai's growth and transformation into a smart city.

The Origins of the Dubai E-Government Initiative

The DeG was launched with an ultimate goal of delivering the government's core services through electronic means in eighteen months, focusing on the following specific objectives:

- Streamline government services by utilizing information technology.

- Make the provision of government services customer-centric by increasing effectiveness and efficiency.

- Consolidate existing government services through information and communication technologies.

- Streamline and standardize internal administrative services, including procurement, finance and accounting, and human resources.

As a first step, a strategic audit and a benchmarking exercise were conducted in 2000.[3] The purpose of the strategic audit was to define the existing gap between Dubai's government and the objectives stated by the DeG. The purpose of the strategic benchmarking exercise was to identify and analyze successful e-government initiatives globally to highlight good practices, note the key lessons learned, and study the undertaken approaches. This project covered e-government initiatives in more than ten countries leading in e-government at the time.

Developing a Vision. Having audited Dubai's current status in e-governance and benchmarked its position with respect to similar initiatives, the DeG team then defined its vision, highlighting three main components: 1) "core purpose," 2) "core values," and 3) "envisioned future." The "core purpose" represented the organization's ultimate driving goal. It was set as a guiding principle that—by design—endures the test of time and can never be completely achieved but, rather, only pursued. The "core values" described the shared beliefs, values, and main characteristics of the DeG that hold its members together. Together, the first two components were referred to as the core DeG "ideology." Finally, the "envisioned future" highlighted short- and medium-term concrete objectives pursued by the DeG in its early stages. The three components of the vision determined the objectives and aligned the goals of the DeG team.

Defining the Strategies. While the DeG vision defined what needed to be done at a high-level in the medium- to long-term, the DeG strategies attempted to define how to pursue the vision. For this purpose, the DeG team developed five guiding strategies: 1) the operational strategy, 2) the organizational strategy, 3) the financial strategy, 4) the information technology strategy, and 5) the legal strategy.[4] Defined in early 2001, those strategies were adopted as a holistic framework that guided the DeG project in its initial few years.

The DeG team later derived the operational framework from the DeG strategies to guide it through the implementation stage. It emphasized two main components, namely "customer focus" and "operational efficiency." The objective of this framework was to assist the DeG in adopting a customer-focused approach while simultaneously enhancing operational efficiency. Additionally, linking customer focus with efficiency within the operational framework enabled the team to flexibly and explicitly make tradeoffs between these two main components throughout the life of the initiative.[5]

The DeG Organizational Structure

The strategy and vision formulation were conducted under an executive committee made up of senior government officials established in 2000. A Strategic Management Office (SMO) was then formed, consisting of three members of the executive committee dedicated full-time to handle the implementation tasks in the first eighteen months of the initiative.

The SMO established two departments under the Dubai Ruler's Court. Those were the Government Information Resources Planning Department (GIRP) and the eServices Department, each of which had its clearly delineated roles and responsibilities. The former took charge of the e-enablement of internal government administrative and support services. It was tasked with providing shared administrative and infrastructure services for Dubai's government departments. The latter mainly took charge of the e-enablement of core public-facing government services. It was tasked with providing core shared-services as well as overseeing the implementation of department-specific core services provided to businesses and the public in Dubai.

The DeG was initially implemented under the guidance and coordination of both departments, which together launched the official online portal of the Dubai government and some sample representative services in October 2001. Both entities followed up closely with the respective government departments for alignment and guidance. They grew organically over the years as they undertook shared services implementations in their respective areas of responsibility. The two departments gradually established their statures in the government, overcoming some preexisting silos and cultures among different government departments.

However, synergies surfaced between them in terms of overall infrastructure management, customer management, and support activities. Consequently, the departments were merged in 2009, when Sheikh Mohammad bin Rashid al-Maktoum issued, in his capacity as ruler of Dubai, Law No. 7 of 2009 establishing the Dubai e-Government Department (DeG Department) as a fully independent government department. As such, the two entities, namely GIRP and the eServices Department, were amalgamated into a single entity to ensure alignment and better coordination across the board. According to Ahmed Bin Humaidan, director general of the DeG department at the time, "the institutional structural change in 2009 reflected the future needs of the government of Dubai and ensured better coordination, leading to further efficiency and effectiveness gains."[6]

The new department was tasked with developing "Dubai's e-strategy," ICT-related policies, and monitoring their implementation. This included, for example, public and administrative electronic services, information security, and the management of knowledge, human resources, and financial capital. Given the organic synergies that existed between the two entities, the merger process was largely smooth, with no perceivable adverse impact on the government departments.

The Three Layers of Implementation

In organizational terms, government departments in Dubai conduct three types of services. First, they conduct several shared administrative services. Those are back-office administrative functions that include human resources management, financial and accounting management, procurement, inventory management, asset management, and supply chain management. Next, in addition to those administrative services, each department is the owner and provider of specific core services, which they generally provide to the public. And third, those core services have some common aspects, including, for example: electronic payment, mobile services infrastructure platform, customer care services, web hosting infrastructure, and electronic survey tools. Those shared core services are used by all the departments and aid them in providing their specific core services to the public and businesses. In other words, the three types of services provided by Dubai government were: shared administrative services, department-specific core services, and shared core services.

E-Enabling Shared Administrative Services. During the early stages of Dubai's drive toward e-government, GIRP was tasked with developing a centralized resource planning system referred to as Government Resources Planning (GRP). This was a government-wide, highly complex initiative that involved more than 100 government-level standardization workshops (for various aspects of GRP) and over 300 government "business owners" across the different departments. Consequently, more than

130 main processes were streamlined, standardized, and automated as part of the implementation process, enabling Dubai to adopt government-wide administrative policies, regulations, and processes. Since then, almost all departments in Dubai utilize a single shared IT-based solution for all their human resources management, financial and accounting management, procurement management, inventory management, asset management, and other back-office needs. "For example, if somebody was transferred to another department they will not need any training as they are using the same system. . . . Also, if a law changes we change the services accordingly in one place . . . instead of more than 20, this saves time and money," said Bin Humaidan.[7] Such centralization has improved service levels and enabled significant cost savings by aggregating demand. It has also facilitated government-level budgeting, consolidation, and expedited knowledge-based decisionmaking. In contrast, the previous decentralized implementation approach resulted in replications of efforts.

E-Enabling Shared Core Services. Government departments in Dubai relied on a centralized effort when it came to the implementation and delivery of the common parts of an electronic service (for example, payment, customer care services, mobile messaging, website hosting infrastructure, and electronic survey tools). These centralized common aspects of government services were provided to all departments through a single centralized entity, namely the eServices Department. After each shared core service was developed, it was rolled out to different departments. This created several waves of development and roll-out activities over the years (one roll-out per department per core shared service). The initial roll-outs were followed up by reviews, enhancements, and further refinements.

E-Enabling Department-Specific Core Services. The DeG's official portal (www.dubai.ae) was inaugurated in October 2001, meeting the set eighteen-month deadline for delivering essential services online. Since then, departments continued to work on "e-enabling" the services they offered to the public. Two intermediate e-enablement deadlines were set by the ruler of Dubai. The first target mandated 70 percent of department-specific services to be e-enabled by the end of 2005, and the second pushed for 90 percent e-enablement by the end of 2007. Reaching these targets required creating an inventory of core services provided by all departments, which didn't exist until then. This exercise unified and standardized core service definitions across the government. Various core service attributes and characteristics were defined, and related information was captured using an electronic tool designed with the participation of all departments.

Between 2000 and 2015, the DeG—later branded Dubai Smart Government—led the transformation of government entities across Dubai, leading to the creation of hundreds of online government services, and generating numerous efficiencies. However, this was not without dealing with numerous challenges.

The Challenges of Digital Transformation

Securing the Commitment of All Stakeholders. During the first decade of its life, the DeG was a large-scale, complex initiative involving multiple stakeholders and constituents, sometimes with conflicting agendas. The announcement of the DeG's ultimatum created several uncertainties and, in some cases, sent a wave of panic across government departments. It was, therefore, clear from the start that leadership and commitment at the highest levels in the government were crucial to ensure its success. To overcome this challenge, the ruler of Dubai personally invested in DeG's mission, persistently and publicly aligning it to the overall vision of Dubai over a decade. This ensured inspiration and commitment at all levels within the government. Due to continued high-level political support, DeG projects were rigorously tracked and championed in all government departments.

Balancing between Centralization and Decentralization. In large-scale transformational initiatives like DeG, which encompass almost all government agencies, there is always an inherent challenge in both governing and organizing. The set strategic vision required integration; however, existing organizational cultures favored autonomy. This was a persistent challenge that was perceived to slow down progress in Dubai's digital transformation. In responding to this challenge, the DeG continued to create balances between centralization and decentralization in the implementation of services on the departmental and service levels.

Adjusting Legal and Regulatory Frameworks. One of the main barriers to e-government adoption was the lack of supporting regulatory and legal frameworks.[8] The DeG acknowledged this prerequisite at early stages of development and took the lead in the process of e-enabling traditional paper-based government commercial and legal transactions. A legal infrastructure was also essential for this transformation to be legally valid in the emirate. Therefore, government enacted the Electronic Transactions and Commerce Law No. 2 in 2002.[9] This law rendered electronic transactions and electronic commerce legally valid in Dubai. To be acceptable in other jurisdictions in the country, a federal legal infrastructure was necessary as well. This further enabled electronic commerce and electronic government while aiming to deter cybercrime across the UAE—extending the legal basis for electronic transactions beyond Dubai.

Filling the Skills Gap. The introduction of e-governance tends to pose substantial skills challenges for governments. Up-to-date ICT skills are required for e-service design, implementation, and delivery, skills that are largely lacking in traditional governments. Faced with the challenge of acquiring those complex skills in a short period of time, government entities in Dubai had to rely on private sector organizations and public-private partnerships to complement their competencies. Overall, the government established medium- to long-term relationships with public-private partnerships (PPPs) and private organizations that were based on proven results and subject to continuous monitoring conducted by the DeG.

Maintaining Significant Levels of Uptake. During the early phases of digitization, low uptake was a common challenge faced by e-government initiatives regionally.[10] To address this, the DeG formulated community outreach and marketing programs to boost the use and adoption of its services by the public and businesses. The activities included targeted and mass marketing (online and off-line), events, information sessions, campaigns, etc. They were seen as critical in increasing public awareness and encouraging further adoption.

The Evolution of Electronic Government

As Dubai's digital transformation evolved between 2000 and 2014, the previously mentioned challenges continued to reemerge at most developmental junctures. Almost fifteen years after the start of Dubai's digital transformation, Dubai's leadership decided that a substantial strategic review was required to overcome these challenges and to widen the impact of Dubai's digital agenda. Moreover, as the city of Dubai became one of the ten fastest growing cities worldwide, new challenges emerged. This was coupled with chronic urban and developmental problems related to population growth, environmental issues, and increased complexities in responding to sustainable development agendas. Increasingly, many of these challenges affected quality of life and wellbeing in the city. Specifically, the most critical of these challenges identified by the city's leadership can be summarized as follows:[11]

Population Growth. Around 86 percent of the population of the UAE lives in urban areas,[12] 2.6 million of them in Dubai alone.[13] However, given its large economy, the number of those who work in Dubai on a daily basis reaches 3.7 million, with more than a million commuting in and out of the city each day. This reality increases pressure on the city's infrastructure, severely affecting quality of life. For example, during the past decade, traffic congestion remained a chronic problem in Dubai despite numerous multibillion-dollar investments in metro, highway, and modern public transport channels. Moreover, the projected growth in tourists and visitors, especially as the city prepares to host the global Expo 2020, meant that another transformative response was needed. Digital transformation was seen by Dubai's leadership to be essential in managing such future growth challenges.

Environmental Sustainability. Globally, cities occupy 2 percent of the surface of the earth but produce around 70 percent of global CO_2 emissions.[14] The UAE, with its 90 percent-urban population, has one of the highest carbon footprints per capita in the world,[15] one of the critical growth drawbacks acknowledged by policymakers in the country. Dubai, as one of the most populous cities in the country, has a leading role to play in environmental sustainability. Reducing the negative effects of rapid urbanization on the environment is a key priority where digital responses can play a role in the wellbeing of this generation and the next.

Public Expectations. Dubai's population has enjoyed some of the highest technology adoption rates in the region for two decades.[16] Matching public expectations about living, development, and quality of life has pushed the city planners to continuously adopt cutting-edge approaches (see table 6-1). Such a high level of societal embrace of digital lifestyle, technological adoption by the government, not just in terms of service delivery but also holistically in its developmental and governance approaches, was a key contributor to a better quality of life. According to numerous stakeholders in the city's digital transformation plans, this realization was a driving force in putting together the blueprints of Dubai's next phase of digital transformation.

Collectively, these chronic challenges drove key policymakers in the city to actively engage in an ambitious long-term digital transformation initiative with the objective of sustaining development, while ensuring that the challenges of growth are minimized. The ultimate objective of this ini-

TABLE 6-1. Dubai's Technology Adoption in a Comparative Perspective

	Dubai	UAE	Gulf Cooperation Council (GCC)	Arab Region
Internet Penetration	91.2%	91.2%	76.3%	40.3%
Mobile Phone Penetration	235%	229%	184%	109.15%
Mobile Broadband Penetration	N/A	92%	115.6%	46.1%
Social Media Accounts Penetration	129%	105%	82%	42.5%
Daily Active Social Media Users Penetration	65.3%	65.9%	57.3%	51.6%
International Bandwidth per Internet User (Bit/s)	107,914	107,914	84,659	35,087
Mobile Phone Subscription	6,348,125	17,942,571	91,819,483	420,532,558
Fixed Broadband Subscriptions	623,379	1,312,134	7,577,196	18,178,043
Fixed Broadband Penetration	22%	15.1%	12.8%	4.17%

Sources: Based on historical and current data from the following sources:

Fadi Salem, "The Arab World Online 2017: Digital Transformations and Societal Trends in the Age of the 4th Industrial Revolution," MBR School of Government, October 2017, www.mbrsg.ae/HOME/PUBLICATIONS/Research-Report-Research-Paper-White -Paper/The-Arab-World-Online-2017.aspx.

Fadi Salem, "Social Media and the Internet of Things: Towards Data-Driven Policymaking in the Arab World—Potential, Limits and Concerns," 7th Arab Social Media Report, MBR School of Government, 2017.

Telecommunications Regulatory Authority, "Latest Statistics 2011–2017," UAE Government, 2017.

Dubai Statistics Center, "Dubai in Figures 2017," Government of Dubai, 2017.

International Telecommunication Union, "Measuring the Information Society Report," 2016.

tiative was to enhance quality of life in the city. By 2014, a new government-wide transformative initiative started building on DeG's achievements of more than a decade. Smart Dubai was born as the next phase of the city's digital transformation, with the underlying mission statement: "to create happiness, by embracing technology innovation—making Dubai the most efficient, seamless, safe, and impactful experience for residents and visitors." At its early stages in 2014, the initiative was envisioned as a journey toward better quality of life, utilizing digital-age tools to ensure inclusive happiness of the city's inhabitants, as well as its future generations. Since its early stages, Dubai's smart city plans focused on "happiness," a unique philosophy in comparison with the directions of other digital transformation initiatives globally up to that time.

Operationally, a "Smart City Taskforce" was formed under the leadership of Dr. Aisha Bin Bishr, assistant director general of the executive office at the time. In March 2014, Dubai's smart city strategic plan was launched, including six dimensions envisioned for the next phase of Dubai's transformation, including economy, governance, environment, living, mobility, and people. The strategy featured 100 initiatives in areas of infrastructure, urban planning, transport, electricity, communications, and economic services. The ultimate goal was "to bring about happiness to all," as stated by Sheikh Mohammed as he launched the plan.[17] Particularly, the strategy put forward plans for 1,000 government services contributing to smart city development to be launched in less than three years. However, at the time, Dubai's crown prince made it clear that the vision was not about increasing "customer satisfaction," or just developing numerous services, but about changing the way of life in Dubai and contributing to the happiness of the city's inhabitants.[18]

From Dubai E-Government to Dubai Smart City

Effectively, Dubai's initial plans toward a smart city transformation started informally in 2007. The government then initiated a study on the transformation to a "digital city." At the time, the world was just about to get hit by the global financial crisis, which had a major impact on Dubai's economy, creating critical budgetary constraints and changing the government's priorities. Several countries in the region were exploring digital transformation agendas; however, environmental factors brought many of these projects to a halt. In addition to the budgetary and financial limitations, urban transformation in the digital era requires societal readiness and technological maturity. Until recently, not all these ingredients were in place.

Thanks in part to DeG's efforts in digital transformation, Dubai's population was already enjoying impressive levels of "technological trust," or acceptance of technology. On the government side, the structural building blocks of Dubai's smart city were layered systematically over the preceding fifteen years. The top-down initiatives solidly built the technological infrastructure of what later became the smart city plan. Dubai's digital governance drive also influenced the UAE's national digital government agenda. Today, the UAE is globally among the highest ranked countries in different digital governance indicators (see table 6-2). For example, it has consistently held the top position worldwide on indicators measuring "Importance of ICT to Government Vision" and "Government Success in ICT Promotion" by the World Economic Forum (WEF).[19] Similarly, the UAE has consistently risen in the UN rankings of digital governance measures, currently holding the fourteenth spot worldwide in "Online Service Delivery."[20]

In contrast to previous major digital transformation initiatives in the city, when the Smart Dubai initiative was announced, none of Dubai's government entities seemed to have been taken by surprise. Members of the

TABLE 6-2. UAE Rankings on Digital Transformation Indicators

Indicator	Rank/ Number of Countries	Year	Source*
Importance of ICT to Government Vision	1/139	2016	WEF
Government ICT Procurement	1/137	2017	WEF
Government Success in ICT Promotion	1/139	2016	WEF
Global Competitiveness Index	16/138	2016	WEF
Networked Readiness Index	26/139	2016	WEF
Online Service Index	14/193	2016	UN DESA
E-Government Development Index	29/193	2016	UN DESA
E-Participation Index	32/193	2016	UN DESA
ICT Development Index	38/175	2016	UN ITU

*World Economic Forum (WEF); United Nations Department of Economic and Social Affairs (UN DESA); United Nations International Telecommunications Unit (UN ITU).

Smart Dubai's leadership team repeatedly express pride—and relief—in that fact. This was a stark contrast to electronic services transformation in 2000, when the crown prince of Dubai at the time announced that government entities had eighteen months to shift gears and transform their traditional, old-fashioned, manual ways of delivering services into electronic government services. At the time, that tight deadline and the many uncertainties around such a transformation sent a wave of panic across government entities. This time around, everyone seemed prepared. The foundations laid down by the digital government drive during the past fifteen years meant that both the government and society were largely ready to adopt a new transformation. However, naturally, this new disruptive transformation created a new set of challenges. In the first phase of Smart Dubai's journey, the following key challenges emerged, requiring a combination of policy, regulatory, and organizational responses.

The New Challenges of Urban Digital Transformation

"After 15 years of electronic government projects, we saw that we were living in silos on multiple dimensions: 1) cross-government silos, 2) silos between the government and the private sector, 3) silos between these two silos and the third sector, and 4) between the public and these different sectors." That was the key challenge realized as early as 2015 by Dr. Bin Bishr as she took the helm as director general of Smart Dubai Office, which incorporated DeG's successor under its umbrella, rebranded as Smart Dubai Government Establishment, alongside its newly created sister-entity, the Dubai Data Establishment.

Indeed, the working culture within government departments in Dubai during the decade preceding the establishment of the Smart Dubai Office was largely characterized as "competitive." Government entities were institutionally competing in a race for excellence. While that competitive culture advanced numerous efficiencies related to doing business in government, it also enforced a strong perception of data, information, knowledge, and innovations as the key sources of competitive advantage. This competitive view also limited the informal and formal information and data flow across government and—in many cases—reduced the level of trust among competing individuals and institutions. Consequently, this enforced new forms of silos, increased overall government cost of doing business in many cases, and ultimately limited cross-governmental innovations.[21] In Dubai, this competition was institutionalized by norms and regulations over more than a decade. For the Smart Dubai team, these silos were a key barrier at early stages of planning the transition into a smart city and creating the data-sharing culture, a must-have foundation for Dubai's ambitious smart transformation. Most important for the smart city, this created remote and disconnected data islands and numerous repositories. Dr. Bin Bishr said: "In assessing this challenge, we realized that data availability can solve many of these issues. So we looked at this as an opportunity to develop a data infrastructure that can bridge these silos."

Realistically, collaboration has never been the standard approach in governing. Moreover, openness to collaboration and sharing of data, information, ideas, and knowledge is not the *modus operandi* in public sector organizations. According to an earlier UAE-wide government survey, perceptions on the costs of collaboration include "losing ownership of ideas," "losing control," and "undermining managerial hierarchy."[22] As such, in these organizational structures, data, information, and ideas are perceived as sources of power. Hence, barriers to achieving better collaborative government are cultural, structural, and technological. On the other hand, enablers of better collaboration in the public sector of the UAE were perceived to include "sharing common goals," "openness to expressing ideas," and "availability of direct communication channels." Given these enablers and barriers, the Smart Dubai team needed an approach that would connect the government entities in a way that trust was nurtured, openness was exercised, and synergies were created toward a common goal.

The team needed to take bold steps to break these silos and infuse a culture where sharing data and innovation could be nurtured across the city. This could start only within the government. One traditional managerial approach was to break information silos by enforcing rules and norms that forced employees and departments to share data, information, and ideas. In such cases, earlier experiences of enforced knowledge management approaches in government suggested mixed results, where "collaboration"—when it took place—could vary from genuine to cosmetic. Another approach was to create a network of collaboration by applying soft measures instead of hard ones, especially at the early stages of development. In contrast to competition, collaboration cannot effectively be enforced by norms and regulations. The concept of collaborative government emphasizes nurturing trust and thereby triggering willingness to collaborate and share data, information, and ideas. This can create an intrinsic culture based on instilling relationships of trust among groups and individuals, as well as understanding and appreciating the shared mutual benefits of cooperating and data sharing.

Acknowledging the steep road ahead, and realizing the cultural characteristics of the government, the Smart Dubai team adopted an open collaborative philosophy on day one, in the form of cross-governmental committees and teams. As such, a soft approach was selected by the Smart Dubai team to build trust, a culture of openness, and willingness to collaborate, not just between government entities but also between government and private sectors. "The lack of collaboration is a challenge addressed by the Smart Dubai Office in a multi-stakeholder approach across government, with the private sector as well as with international organizations," according to Dr. Bin Bishr. For example, in addition to involving private sector players as partners in developing systems and infrastructure, they are also invited to shape policies. Likewise, government entities are not seen simply as implementers but as partners in shaping policies in almost leaderless roundtable settings.

Commenting on the working environment in the formative months of Smart Dubai, Dr. Bin Bishr said: "The multiple cross-governmental committees that have been shaped are effectively driving this collaborative effort." While designing their roadmap, the approach followed by Smart Dubai's team was to create active committees that included selected members from each of the core government bodies. Emphasis on peer partnerships was instrumental for progress and alignment, while minimizing resistance. For example, on day one, eleven entities were identified as strategic partners for Smart Dubai's first phase of development and engaged at each step of the way. Likewise, members in a newly formed Open Data Committee, tasked with building a roadmap to open, regulate, and de-silo the data islands in government, were drawn from all key government bodies.

As a by-product of this approach, each of the powerful government entities felt ownership of Smart Dubai. This way, the different government bodies shaped movement toward the future of the city together. The outcome of this approach was the creation of what seems to be an effective cross-government partnership and a shift in thinking, from "my department" to "my city." In Dr. Bin Bishr's view, "The organizational structure of the Smart Dubai Office, where the mandate is covering the city overall, not just the government, is an important signal to the government entities and the public overall. It reduced the confusion about the value of the smart transformation, that the wellbeing of the public in the city is the target."[23]

Removing that stubborn barrier that haunted global digital transformation efforts was seen as the tipping point for Smart Dubai to launch numerous multiyear transformative projects, still ongoing at the time of writing this chapter. For example, these include the city's ambitious "happiness agenda," implementations of urban "Internet of Things" (IoT) sensory systems, embedding an ambitious "Blockchain" strategy in government operations, utilizing artificial intelligence applications in public service delivery, applying advanced big data analytics in policymaking exercises, and experimenting with robotics in government operations. Smart Dubai also affects the city's strategies for 3D printing of buildings, institutionalization of autonomous vehicles and driverless cars in transportation systems, and the utilization of unmanned aerial vehicles (UAV) or passenger drones and autonomous aerial vehicles (AAV) in government service delivery and transportation. This is coupled with numerous experimental labs, awards, incubators, "hackathons," and "accelerators" aiming to drive advanced digitization of almost all aspects of governance.[24]

Looking forward, in 2017, the Smart Dubai Office launched its future roadmap under the Smart Dubai 2021 initiative, in alignment with the Dubai Plan 2021.[25] The initiative focuses on six strategic objectives to be achieved by 2021:[26] 1) Creating a smart livable and resilient city, 2) supporting a globally competitive economy powered by disruptive technologies, 3) enabling an interconnected society with accessible social services, 4) enabling transport through autonomous and shared mobility solutions, 5) leveraging cutting-edge innovations toward a cleaner environment, and 6) enabling a cashless and paperless digitally connected government.

Over two decades, Dubai has achieved several milestones in its smart city journey. Beyond the city's electronic services, data law, or its smart pilots, there are deeper cultural and structural changes taking place as byproducts of implementing the smart city roadmap. In addition to the shift from competition to collaboration, at least in terms of realizing the smart city objectives, the findings of this study point to key transformations in the way the city functions today and to a cultural shift within its government. These include a steady shift from data silos to systematic information flows. The operationalization of the Dubai Data Law by the Smart Dubai Office is also leading to tangible openness in government operations as a new normal. In part, these transformations were products of years of digital government transformation, which started almost two decades ago under the DeG.

Conclusion

The digital transformation of Dubai from the early days of its electronic government initiative to its present ambitious smart city plans sheds light on the value of local leadership in delivering successful and sustainable results in a subnational context like Dubai. Through historical process-tracing, the chapter illustrates the different phases of a large-scale digital transformation initiative that was conceived, implemented, and sustained in a hybrid of managerial approaches. Furthermore, the evolution of the drivers of Dubai's digital transformation from economic efficiency and rigid focus on technological implementation toward utilizing digital transformation in service of quality of life, wellbeing, and "happiness" provides valuable lessons in digital-age developmental trajectories within the context of government reform.

DeG was one of the first e-government initiatives launched in the Arab region. Likewise, Smart Dubai became the region's first smart city transformation project, affecting the life of millions of people. On a regional level, there are strong signals of a spill-over effect, where Dubai has historically been a trendsetter and a benchmark in digital transformation. An increased number of cities, where close to 85 percent of the region's population live, are already being influenced through Dubai's digital transformation. While there is definitely room for skepticism when it comes to a region largely in turmoil, for now, Dubai's smart city, and its ability to successfully utilize digital transformation to drive government modernization and raise public wellbeing and "happiness," remains a regional inspiration.

Notes

This chapter primarily covers the period between 2000 and 2017 of Dubai's digital transformation journey. The authors would like to thank the Smart Dubai Office, and specifically HE Aisha Bin Bishr, director general of Smart Dubai Office, for the wealth of data and information provided for developing this chapter. Moreover, we would like to extend our thanks to the Dubai e-Government Department (now Dubai Smart Government Establishment), and Mr. Ahmed bin Humaidan, director general of the DeG Department until 2015, who also provided valuable input on the early phases of development in the department.

1. See www.smartdubai.ae.

2. See "Dubai Strategic Plan 2015," Government of Dubai, 2007; "Dubai Vision 2010," Government of Dubai, 2001. In 2014, "Dubai Plan 2021" was launched, and in addition to its focus on economic development, it specifically put the central vision of the city on people, societal development, quality of life, and wellbeing.

3. DeG, "Strategic Audit and Benchmarking," Internal Report, Government of Dubai, 2001.

4. DeG, "Dubai e-Government Strategies," Internal Report, Government of Dubai, 2001.

5. Okan Geray, "Navigating the Economic Downturn: Strategic Positioning of Public Sector ICT Initiatives," Policy Brief 14, Dubai School of Government, 2009.

6. Interview with Ahmed Bin Humaidan, director general of the DeG department at the time.

7. Ibid.

8. Fadi Salem, "Navigating the Multi-Faceted Challenges to e-Government Development in Arab States," Digital Outreach for a Better Future, International Telecommunication Union, January 2010.

9. Electronic Transactions and Commerce Law No. 2/2002, Government of Dubai, 2001.

10. Fadi Salem, "Exploring E-Government Barriers in the Arab States," Policy Brief, Dubai Initiative, Belfer Center for Science and International Affairs, Harvard Kennedy School, December 2006.

11. Fadi Salem, "A Smart City for Public Value: Digital Transformation through Agile Governance—The Case of 'Smart Dubai,'" Mohammed Bin Rashid School of Government, World Government Summit, 2016.

12. The United Nations Populations Division's World Urbanization Prospects, "Urban Population (% of total)," World Bank Statistical Database, 2016, https://data.worldbank.org/indicator/SP.URB.TOTL.IN.ZS.

13. Dubai Statistics Center, "Dubai in Figures," Government of Dubai, 2016, www.dsc.gov.ae/Publication/DIF16.pdf.

14. International Energy Agency (IEA), "CO_2 Emissions from Fuel Consumption," 2015 World Bank Statistical Database, "World Development Indicators (Time Series)."

15. IEA, "CO_2 Emissions."

16. Fadi Salem, "Building a Smart City: Overcoming the Challenges of Digital Transformation—The Case of 'Smart Dubai,'" in UAE Public Policy Perspectives, edited by Melodena Stephens Balakrishnan et al. (Bingley, UK: Emerald Publishing, 2017), pp. 139–76.

17. Jesse Berst, "Dubai Chooses Starter Apps in Bid to Become World's Top Smart City," Smart Cities Council, March 12, 2014, https://smartcitiescouncil.com/article/dubai-chooses-starter-apps-bid-become-worlds-top-smart-city.

18. "Mohammed Launches Dubai Smart City; Smartphone to Be Key Pivot," Emirates 247, March 5, 2014, www.emirates247.com/news/government/mohammed-launches-dubai-smart-city-smartphone-to-be-key-pivot-2014-03-05-1.540576.

19. WEF, The Global Information Technology Report 2016: Innovating in the Digital Economy, Geneva: World Economic Forum, 2016.

20. UN DESA, UN E-Government Survey 2016: E-Government in Support of Sustainable Development, United Nations Department of Economic and Social Affairs, 2016.

21. Fadi Salem and Yasar Jarrar, "Government 2.0? Technology, Trust and Collaboration in the UAE Public Sector," *Policy and Internet* 2, no. 1 (August 2012), p. 34, doi: 10.2202/1944-2866.1016.

22. Ibid.

23. Fadi Salem, "Building a Smart City: Overcoming the Challenges of Digital Transformation—The Case of 'Smart Dubai'" in *UAE: Public Policy Perspectives*, edited by Melodena Stephens Balakrishnan et al. (Bingley, UK: Emerald Publishing Limited, 2017), p. 173.

24. Additional details on these projects are provided in Salem, "A Smart City for Public Value."

25. Government of Dubai General Secretariat of the Executive Council, "Dubai Plan 2021," Government of Dubai, www.dubaiplan2021.ae.

26. More details are available at Smart Dubai 2021 (website), 2021.smartdubai .ae.

SEVEN

Enhancing Transparency in
Post-Revolutionary Tunisia

TRISTAN DREISBACH
Princeton Innovations for Successful Society Program

SECRECY WAS THE WATCHWORD in Tunisia's government during the twenty-three-year reign of President Zine el-Abidine Ben Ali. Many Tunisians could name the people who belonged to the country's tight leadership circle, but they knew little about what happened inside the halls of power. The public had limited access to information about how the budget was formulated, how much the government earned from oil wells and mines in poor rural areas, or how ministries used tax revenues. Nor could entrepreneurs easily gain access to the rules and procedures for starting a business. Even signing up for basic services was hard. Policy conversations took place behind closed doors, and decisions often benefited members of Ben Ali's family. In highly regulated parts of the economy, the small number of firms connected to the president's family accounted for as much as 55 percent of net profits, while the many other companies in these same sectors barely broke even.[1] Security forces protected the regime's policies by suppressing political dissent and punishing citizens who spoke out against the ruling party.

After popular protests unseated Ben Ali in January 2011 and launched a wave of uprisings across the Middle East and North Africa, politicians became more responsive to citizens' demands, and transparency advocates worked to overturn the policies of administrative secrecy. Tunisia started to redefine the relationship between citizens and the state. Interim leaders dissolved the parliament, called for new elections, and began work on a new constitution.

The transitional government of Beji Caid Essebsi, who became interim prime minister a month after Ben Ali fled the country, scrambled to respond to popular sentiment. "There was a demand for transparency and accountability," recalled Nejib Mokni, a lawyer who worked in the office of the prime minister's legal adviser.[2] With unemployment over 18 percent in 2011, economic grievances dominated protesters' complaints.[3] But citizens also railed against corruption. Tunisians commonly used the Arabic word *wasta* to refer to the use of nepotism and cronyism to derive jobs, contracts, or benefits from the state. The 2011 Arab Barometer survey conducted shortly after the revolution reported that 62 percent of Tunisian respondents believed obtaining a job through such connections was "extremely widespread," and 68 percent saw corruption in state institutions and agencies.[4] Dissatisfaction was especially strong among Tunisians living outside coastal population centers, where the poverty rate was twice that in large cities.[5]

Fortuitously, circumstances outside Tunisia were pushing the country in the same direction. The revolution took place amid an expanding global movement toward open government. The number of countries with access-to-information laws was increasing every year.[6] Drawing partly on models in other parts of the world, Mokni and other officials in the legal adviser's office drafted the text of a decree that established the right of citizens to access administrative documents produced by the executive branch of government. The 2011 access-to-information decree "was part of a pack of projects related to the political aspects of the democratic transition, about how to pass from a despotic regime to a regime oriented toward openness in dealing with society," said Kheireddine Ben Soltane, legal adviser to the prime minister.[7]

Shortly afterward, the prime minister's office created a steering committee that included representatives from the National Institute of Statistics—an agency that developed demographic, social, and economic data under the supervision of the Ministry of Development and International Cooperation—along with the legal adviser's office, the administrative reform office in the prime ministry, the finance ministry, and the national archives. The group began to plan how to transform the theory of open government into practice. Committee chair Fares Bessrour—a government auditor who had briefly headed the prime minister's e-government unit before becoming director general of administrative reform—had to figure out how to build collaboration and draw Tunisia into the global open government conversation.

The Challenge

At the time of Tunisia's revolution, government information was still a scarce commodity for citizens of MENA countries. In 2007, Jordan had become the first country in the region to pass access-to-information legislation. "It was an incredibly weak law," said Toby Mendel, a consultant to Tunisia's prime minister and the founder and director of the Canada-based Centre for Law and Democracy, a nongovernmental organization that promoted freedom-of-information legislation.[8] The Jordanian law provided government with too much leeway to deny citizen requests for information; it lacked an access-to-information oversight body that was independent from the government; and it did not include essential procedural details. The region's other countries made even less progress.

Because Tunisia had no parliament to vote on legislation in early 2011, changing access-to-information rules required only a presidential decree that had the force of law. Mokni's office had reached out to Mendel for advice and assistance, and after consulting broadly within the government, Mendel helped Mokni's office produce a text that became the first step toward greater transparency. The draft decree established a right of citizens to access documents related to the executive branch of government. The president issued the access-to-information decree in May 2011.[9]

Although Tunisia shared some of the problems that vexed its neighbors, the country enjoyed advantages that eased the drive toward transparency and cooperation between citizens and government. An important factor was the presence of civil servants who supported greater transparency. Mokni said a younger generation of government employees had started to chip away at the culture of secrecy even before the 2011 revolution. Connected to the outside world through the internet and social media, they valued transparency. They achieved minor successes in opening up government—creating, for example, a more transparent process for registering corporations, an e-government platform offering access to some government services, a website providing information important to investors, and a website to collect public comments on legislation drafted by the government before bills went to parliament. But until the ouster of Ben Ali, any initiative that might affect high-level decisionmaking was doomed by a lack of political will, Mokni argued.

Two other favorable factors for Tunisia were a relatively high level of education and media use. The adult literacy rate in 2011 was 78 percent, higher than Egypt (72 percent), Yemen (64 percent), and Morocco (56 percent).[10] Internet access in Tunisia was steadily growing, meaning that more citizens could use data if the government published them online. In 2011, 39 percent of citizens used the internet, up from 17 percent in 2007 only three years earlier.[11] After the revolution, a burgeoning free press provided a market for information.

Crucially, Tunisia soon established an elected parliament that was no longer beholden to the wishes of an autocratic regime. The transitional government dissolved the previous parliament and scheduled elections in October 2011 for a National Constituent Assembly. The assembly, which served as a transitional legislature and was responsible for drafting a new constitution, gave citizens influence over the policymaking process they had lacked under Ben Ali.

These factors inspired hope among Tunisians that the country would progress in opening the government to public scrutiny. But translating the decree into action would still take ingenuity. It required coordination across government to bolster capacity, to create online open-data websites, and to develop systems for gathering and storing information. Further, the proactive disclosure of information would be meaningless unless citizens downloaded and used data. Building public awareness was key.

The prime minister's steering committee, with Bessrour at its helm, had to contend with some deeply rooted challenges. The first was that open government required a new way of doing business. Most ministries and agencies had no policies or procedures for responding to queries from the public. There was no culture of proactively sharing information with citizens. Even the flow of data among government offices was slow, with each ministry guarding its work instead of collaborating with others. Changing mindsets and teaching new procedures to civil servants, many of whom had worked for years in a system that valued secrecy, would be a challenge. Overall, the government was "very hierarchical, very conservative, and closed," said Karim Belhaj, president of the Tunisian Association of Public Auditors.[12]

Mokni said the extent of internal resistance to new ways of working varied from ministry to ministry and from department to department. Although some civil servants understood the need for change in postrevolution Tunisia, others did not immediately accept the need for openness and accountability. Most had built their careers during the Ben Ali government and had worked under strict regulations regarding privacy and confidentiality. Overcoming this challenge required new guidelines and principles.

Advocates of open government also worried that the transparency initiative might falter while national leaders focused on navigating the postrevolution environment and moving the country toward new elections. The decree was just the first step in a lengthy process. The government and incoming parliament had to work on legislation to strengthen the decree and to enshrine the right to information in the new constitution. Keeping the project on the agenda was essential.

Frequent turnover in ministerial posts added to the difficulties of maintaining a focus on transparency issues; the government changed five times in the succeeding three years. With such fractured attention, champions of change had to come from within government offices. The steering committee had to assemble a coalition to push for new governance statutes as well as effective implementation of existing laws.

Developing capacity to reach the citizenry presented another challenge. "Open data means that data is available and in a standard format that can be used by others," said Mouna Zgoulli, central director of information diffusion and coordination at the National Statistics Institute.[13] Proactively sharing information required not only easy-to-follow online guidance about how to use services but also access to large datasets in formats that were easy for citizens to use. There was some know-how about how to create such websites, but it was scattered across ministries and the statistics institute, which had pioneered this type of data access in 1999 on a limited scale. There was also an e-government unit in the prime ministry, established in 2005, to provide online access to services such as university registrations, tax declarations, and applications for public sector jobs. Khaled Sellami, who had been instrumental in bringing the internet to Tunisia in the 1990s and had become head of the office three weeks before the revolution, was an important resource.

The final challenge was building public awareness of the right to access information and cultivating demand for government data. Jazem Halioui, a Tunisian internet entrepreneur, said Essebsi's original access-to-information decree had stunned many because no one outside the top levels of government knew it was coming. Still, most Tunisians remained unaware of the opportunities open government could bring. Immediately after the revolution, civil society was not well organized around the issue. As officials within government took the lead in developing an access-to-information regime, citizens had to come together to influence government and assure the legal framework was responsive to the needs of the Tunisian people.

Framing a Response

Responding to these challenges required action from people in many parts of government and in civil society. There was no single office or individual with a mandate to lead the whole campaign, though Bessrour's steering committee provided general direction and was mandated to track progress. Because the concepts of transparency and openness were novel to many in Tunisia's government, it was important to get them right from the beginning. Mendel and staff from the World Bank convened instructors at the National School of Administration, a government-run training institute, to explain the provisions of the 2011 decree. The school then added an access-to-information module to the curriculum.

Ben Soltane, the prime minister's legal adviser, organized additional preparatory workshops for officials in several ministries. "It was not easy to change the mentality of the administration and establish the general principle of access to information," he said.[14] Later, in May 2013 and again in 2014, Ben Soltane, Bessrour, and Mendel conducted a seminar for the access-to-information officers from all ministries on how to implement the access-to-information decree and guidelines. Developing standards and procedures to implement the access-to-information decree took place after the first classes and workshops had started. In late 2011, Ben Soltane's team focused their attention on this crucial step. Drawing on Mendel's help, Mokni and Chahreddine Ghazala, who both worked in Ben Soltane's office, took on primary responsibility for drafting guidelines.

Access-to-information systems had two main elements. The first was *supply-driven disclosure*—proactively publishing information in a useful format. Due to limited resources, it was impossible in the short term for most parts of government to publish all the data citizens had a right to see. Because many agencies had primitive websites or no internet presence at all, Mokni and Ghazala could not be too ambitious. The guidelines required each agency to have its own website before May 2013 and to publish certain information on that website, including the agency's responsibilities and organizational structure, decisions and policies of importance to the public, contact information for civil servants responsible for processing access-to-information requests, legal texts governing the agency, and a list of forms and specifications related to the provision of services. Ben Soltane's team took international standards into account as they developed these provisions.

The guidelines did not include any provisions about how agencies should build the websites. They did not aim to standardize content management systems or file formats. Many agencies were starting from square one. Mokni and Ghazala focused on creating very basic expectations for all agencies to meet. The guidelines stated that the e-government unit in the prime ministry could later develop more specific criteria for putting information online.

The second element of an access-to-information system was *demand-driven disclosure,* or rules for how to respond to citizen requests for information. This disclosure did not require a large amount of money or specific technical skills, and the guidelines were very specific about how agencies should collect and respond to information requests. The team created a model information request form and set standards for processing the forms. The guidelines also underscored the decree's fifteen-day deadline for responding to most requests and set out an appeals process for denied requests, including a provision to take disputes about release of data to an administrative court. The draft included guidance on how civil servants should interpret their open-data obligations in the context of existing laws that applied to personal data, secrecy, and related matters.

Mendel met with officials from different ministries to discuss their specific responsibilities under the new rules, including requirements that each unit appoint a dedicated access-to-information officer. The information officers played crucial roles because they carried most of the responsibility for deciding each agency's response to requests for information. This arrangement reduced demands on rank-and-file civil servants, who no longer had to worry about whether they could answer questions without violating restrictive public rules regarding the confidentiality of official information.

Ghazala and Mokni consulted with the access-to-information steering committee to assure support for the new rules throughout government. Mokni said the steering committee generally accepted their proposals. Hamadi Jebali, who became head of government (the new name for the prime minister) in December 2011 after the elections, issued the guidelines in May 2012.

Mokni and the legal adviser's office then created a detailed action plan that used the 2011 decree and the 2012 guidelines to lay out clear instructions for civil servants throughout government. It broke down the guidelines into implementable actions and required every ministry and agency to perform several important tasks, including: appointing an access-to-information officer; publishing information request forms on its website; putting essential information online by May 2013; preparing an agency-specific implementation plan; designing a manual for processing information requests; establishing a mechanism to handle complaints from people dissatisfied with the response to their requests; reporting progress quarterly to the prime ministry; and developing educational outreach programs to enhance public understanding.

The action plan placed specific responsibility for proactive disclosure of data with the e-government unit in the prime minister's office. The plan tasked the office with providing technical assistance to agencies; developing criteria for the publication of administrative documents; and creating a national open-data portal in collaboration with ministries. That portal would be a central source of information and statistics from across government and public agencies.

The action plan also called for setting up an independent commission to oversee information requests, a body that Mendel considered vitally important even though the 2011 decree did not specify its creation. The commission would design a model protocol for handling these responsibilities; make decisions regarding appeals and complaints from citizens; develop a database of information requests throughout government; and lead communication. The action plan assigned the legal adviser's office the job of preparing the legislation required to set up this new institution.

The prime minister issued the action plan in July 2012. At that point, the action shifted to Bessrour's Directorate General of Administrative Reform, which managed the civil service. Implementation would be the directorate's responsibility. Meanwhile, a civil society coalition had started to emerge as citizens embraced the idea of access to information and open data. This new network began to publicize the principles of open government.

Getting Down to Work

Developing and implementing open-data policies required the cooperation of a diverse group of officials and citizens. Tunisian civil society and international organizations helped government offices fill capacity gaps. The emergence of a strong civil society coalition helped keep transparency on the government's agenda even as national crises consumed attention. Tunisia had seven governments between January 2011 and August 2016. With each new government, there was a risk that progress would freeze as civil servants spent weeks educating new ministers about open government and Tunisia's commitments to international donors.

ACTION PLAN IMPLEMENTATION

The Directorate General of Administrative Reform began to coordinate implementation in 2012. Its director, Bessrour, organized quarterly small-group meetings for access-to-information officers from more than twenty ministries to discuss problems and share solutions. He tried to instill a sense of competition among the officers to motivate progress. Despite Bessrour's attempts to implement the action plan, progress on the plan and the quality of reporting were uneven across the government. Some ministries or agencies provided incomplete progress reports. Others failed to submit any results to Bessrour's office, even if they had released information during the reporting period. Some agencies did not appoint access-to-information officers or replace officers who left their positions.

Bessrour sought help from the steering committee, which he chaired. A 2012 directive from the prime minister turned the steering committee into a formal body tasked with following up on implementation of the 2011 decree and the action plan. Bessrour used the committee as a forum to discuss concerns about failure to comply with the action plan. The committee could also provide technical assistance, such as helping ministries create dedicated offices to support their access-to-information officers. The steering committee could not order any agency to take a specific action, however.

Part of the problem was keeping open government on ministers' agendas. A weak economy, militant activity in parts of the country, and a growing crisis in neighboring Libya were a few of the many problems facing Tunisia's leaders in 2012. Ministers tended to put little effort into holding agencies accountable for fulfilling their access-to-information obligations. The low compliance also reflected Bessrour's relatively weak position as head of the Directorate General of Administrative Reform. Although his directorate was part of the prime ministry, the law still vested political authority in the presidency, and the prime minister had little clout over ministries. Bessrour could not directly sanction offices that fell short of their action plan goals or failed to submit reports.

LEADING THE WAY: EARLY ADOPTERS

Publishing data online depended heavily on the initiative of information officers and people working within each agency or ministry. The National Statistics Institute, which became the first government agency to develop its own open-data website after the revolution, was a case in point. Although the institute had developed an online presence in 1999, its website initially provided only basic countrywide economic and social data in text format. The relatively small scope and the lack of downloadable datasets made it difficult to find specific information and conduct analysis.

In some respects, the office was better placed than any other to take the lead. Its mandate was to collect and maintain important social and economic information, and it participated in annual meetings of the UN Statistical Commission, which had become the base for a global professional community. It also partnered with Eurostat, the European Commission's statistics office. Zgoulli, central director of information diffusion and coordination, had participated in international working groups that set standards for data presentation and statistics and led the open-data project. Individual initiative and energy were still crucial for generating the momentum to reach project goals. Zgoulli said that in 2010, prior to the revolution, she and several colleagues had "wanted to reinforce the website as a platform for dissemination of information and to maximize the access of citizens to information."[15] They began to standardize the variables in the surveys they used to gather data, and they had converted all existing data into XML (Extensible Markup Language), from which it was possible to export into any other file format.

As political change swept across the country, Zgoulli believed that making more data accessible would help address the transparency concerns the revolution had laid bare and bolster the institute's credibility. But it took time to win allies in an agency where workers were accustomed to decades of secrecy and tight control. Zgoulli's team told their colleagues that proactive disclosure and a culture of openness would enhance the organization's reputation and even reduce workloads. If data were easily available, Zgoulli said, fewer people would need to contact the institute with personal requests for information. For the institute's open-data project to be a success, however, information had to flow efficiently and automatically from the institute's various departments to a central database. Achieving this goal required a new information system, staff training, and some website redesign, but Zgoulli had only four employees to work on the project. The additional capacity soon materialized when the African Development Bank offered to help Tunisia become the pilot for a project to increase statistical capacity across African governments. The bank provided software that allowed users to search statistical and census data, create datasets on the website, and export the information in a variety of document formats. Tunisia's site went online in 2013. A year later, after the publication of new census data, the site contained more than eighty categories of information.

Challenges remained, however. The laws governing collection and dissemination of national statistics restricted access to some data. Another problem was that Zgoulli's team had to compare the data from different agencies and merge them into a single dataset. Then they had to assure that the data complied with international standards. Zgoulli also cited a lack of capable personnel in other agencies as a major difficulty. "There is cooperation, but we haven't achieved harmony," she said.[16] To improve coordination, Zgoulli favored a legal change to make the institute independent of the Ministry of Development, Investment, and International Cooperation. This would give the institute the capacity to set data management guidelines for public agencies. However, this change did not materialize.

Another early adopter was, surprisingly, the Ministry of Interior. Considered a symbol of police repression and secrecy under the Ben Ali regime, it was the first ministry to launch an open-data website, which went online in 2013. The site provided data on criminal charges, border crossings, issuance of identification cards, traffic safety, and other areas of the ministry's responsibility, all downloadable in open-source formats. The proactive release of information online caught the rest of the government by surprise, although some types of information, especially concerning police functions, were not part of the package.

SUPPORTING THE MINISTRIES

While projects like the statistics institute's open-data site evolved independently, Bessrour's team tried to encourage similar activities across the government. Letting agencies build on what they had was one part of the strategy to win adoption, though this approach created a longer-term coordination problem. Sellami's e-government unit offered assistance on ministry-level initiatives. For example, by helping agencies adopt standards for publishing metadata and providing technical advice on building open-data websites, the team tried to lower the costs of reaching action plan goals.

Further, as each ministry or agency created a website, the e-government team also developed plans for a central open-data portal, data.gov.tn, as called for in the action plan. Sellami invited an official from Kenya, which had embarked on its own open-data project, to visit Tunis and share that country's experience.[17] This project was challenging because standards, operating systems, and software varied across ministries, frustrating efforts to create a unified system for the entire government. It was difficult to share information across platforms or house files in a central government database as envisioned by the action plan.

Nonetheless, Sellami's office was able to launch the data.gov.tn site in late 2012. The initial version simply allowed users to access documents or datasets that ministries had submitted to the e-government unit. Users could click on a category, such as regional development, social affairs, or water resources, and choose from a small number of files available for download. Examples included annual expenditures on social security or spreadsheets containing information on development spending by region. The site did not provide large datasets in user-friendly formats. Instead of providing direct access to statistical data, the site designers simply included a link to the statistics institute's own site.

The staff in Sellami's office aimed to create a fully-integrated site that would allow access to information from across government. Information from ministries and agencies would flow into a central database, where businesses, civic groups, individual citizens, or government employees could browse to find what they needed. Ministries that did not host their own data could choose to host data on the central government website.

The project developed slowly, however. The e-government team had few people and little money. Sellami could spare only one technician in the office to develop the portal. Because the e-government unit lacked the funds to support other open-data projects, it could not provide any financial incentives to ministries to collaborate or deliver on their commitments. Tunisians were stuck with the basic version of the site until the e-government unit could gain additional resources. The e-government team presented the project to the African Development Bank, which agreed to fund an outside company to create the site and an information system that could connect ministries and agencies to a central open-data portal. In 2014, Deloitte, a UK consulting firm, won the contract, and the e-government unit expected the site to launch in 2017.

JOINING THE EFFORT: THREE MINISTRIES GO ONLINE

As the e-government unit tried to coordinate open-data initiatives and pressure built for citizen's to have access to government information, officials in three other ministries started their own projects. For each, capacity was a significant issue, in terms of both money and people.

Ministry of Finance. At the finance ministry, internal advocates of open government had begun to make data available soon after the revolution. The ministry's information technology personnel had digitized the budget process and improved the flow of information prior to 2011, with the goal of quickly responding to budget-data requests from other parts of government. The ministry's public website primarily featured news about the minister, however, and fell short of providing significant information on government financial matters. Publishing the budget and spending information would allow civil society groups, businesses, international development agencies, and citizens to clearly see how the government was raising and spending public funds. Users could check whether government spending was in line with the stated policy goals of government officials. If citizens could easily discern how much the government was spending on projects that impacted their lives and communities, they could more easily hold their government accountable.

Aicha Karafi, director general of the finance ministry, saw an opportunity. Before the revolution, citizens were kept in the dark about government spending. Karafi and her colleagues thought a more transparent budget would remove an important barrier between citizens and government and established a small group to create a plan of action. Assad Khalil, the director of information technology services at the ministry, invited the International Budget Partnership, a U.S.-based NGO, to advise them about how to improve transparency.

Posting the government budget online was a first step, but even this small step presented big challenges. Karafi's group initially made the 2011 budget available as PDF files that were collectively hundreds of pages. For civic leaders, journalists, and ordinary citizens, this format made the budget hard to use. Civic groups such as OpenGovTN asked for budget information in an open format that allowed them to reuse data and analyze information via third-party computer applications.

But the finance ministry wanted to go beyond simply providing a dataset in an open-data format. Karafi wanted to present data online in user friendly formats that would break down different elements of budget data as simply and clearly as possible. For help, Karafi and her colleagues approached the World Bank, which shortly after the revolution had expressed interest in a project to make budget data more accessible and useful. The World Bank made the development of an open-budget platform a part of its loan package to Tunisia. The World Bank also contributed a software tool called Boost, a dynamic spreadsheet program that other countries had used for their open-budget projects.

To oversee implementation and expand these reforms, the ministry created a commission that included specialists in budgeting, public finance, information systems, and auditing. The commission set goals and standards for digitalizing data that existed on paper or in incompatible formats. Public consultation was a key part of the process. Employees of the ministry's IT department began to meet with civil society representatives and the media to ask how an open-data website could serve the needs of citizens and organizations. Among other things, the meetings highlighted the need for a glossary to help users understand data definitions. There was also strong interest in information on government subsidies.

Organizational culture within the ministry initially slowed the effort to meet the goals the commission set. Changes in procedures for processing data often required changes in work habits and mindsets among ministry employees, a sensitive issue for veteran workers who had to accommodate new ways of doing things. To build internal support, Karafi's team invited ministry employees to workshops and demonstrated how the new procedures would simplify their work. The team highlighted how the automatic updating feature that a central database made possible would save employees time in other aspects of their work. "We also reassured them they would keep their jobs," Karafi said.[18]

The team worked to create a user interface that was accessible, flexible, and easily understood. The open-data application the team developed provided users year-to-year budget data in multiple formats: machine-readable data from all budgets since 2008; PDF files of each agency budget; and interactive tools to help citizens explore budget data. One part of the site, called Where the Money Goes, displayed the annual budget in colored blocks, each representing a function or service, with the size of the block proportional to the amount allocated. Clicking on one of the blocks gave users a new set of blocks with more specific details on expenditures in that area. The intuitive format made it possible for users with no financial experience to find data on budget allocations and expenditures quickly and easily. The ministry launched the new public site in late 2015 under the name Mizaniatouna, "Our Budget" in Arabic.[19]

Ministry of Energy and Mines. Officials in this ministry began to discuss the creation of an open-data website in 2014. At the time, much of the ministry's data was either confidential or shared only with industry professionals or other government agencies. The issue was politically sensitive because the oil and mining industries operated mainly in poorer areas of southern Tunisia, where residents claimed their communities did not receive an adequate share of the tax revenue received from businesses. One active civil society organization, the Tunisian Coalition for Transparency in Energy and Mines, demanded the release of financial data related to contracts awarded to mining and oil companies.

Kais Mejri, a lawyer who joined the civil service in 2000, headed the ministry's governance unit and supported publishing the data. This step would both address public demand and facilitate the sharing of information among ministry staff. Mejri also hoped Tunisia would sign on to the Extractive Industries Transparency Initiative, a global standard for open and accountable management of oil, gas, and mineral resources. Putting more information online would bring Tunisia closer to that standard. With a small team and no funding to hire new employees or buy software, Mejri had to find resources. He turned to members of the OpenGovTN group for expert advice and encouraged the ministry to use CKAN, an open-source data management system that governments around the world had used to create public open-data websites.

Additionally, Mejri looked to examples from Tanzania, the United States, the United Kingdom, and France to refine his vision of the ministry's open-data site. The final proposal was a modified version of the CKAN platform that displayed visually appealing graphs when users logged on rather than a mass of numbers. It also identified more than 150 datasets on oil production, energy consumption, carbon emissions, and other subjects for inclusion. They also planned eventually to automate the entry of new information directly to the site.

Volunteer technical assistance came from civil society activists like Hatem Ben Yacoub, a Tunisian expatriate engineer and e-government consultant who, in 2009, began meeting with government officials to share ideas during his frequent trips home. Help also came from IT students at universities, the Natural Resource Governance Institute, a U.S.-based NGO that organized workshops to increase the technical capacity of Mejri's staff, and Open Knowledge International, a UK-based nonprofit network that advocated for cost-free sharing of information.

Adopting CKAN to manage all information in one system triggered some internal resistance because the change required new policies and procedures. Mejri launched a communications blitz to win internal support. "We tried to market the platform as a tool for the administration, not just something dedicated to the citizens," Mejri said.[20] He organized training sessions in the ministry and emphasized that although the new procedures could be burdensome at first, they would ultimately lighten workloads and reduce the loss of information. Mejri's efforts came at a crucial time. In June 2015, a new wave of protests swept Tunisia under the slogan, "Where is the oil?" Citizens in southern cities near oil fields demanded to know more about the oil extraction; the amount of revenue the government obtained from it; and the nature of revenue distribution. These protests added pressure to complete the site. There were many ways the project could go awry. To ensure the completed site would not break, Mejri recruited help from civil society and universities to conduct a stress test and security audit.

The site's launch helped meet protestors' demands. However, the site lacked one content element the public wanted: the contracts between the government and resource-extraction companies. Mejri had focused on putting all publicly available information online, but neither the ministers involved nor state-owned oil and mining companies had agreed to make contracts available. In 2016, after the launch of the open-data website, civil society members, including Mohamed Ghazi Ben Jemia of the Tunisian Coalition for Transparency in Energy and Mines, called on Minister Mongi Marzouk, who took office in January of that year, to make the contracts public. Marzouk, who had a background in information technology, supported the measure. Mejri's team posted the contracts on the site later that year.

Ministry of Culture. Because of its policy scope, this ministry was central to neither core economic activity nor to safety, work permits, or other essentials. The ministry provided grants for cultural centers and activities and kept track of production and consumption of books, films, and other cultural products. But during Tunisia's years under dictatorship, citizens had viewed the ministry as "corrupt, opaque, and self-serving," according to journalist Sarah Souli, and suspected ministry officials of nepotism and misuse of public funds.[21] The ministry's new leaders wanted to revamp its public image.

Saloua Abdelkhalek, the ministry's deputy director for organization and method, was responsible for the open government program. In late 2012, she had a small group of three or four people to work with her on the project. They looked to the experiences of other culture ministries, in countries such as Finland and France. Ben Yacoub, the OpenGovTN member who had worked with Mejri, arranged for the Ministry of Energy and Mines to share its experiences with the culture ministry. Abdelkhalek's small team spent the first nine months training and educating ministry staff about the open-data initiative. As with other ministries, changing mindsets and building skills was challenging. Abdelkhalek first engaged the offices within the ministry that were most enthusiastic and then moved toward those that were more resistant. Over roughly two years, her team collected information from all offices within the ministry, structured that information in open-data formats, developed the website, and ensured that data flowed freely among offices.

The ministry's site went online in 2016 and included basic information about budgets, award programs, and culture-linked commerce. Abdelkhalek's team placed a premium on responsiveness and decided to publish any information that three or more citizens requested. Abdelkhalek wanted the ministry site to use the same CKAN content management system utilized by the Ministry of Industry (which consolidated with the Ministry of Mines and Energy in 2016) to ensure compatibility and interoperability. She drew on help from other parts of the government and from civic groups to build this capacity, gradually moving to put the new system in place.

MAINTAINING MOMENTUM

High-level support was crucial for the open-data initiative to flourish. In 2012, Sellami attended a World Bank–organized conference in Brazil to discuss the Open Government Partnership (OGP), a multilateral initiative that advocated for the adoption of open government principles. He quickly became convinced that membership in the partnership would bolster and sustain political support for greater transparency. Joining the organization would also increase Tunisia's international recognition and access to financial or technical assistance. The government agreed to apply for membership.

Tunisia joined the partnership in January 2014, and OGP affiliation provided additional impetus, coordination, and monitoring capacity to support open-data efforts, independent from the work of the access-to-information steering committee and Bessrour's office. Joining the OGP required government to work with civil society to create a two-year national action plan to implement concrete commitments, conduct annual self-assessments, and submit to an independent review every two years. Sellami chaired a joint steering committee consisting of five representatives of government and five civil society representatives. The committee solicited hundreds of proposals from citizens and government and narrowed the list to twenty, including: an improved open-data portal; building civil servants' capacity to implement open governance; an open-budget system; and an open-data platform for mining and oil extraction. Many of the commitments in the action plan involved projects that had been discussed or initiated earlier, such as the Ministry of Energy and Mines' open-data project.

The joint OGP committee coordinated and tracked the progress of projects throughout the government. The committee members met monthly with representatives of ministries and agencies included in the action plan and issued a public statement after every meeting. The meetings provided a forum for leaders of government units to report on progress and request advice or technical assistance from the head of government or from another unit.

RAISING AWARENESS AND BUILDING USAGE

Any open government initiative depends on public awareness and engagement, and especially on private entrepreneurs and civic innovators developing apps or analyses that transform data into practical tools. If people did not use the services and information made available, the programs would have little or no impact, except to make some types of intergovernmental operations more efficient. The statistics institute became a model for building relationships and usage. Before the 2014 census, Zgoulli's group met with journalists, professors, and civic leaders and asked them about the information they wanted and the format that would be helpful.

In response to the ideas offered, the institute broadened its outreach through workshops with universities and civil society groups. IT published brochures for each of the twenty-four governorates (administrative regions) identifying available information and how citizens could find and use it, and assembled a four-page glossary explaining each statistical indicator it used. Other ministries followed suit. For example, Mejri of the Ministry of Industry, Energy, and Mines participated in training sessions with journalists, civil society members, and members of parliament to talk about the ministry's website and data on natural resource use. Eventually, the finance ministry also advertised the information available on its website.

The public's use of the information-request system, as well as the open data, increased slowly. Tunisian NGO iWatch set up a website, ma3louma .org, to help citizens who had trouble obtaining information from the government. iWatch recruited Tunisians around the country to file requests for information. "We told people if they don't get access to the document they wanted and didn't have a lawyer, we'll give them one," said Aly Mhenni, the iWatch parliamentary lobbyist.[22] The NGO followed up on all requests and posted the progress of each request online. By 2016, iWatch had handled more than 100 cases through this service but reported that ministries and agencies had fulfilled only twelve requests. Information officers were still processing requests in most cases. One problem was a lack of knowledge in government offices about their responsibilities under the law, Mhenni said.

Legislating Information Access

Although Essebsi's 2011 decree gave citizens the right to access official information, and the guidelines and action plan had laid out the responsibilities of civil servants and officials, the legal framework for open government remained relatively weak in relation to the international standards promoted by organizations such as Toby Mendel's Centre for Law and Democracy.

First, Tunisia lacked an independent commission to oversee the development, maintenance, and improvement of public access to information. Second, a broad list of exceptions gave the government considerable leeway to deny requests. Third, although the decree had the force of law, it did not have the approval of Tunisia's elected parliament. Fourth, the decree provided no strict sanctions for civil servants who failed to comply with requests for information.

In March 2013, the office of the legal adviser worked with the steering committee to create a new law that the head of government could submit to parliament. Legislation not only would buttress the concept of access to information but also would give political parties an opportunity to debate the issue in parliament. The drafters consulted regularly with the steering committee and similar statutes in South Africa, the United Kingdom, Mexico, and India. Mokni and other officials believed that any law on access to information should create an independent commission to provide citizens with an avenue to appeal unfulfilled information requests and avoid a cumbersome judicial process. Citizens would be more likely to pursue appeals if they did not have to spend time and money navigating the courts. In addition, such a commission could monitor the compliance of public agencies with the access-to-information law. Commission members would have the power to issue sanctions for noncompliance. The standards created by Mendel's organization emphasized that the commission be independent from government so that it could make impartial decisions about information requests. By June 2013, Bessrour's office posted the draft law online for public consultation.

Overcoming Obstacles

Political upheaval and civil unrest delayed parliamentary approval of Tunisia's access-to-information law for more than three years. The month after Bessrour posted the draft law, a gunman assassinated Mohamed Brahmi, a left-leaning opposition politician. The event aggravated existing tensions between the ruling coalition, led by the Islamist Ennahda party, and the opposition. Protesters filled the streets, and many opposition politicians put aside their work in the legislature to join the protests, demanding that parliament dissolve and the government resign. Work on the new constitution stopped.

Although Bessrour's office submitted the draft law to the council of ministers for approval in August 2013, the council, consumed by the national crisis, took no immediate action. In October, four civil society organizations intervened and mediated political talks between the two sides. Under the terms of the resulting deal, the assembly agreed to resume its work and to appoint a new prime minister to run the government. That month, Bessrour's office resubmitted the law to the council of ministers. In December, the parliament refocused its efforts on finalizing the new constitution, and thanks in part to the advocacy of the OpenGovTN network, Article 32 of the constitution, approved in January 2014, enshrined access to information as a fundamental right of Tunisian citizens. "Constitutionalization of this right was an important step," Mokni said. Any rules or laws that contradicted the right of access to information "were now in contradiction with the constitution."[23]

A few months later, Tunisia secured a US$250 million World Bank development policy loan contingent on finalizing the access-to-information law and the council of ministers finally sent the draft law to parliament.[24] After the adoption of the constitution and the election of a new parliament (known after December 2014 as the Assembly of Representatives of the People) later in the same year, the parliament's rights and liberties committee took up the draft law in May 2015. Civic groups, which had gained strength since the revolution, began to lobby the committee to strengthen the draft legislation.

Mokni, who left his position in the legal adviser's office in 2013 to work for the Tunisia office of Article 19, the British NGO, brought international experts to Tunisia to discuss the law. He wanted to ensure the list of exceptions was as narrow as possible. iWatch, the local Transparency International affiliate, was also concerned that the proposed law contained too many broad exceptions. The draft legislation stated that public bodies could withhold information that "could be harmful" to the confidentiality of deliberations; national defense; foreign policy; state security; monetary, economic, and financial policy; the administration of justice; prevention of crime; individuals' fundamental rights and freedoms; and several other categories.[25]

Mhenni wanted the law to allow public authorities to withhold information only when its release would explicitly harm a narrowly defined set of state interests. The parliamentary committee listened, shortened the list of exceptions to include just national security, public safety, and international relations, and sent the bill forward in June 2015. But the government withdrew the proposed legislation the next month, citing concerns about a too-narrow list of exceptions and lack of proper safeguards for sensitive information. The steering committee reframed the exceptions once again, giving the government more freedom to refuse requests for information. But when the head of government returned the draft to parliament in August, Mhenni and other civil society representatives found it unacceptable.

In early 2016, the proposed law went to a consensus committee, which became the focus of intense scrutiny by media and civil society. The consensus committee for any piece of legislation consisted of the members of the relevant parliamentary committee, representatives of the ministry that had ownership of the proposed law, and other interested members of parliament. Such committees were not part of the formal legislative process but had evolved to iron out disagreements before any final vote. Mhenni and other civil society representatives met regularly with sympathetic members of the consensus committee to review the law as it underwent final revisions. The Union of Parliamentary Journalists and the national journalists' syndicate held a press conference urging the committee to adopt a law with minimal exceptions to the right of access to information. Civil society groups launched an online campaign to put public pressure on the consensus committee members.

Three days of discussion yielded a compromise. Mokni said that the solution was to model the exceptions after Article 49 of the new constitution, which defined general conditions in which limitations on constitutional rights and freedoms were permissible. The final text in the draft stated that authorities could deny access-to-information requests only if the release of that information could damage public security, national defense, international relations, or certain individual rights. Government, parliament, and civil society also agreed that the compromise should include a "harm test" provision that required ministries and agencies to consider the potential costs of sharing certain information against the value of doing so. The independent commission would apply the same test in case of an appeal. Mhenni said the harm test allowed for the narrowest possible understanding of the exceptions because the commission could choose to grant requests in those categories if it deemed the harm to be minimal.

The legislation passed in March 2016 and had a one-year implementation deadline that required the head of government to take several steps by March 2017, including appointing a commission to create a strategy for improving access to information, oversee the government's access-to-information activities, and adjudicate complaints from citizens whose information requests had been denied. The commission included both government representatives and civic leaders.

Assessing Results

With the adoption of the 2011 access-to-information decree, Tunisians gained the power to request data from their government. Government officials, members of parliament, and civil society groups all contributed to creating guidelines, a constitutional amendment, and a new law, adopted by parliament in 2016, to enhance access to information. The Centre for Law and Democracy rated Tunisia's right-to-information law as the eleventh best in the world and commended its broad scope and limited exceptions. The NGO's few criticisms focused primarily on the lack of specific legal sanctions for institutions that systemically failed to comply with the law and the lack of legal immunity for members of the oversight commission.[26]

Putting the new law into practice was no simple exercise. Zgoulli, of the national statistics institute, said the government lost focus on implementing the original action plan when it began drafting the new legislation in 2013. Progress on the development of information systems, training, and building public awareness was slow. Limited awareness of the access-to-information decree and the subsequent law among civil servants was a persistent obstacle.

Nonetheless, several government departments built their own open-data websites and made a substantial volume of information available to Tunisian citizens. The statistics institute presented a wealth of demographic data as well as economic data on industry, agriculture, and other sectors. The finance ministry, which had not published budget data prior to 2011, made its data usable by citizens. The industry ministry, which consolidated with the Ministry of Energy and Mines in 2016, enabled open access to natural resource extraction contracts. The interior ministry and culture ministry also created open-data sites. Karafi, of the finance ministry, said that the open-data project improved internal operations. The open-data platform eliminated problems with information redundancy between offices in the ministry and made it easier to search for specific pieces of budget data.

In 2017, Tunisia's national open-data portal remained a work in progress. Much of the data available on the portal was outdated. A 2017 study from the University of Pardubice in the Czech Republic ranked seventy national open-data portals based on their technical dimensions, ease of access, level of communication with users, and the characteristics of the dataset. Tunisia's data.gov.tn site ranked second to last.[27]

Nevertheless, civil society groups capitalized on published information to hold the government accountable for irregularities. When citizens came to iWatch to report potential acts of corruption, the organization used the access-to-information decree to determine the facts of the case. In one instance, iWatch also issued a request for the text of a controversial arbitration agreement between the country's post-revolution Truth and Dignity Commission and a relative of former president Ben Ali, who had profited under the old regime. "We took [the commission] to court," Mhenni said. "The court gave us the right to have it."[28]

However, overall public awareness remained low. Mhenni said Tunisia had no tradition of access to government information, and few citizens knew they had acquired the right. "Even the media, who can use the law to access information, don't use it," Zgoulli said.[29] Belhaj said citizens lacked trust in government, and people were not aware of "success stories" in which citizens asked for important information and received it. Utilizing published government data was "the most important thing," Belhaj said. "We have to show people that the use of this information can help transparency and hold government accountable."[30]

The government did not post details about the total number of information requests submitted to access-to-information officers across all ministries. The statistics institute alone recorded more than 500 requests for information in both 2014 and 2015. Most ministries found that citizens submitted no more than a handful of requests for information to their access-to-information officers. The culture ministry had only five inquiries the first year and eight the next. After the passage of the access-to-information law in March 2016, requests for information from the culture ministry rose. The requests made in the first six months following the law's passage matched the total number received up to that point. Abdelkhalek of the culture ministry ascribed the new interest to the publicity that surrounded the access-to-information law.

Some ministries and agencies reported promising data on the number of users accessing open-data websites. The statistics institute's open-data site received over 5,700 hits per month, although the majority of users were located outside Tunisia, Zgoulli said. The industry ministry received about 115 visitors a day, Mejri said, although about half came from outside Tunisia. Visits increased after the oil and mining contracts went online in 2016. The finance ministry reported that its website usage numbers were small, but as of late 2016 the ministry had not conducted an outreach program to educate citizens about the open budget site. Abdelkhalek argued that, "When we diffuse information in public, that leads to a decrease in protests and fewer doubts from people using government services." She also said, "When they see that everything is open, they don't suspect corruption."[31] Abdelkhalek also believed open-data gave civil servants a greater sense of accountability to citizens.

Reflections

Tunisia's open government initiative succeeded where many other countries failed, for several reasons. The 2011 revolution created a moment of opportunity. Leading members of the Ben Ali regime who benefited from a lack of transparency left the government in 2011. A new parliament was responsive to public concerns and had no vested interests in the old regime's restrictions on sharing information. Fabian Seiderer, a senior public sector management specialist at the World Bank and part of the Bank's team in Tunisia, said it was vital to initiate reforms quickly after the 2011 revolution. Waiting until a new government came to power after the October elections could have made the process more difficult. Experience taught him that the window for implementing politically difficult changes to administrative practices after regime change was six to twelve months.

The presence of internal champions of reform in various agencies was another reason Tunisia succeeded. The Ministries of Industry and Culture, as well as the statistics institute, benefited from dedicated personnel who believed in transparency and were determined to secure the political support and necessary resources. Those reformers sometimes had to pursue projects without top-level backing. They had to engage with their superiors to educate them on the importance of open government; legal requirements; obligations under the Open Government Partnership; and agreements with international donors. The message had to be repeated whenever there was turnover among ministers.

Aicha Karafi and Assad Khalil, part of the finance ministry's open-budget team, and Kais Mejri, who led open-data efforts at the Ministry of Industry, Energy, and Mines, stayed focused through multiple governments. They harnessed external financial and technical assistance to achieve objectives despite limited support from within their ministries. These champions valued transparency and wanted to bolster the credibility and reputation of their ministries both within Tunisia and abroad. Their individual commitment to open government may have been as important as official decrees or regulations in providing citizens with information.

International donors and NGOs not only assisted agencies' access-to-information efforts but helped civil servants keep open government on politicians' agendas. The World Bank included provisions on development of the legal framework and creating an open-budget website in its development policy loans, which were important sources of financial support in the years following the revolution. The Bank had also introduced Tunisian officials to Toby Mendel, the Canadian adviser who helped Tunisia draft its legislation. Other organizations provided financial assistance or training to specific aspects of agencies' open government projects.

Tunisia also benefited greatly from an independent parliament. Civil society groups enjoyed influence on the legislative process and lobbied members of parliament to keep exceptions to the right to information as narrow as possible. Although the parliament was at times slow to act on legislation, it approved a law that earned international acclaim. Civil society groups became a stronger force for change as the open government movement grew during the years following the revolution. In the immediate aftermath of Ben Ali's departure from office, there was no strong civil society presence working on access-to-information issues. The work mainly was done within the offices of the president and prime minister. But as civil society organization improved, civil servants turned to them for technical guidance on open-data projects, and parliament began to respond to civil society demands for greater openness.

However, proactively publishing information and giving citizens the right to request information from the government did not unleash the pent-up public demand that some proponents expected. Although Tunisia made significant progress on the supply side of the information equation, gains were lean on the demand side. Mendel acknowledged this concern but said that the priority was to take advantage of the window of opportunity presented by the revolution to develop the legal framework. Citizen demand would grow once citizens understood their new rights. By 2017, such progress was apparent. Ben Yacoub acknowledged that much of the data might be useful or interesting only to a small group, but that group was an important one. "There are citizens active in civil society who are interested in data," he said. "There are businesses using the data." It even helped spread information to other government officials who previously did not know how to access useful information. "When the ministry of finance published the budget of the municipalities for the first time, we found that people in government were asking us for the link."[32]

Finally, public engagement was an important element of this open government effort. In October 2011, Jazem Halioui, an internet entrepreneur, reached out to Mabrouka M'barek, a newly elected member of parliament who represented Tunisians living in North America. Together with Tunisian blogger Houssein Ben Ameur, they worked with a small network of Tunisians to create a Facebook page called OpenGovTN to share ideas and coordinate actions. The group had two goals: to include the principle of open governance in the constitution, and to promote access to information, public participation, and open data in government. The group's membership grew to include thirty-four members of parliament from all major parties, members of civil society groups, and thousands of citizens. In March 2012, OpenGovTN published a short electronic book (e-book) called *Open*, which Halioui said was the first Arabic-language book on principles of open governance. As citizen interest grew, civil society groups began to ask for information on topics such as the amount of money the government earned from the oil and mining industries and the cost of government subsidies for staple foods and fuels. Groups like OpenGovTN played a crucial role in promoting citizen participation and open governance through public engagement.

Notes

1. Caroline Freund et al., *All in the Family: State Capture in Tunisia*, World Bank, March 1, 2014, http://documents.worldbank.org/curated/en/440461468173649062/All-in-the-family-state-capture-in-Tunisia; Tristan Dreisbach and Robert Joyce, "Revealing Tunisia's Corruption under Ben Ali," *Al Jazeera English*, March 27, 2014, www.aljazeera.com/indepth/features/2014/03/revealing-tunisia-corruption-under-ben-ali-201432785825560542.html.

2. Interview with Nejib Mokni, legal adviser to Beji Caid Essebsi, Tunisia's former prime minister.

3. World Bank data: http://data.worldbank.org/indicator/SL.UEM.TOTL.ZS?end=2014&locations=TN&start=2009.

4. Arab Barometer data: www.arabbarometer.org/content/online-data-analysis.

5. Mongi Boughzala and Mohamed Tlili Hamdi, *Promoting Inclusive Growth in Arab Countries*, Brookings, February 2014, www.brookings.edu/wp-content/uploads/2016/06/Arab-EconPaper5Boughzala-v3.pdf.

6. A transitional government sought funding from the World Bank. The terms of a US$500 million development loan committed the country's new leadership to opening up government and providing citizens with access to information.

7. Interview with Kheireddine Ben Soltane, legal adviser to the prime minister.

8. Interview with Toby Mendel, a consultant to Tunisia's prime minister and the founder and director of the Canada-based Centre for Law and Democracy, a nongovernmental organization that promoted freedom-of-information legislation.

9. The president first issued the decree in May 2011, then issued a revised decree several weeks later to lift some of the restrictions contained in the original language. In June 2011, the World Bank approved a development policy loan to support Tunisia's efforts to strengthen governance, transparency, and accountability. "Bank Approves US$500 Million for Governance Reforms and Economic Opportunities," World Bank, June 21, 2011, http://web.worldbank.org/WBSITE/EXTERNAL/COUNTRIES/MENAEXT/0,,contentMDK:22945865~menuPK:247611~pagePK:2865106~piPK:2865128~theSitePK:256299,00.html.

10. UNESCO data: http://data.un.org/Data.aspx?d=SOWC&f=inID%3A74.

11. International Telecommunication Union data, www.itu.int/en/ITU-D/Statistics/Pages/stat/default.aspx.

12. Interview with Karim Belhaj, president of the Tunisian Association of Public Auditors.

13. Interview with Mouna Zgoulli, central director of information diffusion and coordination at the National Statistics Institute.

14. Interview with Ben Soltane.

15. Interview with Zgoulli.

16. Ibid.

17. Rushda Majeed, "Disseminating the Power of Information: Kenya Open Data Initiative, 2011–2012," Innovations for Successful Societies, September 2012, https://successfulsocieties.princeton.edu/publications/disseminating-power -information-kenya-open-data-initiative-2011-2012.

18. Interview with Aicha Karafi, director general of the finance ministry.

19. World Bank promotional video for Mizaniatouna project, www.youtube.com/watch?v=rk_o0Aq4jpA.

20. Interview with Kais Mejri, lawyer in the civil service.

21. Sarah Souli, "New Outlook on Culture Raises Tunisian Hopes, Fears," Al Monitor, June 9, 2016, www.al-monitor.com/pulse/originals/2016/06/tunisian -culture-shift.html.

22. Interview with Aly Mhenni, iWatch parliamentary lobbyist.

23. Interview with Mokni.

24. World Bank Report 86052-TN, April 1, 2014, http://documents.worldbank. org/curated/en/624771468113095561/pdf/860520PGD0P132010Box385177B00 OUO090.pdf.

25. "Tunisia: Draft Law on the Right of Access to Information," Article 19, September 2013, www.article19.org/data/files/Tunisia_RTI_Law_23092013_FINAL_ GG_bb.pdf.

26. Center for Law and Democracy Global Right to Information Rating, www .rti-rating.org/view_country/?country_name=Tunisia.

27. Renata Machova and Martin Lnenicka, "Evaluating the Quality of Open Data Portals on the National Level," *Journal of Theoretical and Applied Electronic Commerce Research* 12, no 1, 2017, www.scielo.cl/scielo.php?script=sci_arttext&pid =S0718-18762017000100003.

28. Interview with Mhenni.

29. Interview with Zgoulli.

30. Interview with Belhaj.

31. Interview with Saloua Abdelkhalek, deputy director for organization and method at the Ministry of Culture.

32. Interview with Hatem Ben Yacoub, a Tunisian expatriate engineer and e-government consultant.

PART II

IMPROVING SERVICES IN LINE DEPARTMENTS

EIGHT

Facilitating Investment through the Cairo One-Stop Shop

ANDREW H. W. STONE
ADELE BARZELAY

ZIAD BAHAA EL-DIN REFLECTED on his task. In his earlier work, he had written about and consulted on public sector reform projects. Now he had to not only create a plan for reform but also to implement it. As the new chair of the General Authority on Investment and Free Zones (GAFI), he had been asked to create a modern one-stop shop in Cairo, the heart of the Egyptian economy.

He had to take Egypt's complex registration and licensing procedures and simplify them for investors—turning hundreds of steps and dozens of agencies into a single stop. He had to take an unproductive, process-oriented, and sometimes corrupt bureaucracy and turn it into a customer-oriented, results-oriented, high-integrity, and high-productivity team. He had to contend with traditional ways of doing things, with the aim of changing them completely. He had to overcome vested interests, ranging from comfortable lawyers who earned hefty fees navigating the complex business start-up process to notaries who, ensconced in their comfortable offices, enjoyed a reliable income from their monopoly rights in legally certifying documents and signatures. And he had to act fast and show results.

On the one hand, reforms were profoundly threatening to a variety of established politicians, bureaucrats, and businesses. On the other, the government was under increasing pressure both domestically and internationally to show results. To prove the value of reform, there would need to be quick and visible results—new investments, more investment, and the formalization of unregistered firms. Yet this was not the first effort to reform business start-up procedures.

Genesis of the One-Stop Shop

By 2001, Egypt knew it faced a serious challenge in attracting investment. Foreign direct investment (FDI) had sharply declined since its heyday in the 1980s, falling from 2.5 to 3 percent of GDP to less than 1 percent (figure 8-1). Total private investment was stagnant, hovering just above 10 percent of GDP. One clear deterrent to new investment was the bureaucracy, discretion, and uncertainty surrounding the business environment. Egypt's bureaucracy was legendary for its size, complexity, and intransigence.[1] One study described the process as it existed in the 1990s in this way:

> Companies wanting to obtain a business license in Egypt can expect to wait up to one year while wading through a mountain of paperwork. Entire files are often lost and companies have to make special arrangements including under the table payments of up to 5,000 LE to obtain a license. The time spent by an individual business man to obtain the license and the associated cost cannot be readily determined. Business owners, however, have to visit the various departments at different times for an average of 25 visits to obtain a license.[2]

Delays, discretion, and a lack of transparency also encouraged the practice of "speed payments," where bureaucrats would demand, or investors and their agents would willingly offer, informal payments to obtain a quick approval.

The idea of creating a one-stop shop (OSS) for investor services in Egypt dated to 2001, a time when the idea was being contemplated elsewhere in MENA (box 8-1). A study carried out by the Ministry of State for Administrative Development suggested enormous delays but was seen by officials as exaggerated. To verify, GAFI undertook a careful follow-up study that looked at the number of ministries and affiliated agencies an investor must deal with, the services they provide, and the regulations governing investment. After finishing the study, GAFI sent a copy to all con-

FIGURE 8-1. Investment and FDI as Percent of GDP, 1990–2018

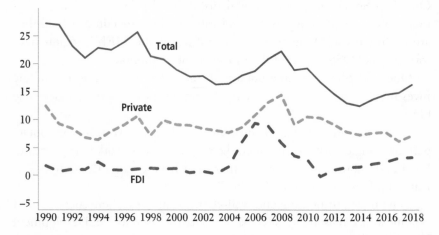

Source: World Development Indicators.

cerned ministries to double-check on their findings, then integrated their feedback. GAFI's study concluded that launching a new investment could involve as many as twenty-two ministries and seventy-eight governmental entities:

- Administrative procedures were far too numerous and time consuming, many were redundant, and some were inconsistent with each other.

- Investors required 349 services (including approvals/permits and licenses both in the establishment and operating phases).

- There were 200 regulations for business licensing.

The First One-Stop Shop Attempt

Spurred by these alarming findings, the Cabinet of Ministers decided in June 2001 to establish an OSS that would assemble officials from all relevant government entities in one place. Presidential decree 79/2002 established an OSS in GAFI in 2002, as well as branches of the OSS in governorates and the new urban communities. According to the decree, the OSS was to provide "all investment-related services," which included

BOX 8-1. One-Stop Shops: Possibilities and Pathologies

One-Stop Shops are one of several institutional substitutes that governments often adopt to bypass or accelerate existing procedures where they are dysfunctional. At least fifteen countries in the MENA region have some kind of OSS as part of their investment promotion efforts.

One-Stop Shops became popular in the 1980s as a means to promote investment, often as an adjunct to investment promotion agencies (like GAFI).

"The basic idea is that an investor would only have to be in contact with one single entity to obtain all the necessary paperwork in one streamlined and coordinated process, rather than having to go through a labyrinth of different government bodies."

"The most outstanding and well-known examples where such an OSS system works reasonably successfully are the Economic Development Board (EDB) of Singapore, the Malaysian Industrial Development Authority (MIDA), and the Industrial Development Authority (IDA) of Ireland. In all three cases, investors can rely on the agencies to provide practically all the approvals and clearances needed."

"Practically all governments that tried to implement this form of an OSS encountered significant resistance by the various government agencies responsible for the different administrative procedures. Most importantly, other ministries and agencies fear that the creation of such an OSS would result in curtailing their authority and mandate, quickly leading to intensive turf battles within the government bureaucracy. But more relevant than whether such an OSS is politically feasible is the question of whether a single agency should actually have this much authority and power. . . . Governments therefore typically shy away from establishing such an OSS in the narrow sense. Instead they tend to rely on some form of coordination mechanism where the various authorities maintain their existing mandates and responsibilities."

"In many cases . . . authorities . . . only delegate junior staff to the OSS who do not have sufficient authority to actually grant approvals. This, in fact, means that [t]he OSS is simply a mailbox operation, where the investor submits his paperwork just to pursue it directly with the relevant authority in order to see his application through. The 'One-Stop Shop' has actually turned into a "one more stop.""*

---

*Quotations from Frank Sader, "Do 'One-Stop Shops' Work?" World Bank Foreign Investment Advisory Service, September 21, 2000.

giving the approvals, permits, and licenses necessary to start and operate a business.

Presidential decree 79/2002 organized the work of the OSS and created a system of delegation and liaison officers for ministries and other affiliated entities. The decree legally authorized some of the government entities represented at the OSS to perform the services of their agencies and give approvals on their behalf without having to refer to a higher authority.

The Cairo OSS was housed in a temporary office while a permanent headquarters was being constructed. The government also inaugurated branches in Alexandria, Ismailia, and Assiut. At that time, firms of significant size could register under either the Company Law at the Companies Authority or the Investment Law (also called the Guarantees and Investment Incentives Law) at GAFI.[3] Egypt accords national treatment to both foreign and domestic investors with very few exceptions.

This first iteration of a Cairo OSS largely failed. Its effectiveness was constrained by several key challenges. Although the Cabinet of Ministers intended to unify investment management by making GAFI the administrative authority responsible to serve investors, its power and scope of authority were limited. A key problem for GAFI and the nascent OSS between 2002 and 2004 was the lack of a stable home. During this period, the affiliation of GAFI and the OSS varied. Sometimes it reported to the prime minister, sometimes to the presidency, and at other times to the Ministry of Economy. In 2004, the Ministry of Economy was eliminated and a powerful new Ministry of Investment took over a broader range of functions.

Second, the OSS lacked the practical authority to override existing procedures. It was assigned the task of collecting necessary approvals, permits, and licenses from the appropriate jurisdictions corresponding to the investments. However, on a practical level, the establishment procedures under the two laws remained the same, making the OSS a "one-more-stop shop." The staff of the OSS lacked knowledge, competency, training, and authority to grant approvals or licenses, so they were not able to help investors accelerate the process. Representatives from official entities did not have the necessary competencies or authority to grant approvals or licenses. Thus, they essentially functioned as forwarding agents for their agencies and, in some instances, the liaison officers did not have sufficient legal knowledge to respond to investor inquiries.

Third, the OSS at GAFI served only one group of investors—those applying for incentives spelled out under Investment Law 8 of 1997. In this case, business registration also entitles investors to incentives detailed in the law.[4] Establishment procedures required that the investor complete the establishment contract in front of a lawyer and that the investment activity fall within the activities stipulated in the law.

Other investors continued to have to establish their firms with the Companies Authority (in a different location) under Law 159 of 1981 (with different procedures). In this case, registration under the Companies Law required the investor to apply directly to the Companies Department, and an approval did not lead to the automatic application of benefits. Also, establishment procedures relied on "the notification system," where the investor presents a request and, if he is not rejected within fifteen days, his request is approved.

Fourth, of the many entities whose approvals were required, there were only between nine and eleven entities represented at the OSS between 2002 and 2004. The initial OSS brought together only a limited number of relevant entities, including the Public Notary, the Commercial Registry, the Syndicate of Law, and the Passport Department. There were also no concrete accompanying efforts to streamline or simplify procedures or to change the underlying bureaucratic system.

Overall, the OSS was merely a concentration of some of the relevant entities, which continued to have overlapping and sometimes duplicative responsibilities. The net effect was that the early OSS did not ease the burden of business registration for the investor. According to users of the old OSS, it could take anywhere from 10 to 140 days to establish a business.

In addition to the delays, there was an issue of culture. The dominant culture in GAFI and other entities involved in approvals had always been that of regulators, carefully screening out unworthy or unwise projects and cautiously avoiding potential deviation from the rules. The notion of customer service remained largely alien.

A New Beginning for the Government and GAFI

The year 2004 was significant for reform in Egypt. It was a year of new laws and policies, a new government, and new leadership. Following sluggish economic growth, a large and growing fiscal deficit, uncoordinated monetary and exchange rate policies, and a low degree of business confidence during the five-year term of the previous prime minister, a new government was formed in July 2004. The reshuffle brought in Prime Minister Ahmed Nazif, the former Minister of Telecommunications and Information Technology. It also replaced several older politicians with young economic liberals and prominent businessmen, especially in key economic posts. This reformist economic team included:

- Youssef Boutros-Ghali as Minister of Finance. Boutros-Ghali was previously Minister of Economy and Foreign Trade, economic advisor to the prime minister, and an IMF senior economist.

- Mahmoud Mohieldin as Minister of Investment (a new post that subsumed many economic and investment functions), who was formerly an economic advisor to the government.

- Rachid Mohamed Rachid as Minister of Foreign Trade and Industry, who was formerly in the private sector.

This new group shared common goals and culture, valued teamwork, and had always advocated economic policy reform. They launched tariff and tax reforms early on, signaling a sea change in policy.

Just prior to the change in government, a new law (14/2004) had been introduced amending Investment Law 8 of 1997, which fundamentally changed GAFI's mandate and business establishment procedures. The law reoriented GAFI from its mix of regulatory and promotional functions into an investment facilitation and promotional agency. With this change, GAFI became the sole body that all investors—domestic and foreign, large and small—need to address to establish their companies. GAFI's mandate called for assisting investors in a variety of ways and acting on their behalf at related governmental agencies, for example:

- Providing all licenses and approvals required for the establishment and operation of a project on behalf of the investors; for example, notarization of related deeds, and issuance of residence and work permits.

- Providing investor assistance for site selection and land acquisition, whether for agricultural, industrial, or tourism activities.

- Certification of the dates of commencing production and helping investors take full advantage of the tax holiday granted according to location.

Under this reform, the Companies Authority, which used to establish companies under Law 159/191, was abolished, and GAFI was mandated to perform the registration procedures of both Law 159 of 1981 (non-incentive) and Law 8 of 1997 (incentive) companies. Other functions included issuing licenses on certain tax and custom exemptions granted to investors. These licenses were to be considered final and operative and would not need approval from another entity. The law required all state entities to provide GAFI with all necessary data and information, as well as maps for available investment locations.

A NEW LEADER

A presidential decree provided for the appointment of a new chair of GAFI.[5] The choice was Ziad Bahaa El-Din, a young intellectual and reform-minded lawyer who was to play a catalyzing role in the transformation of GAFI. In his diverse career, he had served as a legal advisor to the government on trade, commercial law, and capital markets, written several key commercial laws, both taught and practiced law, represented many prominent private clients, and published extensively. Bahaa El-Din recognized that red tape was "strangling investments" and promised reforms to cut through it.

The new law also changed GAFI's governance. Three vice-chairs were selected (of whom two were men and one was a woman), each with specific responsibilities. They are all appointed for one-year terms on a renewable basis. GAFI was given an enlarged board of directors with eleven members, including the three vice chairs and eight investors or other experienced persons. Unlike other public agencies in Egypt, and signaling the sea change in thinking, most of the board came from the private sector. GAFI also established a board of trustees that includes representatives of investors, exporters, and entities providing services to investors. This board reviews investment problems and gives advice to GAFI on investment issues related to policies, strategies, laws, and investment promotion.

Bahaa El-Din approached his new job enthusiastically, yet it was hard to underestimate the challenges. On the one hand, he had strong support from the new government, including reform-minded ministers, to remake GAFI and the OSS. GAFI had substantial resources and dedicated revenue from its investment zone operations. Furthermore, it had the authority granted by the new investment law to assume unprecedented responsibility in business registration and licensing.

At the same time, he was working both internally and externally with a bureaucracy more accustomed to regulating the private sector than assisting it. Among the challenges confronting him were: coordinating the functions of the many agencies and ministries still involved in business start-ups; appropriately staffing and motivating a new office; dealing with investors in a way that kept their life simple yet accomplished the regulatory goals of government; reducing corruption and speed payments; and dodging the shortcomings of other OSSs. Arriving at a sound strategy for the new OSS would be critical in facing the challenges ahead.

A New Mission

Ziad Bahaa El-Din clearly understood that for GAFI to improve and promote Egypt's business environment it must make a "transition from regulator to promoter/facilitator that will focus on company registration and licensing, one-stop shops, free zone management, a potential investor facilitation service, investor aftercare, research and information, and policy advocacy."[6] The head of the OSS defined its mission as being "to transform Egypt into an investor-friendly destination."[7] Its main purpose was to facilitate investors' dealings with registration and licensing authorities by concentrating them in the premises of the OSS itself, as well as to streamline and coordinate the process with the different ministries and agencies involved whose approvals are not located in the OSS. For the OSS, a new business model was developed that treated the investor as a client and sought to create the most convenient experience for the client. Thus, the reforms implemented not only took on the complexity and length of procedures that government applied to new businesses and investments; it also vastly improved the investors' experience of dealing with those procedures and the officials who administered them.

Key elements of the transformation included: 1) institutional and legal reform; 2) streamlining procedures; 3) restaffing, re-skilling, and remotivating; and 4) decentralizing.

Institutional and Legal Reform. The most important legal reform shaping the new OSS was the 2004 revision of the investment law, which merged GAFI and the Companies Authority into a single entity responsible for establishing all businesses. At the same time, the change unifies several of the establishment legal procedures. Since 2005, companies' statutes have been published only in the *GAFI Investment Gazette*. Furthermore, the passage of a new code of commerce, customs law, and tax law eliminated many of the existing differences between firms of different types.[8] The

Minister of Justice also issued a decree to unify the two Public Notary offices instead of having a separate office for each law. Moreover, a new unified companies law was under preparation and aimed to unify establishment procedures between the two relevant laws.

Streamlining Procedures. GAFI's revised mission cast many former standard operating procedures in a new light. Bahaa El-Din suggested:

> You must first determine your role and what you are trying to achieve by each step. For example, for 30 years, you had to submit a feasibility study of [an investment] project. Why? As a facilitator, why should I worry? If it's a bank or brokerage firm, there are different regulations. We are here to establish companies, not to establish their viability. What I am trying to achieve by rules—eliminate every step and constraint that has no reason—and to eliminate duplication. Also, any restriction that can be avoided completely by legitimate means should be eliminated . . . [and we should] eliminate any rules or requirements with no foundation in law.[9]

By 2006, GAFI had managed to "deregulate" more than forty different start-up procedures. This did not mean bypassing or abandoning central government functions. "It doesn't eliminate the functions of the state," noted Bahaa El-Din. "The Ministry of Health can't stamp an approval of a new medicine [in the OSS]." But there was a systematic effort to streamline necessary functions, eliminating unnecessary ones.

Before and after the opening of the new Cairo OSS, Bahaa El-Din was engaged in reworking the procedures involved in business registration to smooth the procedural flow. "My work is about pieces. The cumulative effect makes a difference." Bahaa El-Din says that the redesign of procedures is "plumbing work—the details are what kill."

A central innovation introduced in the new OSS was the separation of the "front" and "back" offices. "Investors should stay at the front office. You have to limit points of contact. This has an amazing effect on corruption. It took lots of time [to communicate this concept to officials]—those applying the rules are part of the discussion—you have to understand [their] logic." By matching each investor (or investor's representative) to a single GAFI officer who walks the investor through the entire registration process, providing all services through one window where required documents are submitted, and combining all required payments into a single bank window transaction, the process is greatly simplified for the customer. Most opportunities for requests for or offers of speed payments are eliminated. The approvals are done in the "back" office by officials who now have no contact with applicants.

Easing post-establishment procedures and regulations also helped companies start operations at a much earlier date than anticipated. One of the major improvements was to allow investors to start operating their businesses immediately by granting them temporary licenses before receiving final approval for their companies (pending security clearance).[10] If the investor is granted a temporary license from GAFI, then no entity is allowed to either stop his activities or refuse to grant him any required licenses. The permanent license is to be granted once the security clearance is obtained. In another reform, new rules promulgated by GAFI have allowed amendments in the legal statute of companies (articles of foundation) to be approved within only one week. This is achieved by presenting a final request accompanied with necessary attached documents to the OSS. This is a key step in facilitating company expansions, mergers, and acquisitions.

RESTAFFING, RE-SKILLING, REMOTIVATING

Bahaa El-Din used a combination of new staff and existing staff in the new OSS. New staff were taken on to deal directly with clients in the front office, where a client orientation and excellent investor-relation skills were at a premium. But for many other posts, existing staff were utilized. The key was to use the mechanisms and levers available to encourage a culture of professionalism dedicated to client service and performance. A new promotion system based on merit and qualifications was introduced to replace the old seniority-based system. Nonperforming staff were made redundant or reassigned. "We jump-started a program of promotion of better-qualified people. Of 12 departments, 8 heads are new. I did get some consultants from the outside but didn't create a parallel system—I try to promote people from within." To motivate GAFI staff, Bahaa El-Din took advantage of GAFI's autonomous financial structure to raise salaries "30 percent across the board plus an incentives system of up to 20 percent of salary." To increase output (and justify the higher salaries), he extended the workday by 1.5 hours, from 8 a.m. to 4 p.m. Staff stop accepting new registration requests at 3 p.m. to start finishing up the day's paperwork.

Yet only half the staff of 400 in the OSS worked directly for GAFI; another 200 worked for other agencies. "I don't have administrative authority over the others—if they're not doing their jobs well, I can't fire them," says Bahaa El-Din. "But we can give incentives—for example, buses. I included these 200 people in transport [for OSS workers]. Bonuses—they're part of it. When the FDI figures came out, [the minister] granted one month bonuses." As a result, these officers were more willing to conduct their administrative work quickly and professionally, in line with the OSS's overall objectives.

Decentralization. Finally, the OSS implemented a system of internal quality control. Progress is monitored according to data such as the number of firms registered, enquiries answered, and other key performance elements. This information can then be linked to personnel decisions. Decentralization of decisionmaking has enabled more rapid and responsive customer service. The chair of GAFI has delegated his power of attorney to directors in the second tier of management. For example, in the Cairo OSS, the director of the establishment unit can sign on his behalf on establishment contracts worth up to a maximum of US$8.7 million.

Financial autonomy has facilitated GAFI's ability to offer services and motivate employees. As a quasi-autonomous economic authority, GAFI has its own financing sources that allow the organization to have some discretion regarding hiring, salary increments, and incentives. GAFI is currently financed by free zones receipts, of which a portion is allocated to the management of the OSS. Although the OSS does not collect fees for facilitating business registration, it does collect fees for some investor services, such as publication of company articles in the investment gazette, the ratification of the minutes of boards of directors and of ordinary or extraordinary general assembly meetings, as well as some fees for administrative services such as photocopying. The OSS also collects dispute settlement fees amounting to around US$520. At the same time, the different authorities collect fees for the services they provide (the Commercial Registry, the Public Notary, the Syndicate of Lawyers collect their own fees).

How the New OSS Works

After consulting with private investors early on (and through the newly constituted board), and after broad internal efforts to organize the functions of the OSS, the process of launching the OSS began. The Cairo OSS commenced operations in late December 2004 and moved into its new headquarters in Salah Salem in January 2005. The Cairo OSS is well-organized and features an attractive, modern layout with a welcome center on the ground floor. At the front desk are a staff of multilingual assistants and three legal counselors.

The investor entering the office first encounters the front desk, which responds to investors' inquiries concerning investment guarantees and incentives for both Law 8 of 1997 and Law 159 of 1981. In 2005, the desk received 35,021 inquiries, of which 27,452 were answered at the reception desk and 7,479 were referred to the advice desk. The front desk also provides information on business establishment processes, required documents, and fees. A complaint unit receives investors' grievances, examines them, and redresses the issues across the relevant agencies. It is important to note some complaints are directly addressed to the chair's office. All these complaints are handled by the Central Administration for Investors' Care at no cost to the investor. This unit received 132 complaints in 2005, of which 129 were resolved.

An investor starting a business proceeds from the front desk to the second floor. Hall 1, on the first floor, provides the necessary services for establishing a business. The investor does not need to go anywhere else to start a business and deals with only one window to input the required data in the establishment contract. A single GAFI officer walks the investor through the entire registration process. Services are provided through the single window where required documents are submitted, and the follow-up on the outcome is also provided. Completing documents in the new OSS is automated to reduce the time lost in filling out long, duplicative forms. The digital templates for establishment contracts replaced old handwritten formats, accelerating the process. Prior to this, the investor had to purchase printed forms to be completed manually and then have them revised by a specific department. Hall 2, on the second floor, provides post-establishment services rendered both by GAFI's technical sectors (such as recommendations to issue residence and work permits or exemption from custom duties) as well as those by other entities represented at the OSS.

Representatives from thirty-four government agencies work in the OSS to serve investors.[11] Aside from those involved in registration, GAFI also has encouraged other relevant entities to set up a representation at the OSS premises.[12] In contrast with the old OSS, many more entities are represented, and several of them have delegated authority to make approvals or issue licenses in the OSS that are required for the establishment of a business.[13] In the establishment department, six entities have delegated power to grant approvals or licenses.

There also were twenty-seven entities providing post-establishment services. Examples of these services include ratification of the company's board, its general assembly meeting minutes, and amendments in its commercial legal status, in addition to the issuance of passports, work permits, and taxpayer ID. A representative of the Department of Defense, which must sign off on construction on new land and any project in Sinai, is also on the premises.

In all, representatives of the following nine entities have been delegated approval authority: the Capital Market Authority; the Office of Investment Authentication; the Public Union for Trade Chambers; the Syndicate of Law; the Investment Tax Office; the Commercial Registry; the Sales Tax Office; the Office of Issuance of Work Permits for Foreigners; and the Passport Department.[14]

Other agents lack the autonomy to act or give approvals without resorting to their parent ministry. In these cases, GAFI acts as a window to receive applications and to forward them to the responsible ministry or agency. For example, if the case calls for the Ministry of Interior, the Ministry of Tourism, and the Ministry of Agriculture, instead of having a delegate with approval authority, the relevant entity assigns a liaison officer, who receives the requests, sends them to the ministry, is responsible for the follow-up, and delivers them at the OSS to the investor.

Finally, a committee for dispute settlement has been created to investigate and solve investor complaints and disagreements with other government bodies. The committee, which includes representatives of relevant entities, convenes every week to look into the problems that arise. According to users of the OSS, this fee-based mechanism provides a quick and effective means to solve problems. To ease procedures, the precedents established by recommendations issued by the committee are used for similar cases so they need not be discussed again. Moreover, if the investor faces a problem with an entity that is not represented, the committee takes responsibility for addressing that entity and following up on the problem.

Achievements

The purpose of this reform effort was to produce a simpler and faster process for starting a business—a broadly achieved goal. For Egypt, the administrative changes have yielded an increase in the number of formally registered enterprises. A key achievement is a dramatic simplification of business start-ups. From the investor's perspective, the number of procedures was cut from nineteen to three steps. They are:

1. The investor presents the required documents to the establishment unit to revise the establishment contract with GAFI's lawyer. He or she also manually and separately fills several applications for different entities involved in the registration process.[15]

2. The file is then transferred to the follow-up unit officer to estimate the fees for each entity involved in the registration process. The fees are paid in one lump sum at the branch of the Bank of Alexandria on GAFI's premises. Investors then take their receipts back to the registration desk.[16]

3. The GAFI follow-up officer undertakes and concludes the procedures with the following bodies: Lawyer Syndication; Capital Market Authority; the Public Notary; the Union of Trade Chambers; and the Commercial Registry.

After these three steps, the contract is ready to be signed by the investor or the investor's lawyer. The decree establishing the company is immediately issued, followed by the Commercial Register of the company. Today, an investor can complete all requirements at the OSS in one day and expect to receive the certification by express mail about two days later. In most cases, the investor need not visit any other office.

GAFI records indicate that, since the establishment of the OSS in 2005, the amount of time it took to register a company dropped from an average of thirty-four days (and up to 140 days) before 2004 to three days. This is all the more impressive since Law 8 on company registrations also entails screening of eligibility for fiscal incentives.

As to other services, digital copies of the Commercial Registry are now issued on the same day, while the old handwritten format used to be issued in five days. Ratification procedures (of minutes of board and general assembly meetings) are now obtained on the same day instead of after five days. Over the six-month period from July 1, 2005, to December 31, 2005, minutes of 2,391 general assembly meetings and 4,403 boards of directors meetings were ratified.

According to figures collected by GAFI, the total number of businesses registered in Cairo rose dramatically to more than 5,700 businesses in 2005, declining somewhat in 2006 (see figure 8-2). It is important to note that the OSS did not register companies under Law 159 prior to 2005, as they were established in the Companies Authority. The number of companies established under Investment Law 8 of 1997 (the incentive law) strongly increased between 2002 and 2005 before experiencing a modest drop in 2006, while the number of companies established under Law 159 of 1981 (the non-incentive law) experienced a smaller increase.

Since 2002, the majority of established companies were projects with 100 percent Egyptian participation under both laws. However, the establishment of the OSS in 2005 appears to have triggered a surge in the number of established projects with full Egyptian participation under Law 8 of 1997. One possible explanation is that the OSS encouraged Egyptian firms to formalize. With the elimination of a separate Companies Authority in 2005, companies of all types registered at the GAFI OSS in Cairo. The most popular forms were simple partnerships, sole proprietorships, and joint stock companies.

Under the commercial law, simple partnerships, partnerships, and sole proprietorships can continue to be established at the Commercial Registry's office nearest the company. For many small companies (or for the lawyers representing them), this option proves convenient. Then, the contract must be notarized either in court or at the Public Notary. Finally, the Trade Chamber must give a certificate (approval) so the company can start

FIGURE 8-2. Number of Businesses Established
in Cairo by Investment Law

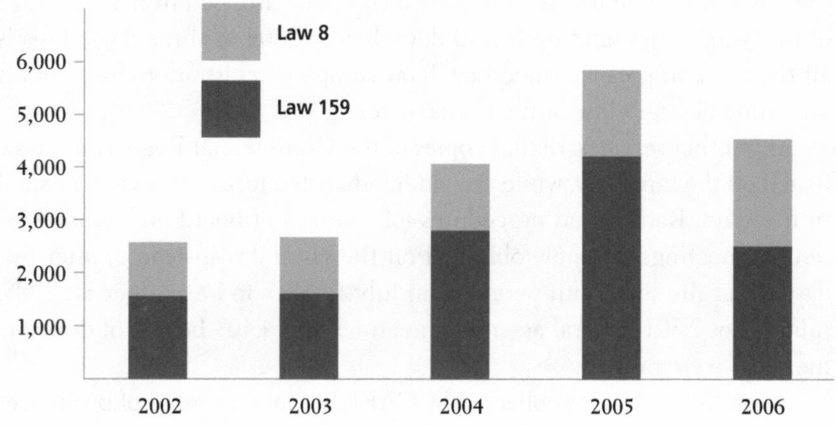

Source: GAFI.

operating its business. As noted, some law firms prefer to register companies locally rather than using the OSS, due to higher fees. Numerically,
the majority of registered firms continued to use the Commercial Registry,
but these firms were generally quite small. In terms of capital investment,
the OSS was the economic center for business entry, accounting for almost
fifty times as much issued capital value of companies in 2006.

Challenges Going Forward

In spite of this progress, as Dr. El-Din's tenure at GAFI drew to a close
in 2007, the OSS reform agenda remained incomplete. Egypt had yet to
undertake a unified investment law, for which there was limited political
support. The OSS was originally conceived and designed to be a one-stop
shop for company *establishment*. However, it was portrayed by the media as
a more comprehensive set of reforms regulating all corporate or company
action. This misconception led the media and public, as well as some politicians, to have unrealistic expectations for GAFI, though it might also
have contributed to increasing the political capital of the agency.

To some observers, such as Dr. El-Din, it appears in retrospect that the
GAFI reforms were more "enclave reforms" rather than a comprehensive
cultural change across the agency.[17] The impetus for reform in 2004 had
benefited from a group of reformist ministers and other senior officials who
had backed the project. Many hailed from the private sector and expended
much energy on reforms to speed up the processes to guarantee faster results. The ministers who were more interested in structural/institutional
reform pushed for deeper reforms that would tackle the foundational flaws
impeding the sustainability of the project. Yet, in the pressure to demonstrate rapid results, many of these deeper reforms were not implemented.

Even with regard to company establishment, although the OSS
achieved an important streamlining of procedures for business start-up,
some challenges to facilitating new investment and company formation
clearly remained. First, some projects still needed prior approval from
other authorities (for example, some tourism and health projects). Some
could not be established at GAFI's OSS, including those partnerships and
sole proprietorships that were investing outside the scope and activities of
Investment Law 8 of 1997 (such as trade and consultancy firms). In addition, GAFI could establish some but not all financial services firms, as
certain firms needed to be established at the Capital Market Authority (according to Law 95/1992), where registration was still very bureaucratic.

Second, while there was a representation of the Syndicate of Law at the OSS, lawyers dealing directly with the local syndicates were allowed to register the businesses at a subsidized rate (up to between 50 and 60 percent of their fees). Actually, a portion of the fees paid by the investor was returned to the lawyer to encourage the latter to register at the local syndicates, thus relieving pressure from the Syndicate of Law.[18] Lawyers who registered at the GAFI OSS did not benefit from this. Therefore, lawyers preferred to register at the local syndicate outside the OSS. The GAFI chair tried several approaches to enhance legal services. GAFI tried to work around this by having the lawyers benefit from this subsidy by giving them a letter they could present to the local syndicate. Nevertheless, in the wake of the reforms, the subsidy given in the Giza syndicate (60 percent) was higher than the subsidy given at the Syndicate of Law at the OSS.

Third, GAFI did not have administrative authority over all the entities represented at the OSS. While the GAFI staff were trained to deal with investors, that is, to serve them in a friendly and time-effective manner and provide them with accurate information they required, some staff continued to display the same bureaucratic mentality, a lack of expertise, or simply an indifference to client service that characterized much of Egyptian bureaucracy before the OSS.

According to OSS users, there were two main bodies that continued to follow the old rules and procedures, subjecting clients to painful red tape. One was the Public Notary. OSS users suggested that notary service became unduly rigid and bureaucratic after moving to the OSS, possibly due to a fear of being held accountable after previous bad experiences. While a notary's main role was simply to verify signatures, some OSS patrons complained that the notary occasionally rejected or refused to verify the signature "if the third middle name of the person is not mentioned in the establishment contract although it is fully written in their ID card." Moreover, these employees examined the documents over again even though GAFI had already revised them, signed the establishment contract of the business, and stamped it. For some post-establishment services, like amendments in the Commercial Registry that need to be documented by the Public Notary, the notary would go so far as to question the validity of the Commercial Registry and would require a recent official copy.[19]

Not surprisingly, many users wanted to see the OSS's administrative authority extended to additional functions and public entities. Where there was only a liaison officer, they would have liked to see a fully delegated agent with approval authority. Utility service connections, needed for business start-ups, were slow and in the hands of independent entities.[20] Local officials were responsible for construction permits and could sometimes impose other demands and delays. (For example, the civil defense sold mandatory fire extinguishers). In spite of the OSS's efforts to coordinate with all concerned entities, some could still take a lot of time to deliver their services. For example, tax cards from the Income Tax Authority could take up to fifteen days to receive. "People over expected," said Bahaa El-Din in 2006. The OSS "doesn't eliminate the functions of the state. . . . Simplification must continue."

After Dr. El-Din left, Egypt's OSS implementation continued to suffer challenges, such as liaising with other state entities for licenses; setting up OSS automation and electronic services; and minimizing licensing procedures.[21] Egypt also continued to rank poorly on Doing Business indicators for contract enforcement (162), registering property (109), and paying taxes (162). Just prior to the 2011 revolution, Egypt's rank improved on Doing Business indicators for contract enforcement (143), registering property (93), and paying taxes (136).[22] Effective implementation of Investment Law 72, and its recently approved executive regulations, will remain important priorities for Egypt to maintain momentum on private sector growth and ease of doing business in coming years.[23]

Nonetheless, within the confines of its authority, the OSS managed to achieve a remarkable sea change in performance and bureaucratic culture. This reform was one part of a set of measures that, combined with highly favorable economic factors, worked to sharply increase investment in Egypt. One sign of this was FDI, which rose from US$2.1 billion in 2003–2004 to US$3.9 billion in 2004–2005 and US$6.1 billion in 2005–2006 (see figure 8-1). Portfolio investment also jumped forward. Market capitalization of the listed companies in the Egyptian Stock Exchange increased from 33 percent of GDP in 2004 to more than 85 percent in 2006. And, as a final indication of success, in 2005–2006 the Egyptian economy recorded a growth rate of 6.9 percent compared to 3.5 percent in the two previous years.[24] As a testament to the success of this reform effort, the OSS has survived the vast political changes wrought by the Arab Spring.

Post–Arab Spring Developments

After 2008, the GAFI reforms faced a host of challenges. Some were related to the external environment. The global financial crisis and Arab Spring turmoil halted Egypt's growth momentum. In the context of civil unrest and an uncertain political future, new entrepreneurial ventures face extraordinary obstacles. FDI declined to US$2.2 billion in 2010–2011, from a peak of US$13.2 billion in 2007–2008.[25] Between 2009–2010 and 2010–2011, FDI inflows as a percentage of GDP declined from 3.1 to 0.9 percent.[26] Real GDP growth also slowed from 5.1 percent in 2009–2010 to 1.9 percent in 2010–2011.[27] Political instability served as a powerful brake on investment. Perhaps as a result, GAFI reports that a total of 632 new companies were established in November 2013, down from 780 new establishments in November 2012. Egyptian government policies also influenced the drop, as attitudes among the Morsi government toward foreign investment were ambivalent, and major privatization deals were halted or cancelled.

Economic reforms aimed at attracting investment and promoting private sector growth were enacted following President El-Sisi's rise to power in 2014. The government declared investment a top priority, showcasing its substantial investment reforms during the Egypt Economic Development Conference (EEDC) held in March 2015. Presidential Decree 17 of 2015 made substantive changes to Investment Law 8 of 1997, setting the foundation for an integrated OSS for business registration.[28] GAFI was mandated to act as a liaison between investors and government agencies. A follow-up unit in charge of coordinating with the tax and labor authority on behalf of companies at the OSS was also introduced. Egypt's Minister of Investment at the time declared the implementation of the augmented OSS within eighteen months. The law also had implications for GAFI's management structure. It trimmed back GAFI's financial and administrative independence, and from 2015 onward, GAFI's board was chaired by the Ministry of Investment (now the Ministry of Investment and International Cooperation).

The 2015 amendments were followed by Investment Law 72 enacted in June 2017, repealing Investment Law 8. The law enshrines new incentives for investment, reduces bureaucratic processes, and reintroduces private free zones. Under this framework, an augmented OSS in the form of an Investor Services Center (ISC) will be established, incorporating businesses, facilitating licensing, and allowing permit approval and issuance.[29]

ISCs will also provide automated services and an updated information portal, and will allow the validation of electronic signatures, documents and forms, and electronic payments. For the first time, Accreditation Offices will be licensed by GAFI to facilitate licenses and ensure technical compliance.

Recent reform efforts are showing initial signs of success. FDI surged to US$8.7 billion in 2016–2017 from US$6.9 billion the previous year. Egypt's ease of starting a business ranking moved up thirty-one places to reach thirty-nine out of 190 economies in 2017, outpacing the MENA region average of eighty.[30] Company registrations increased by 26 percent to reach 15,200 in 2016–2017.[31] The successful creation of the OSS has undoubtedly produced positive results for new entrants into the Egyptian economy.

Dr. El-Din went on to hold several distinguished positions within the Egyptian government, including serving as Deputy Prime Minister for International Development and as Minister for International Cooperation from 2013–2014. As of 2018, he worked for a private consultancy in Cairo and sits on several company boards.

Notes

The author and editors are grateful to Khalid Elashmawy for drafting the epilogue and for other important inputs into the manuscript.

1. Taher Helmy, "Empowering the People," *El-Ahram Weekly*, September 2–8, 2004, issue 706: Helmy, the president of the American Chamber of Commerce (AmCham) in Egypt, said: "Our skill level and institutional reform has not kept up with policy leaps; in fact, we have more bureaucracy today than before. Civil servants are being asked to make decisions regarding complex new market economy concepts and take responsibility for them. They are at a loss, so they create more obstacles to slow things down and protect themselves, knowing that mistakes can cost them their jobs—or worse. The absence of a simple system that is competently executed has proved to be a tremendous impediment for investors large and small, local and foreign." See Andrew Stone, "Establishing a Successful Oner Stop Shop: The case of Egypt," presented at IMF/AMF High-Level Seminar on Institutions and Economic Growth in Arab Countries, Abu Dabi, UAE, December 19–20, 2006, p. 2, https://www.imf.org/external/np/seminars/eng/2006/arabco/pdf/stone.pdf.

2. Salama Fahmy and James Brown, "One-Stop Shop: A Case Study," World Bank Private Sector Development Forum, 2006. In 2001, the Egyptian pound varied between 3.8 and 4.6 to the U.S. dollar. The rate in 2006 was 5.8.

3. The mandatory minimum capital required of a Commandite Company Limited by Shares (CCLS) is LE 250,000 (Article 6[2] of the ministerial decision implementing the Commercial Companies Law). For a joint stock company, the minimum share capital is LE 500,000 if the JSC offers its shares to the public and

LE 250,000 if it is private. The company law is No. 159 of 1981 and the investment law is No. 8 of 1997.

4. Law 8 of 1997 was designed to encourage domestic and foreign investment in targeted economic sectors and to promote decentralization of industry from the Nile Valley area. The law and its executive regulations and amendments provide over twenty investment incentives. It regulates companies (regardless of their legal form) in several specified activities, such as agricultural, poultry and animal production, industry and mining, hotels and tourism, transport, oil, housing and infrastructure, hospitals, some financial services firms, and projects funded by the Social Development Fund. This law allows foreign investors to own any amount up to 100 percent in projects in most sectors. Companies (foreign or domestic) established under this law benefit from tax holidays, reduced custom duties, guarantees against expropriation and sequestration, guarantees regarding foreign exchange, and guarantees regarding repatriation of capital and profit. It also regulates the regime of the free zones (public and private).

5. Presidential Decree No. 316 of 2004.

6. "Egypt: Open for Business," Conference Comments, American Chamber of Commerce, New York City, March 16, 2006.

7. Hadia Mostafa, "One-Stop Investment Shop," *Business Today Egypt*, June 2005. The article quotes Hassan Fahmy, the general manager of GAFI's Investor Reception and Advice Department.

8. For example, the June 8, 2005, Unified Income Tax Law (Law 91 of 2005) reduced the corporate tax rate from 42 percent to 20 percent (except for oil companies, for which taxes are at 4.55 percent). The new legislation eliminated exemptions and tax holidays stipulated in Law 8 of 1997, with the exception of those on cultivation and land reclamation, animal breeding, fisheries, and bee-hiving. The exemption cancellations were not applied retroactively.

9. The quotations in this section, unless otherwise cited, are from an interview granted by Bahaa El-Din, conducted in mid-2006 by Andrew Stone.

10. The new system has been initiated based on Clause 54 of Investment Law 8 of 1997 and its amendment in 2004.

11. Included but not limited to representatives from the Ministries of Industry, Health, Social Affairs, Housing, Agriculture, Water Resources, Tourism, Communication, Electricity, Transport, Finance, Interior, Planning, Labor, and Environment.

12. As provided for in the new Law 13 of 2004 in Clause 51.

13. Initially, the OSS started with a representation with thirty-two agencies, but two more agencies were added later: the Investment Post Office and the General Authority for Social Insurance.

14. As will be seen, not all these entities have the power to perform *all* services on behalf of their entity.

15. These documents include applications related to the Commercial Registry, Capital Market Authority, Investment Gazette, and Chamber of Commerce.

16. Payment is made at this early stage because entities need to receive their money before rendering their service.

17. Dr. Ziad Bahaa El-Din, interview with Khaled Elashmawy, November 1, 2017.

18. Giza, Cairo, or other local syndicates.

19. The Commercial Registry is usually issued every five years.

20. A World Bank survey of manufacturing firms suggested it takes small- and medium-sized enterprises (SMEs) an average of over ninety days to get a telephone connection and over 100 days for an electricity connection, although large enterprises get these services much faster. Obtaining water connections could also be time consuming, although experience varies. See World Bank, "Egypt, Arab Rep. – Enterprise Survey 2016," September 7, 2017.

21. "One-Stop Shop Egypt Case Study: Inter-Ministerial Coordination," Organization for Economic Cooperation and Development.

22. World Bank Group, Doing Business 2011: Egypt, Arab Republic, "Making a Difference for Entrepreneurs."

23. "Egypt's Cabinet Approves Investment Law Executive Regulations," Reuters, October 2017, www.reuters.com/article/egypt-investment/egypts-cabinet-approves-investment-law-executive-regulations-idUSC6N1J801B.

24. The data cited here is from Egypt's Ministry of Investment website, www.investment.gov.eg/MOI_Portal/#.

25. "Egypt Foreign Direct Investment Net Inflows," World Bank Data.

26. "Annual Report 2010/11," Central Bank of Egypt, "Annual Report 2006/2007," Central Bank of Egypt.

27. Ibid.

28. "Egypt Investment Climate," U.S. Department of State, 2015.

29. "Egypt's New Investment Law: A New Legal Framework for Investments and Investors," Zulficar & Partners Law Firm, www.zulficarpartners.com/wp-content/uploads/2017/08/New-Investment-Law-7-2017-ZP-Presentation.pdf.

30. "Doing Business 2017: Egypt Economy Profile," World Bank Group, www.doingbusiness.org/~/media/WBG/DoingBusiness/Documents/Profiles/Country/EGY.pdf.

31. "Egypt—GAFI Launches Investment Map before the End of 2017: CEO," Daily News Egypt, 2017.

NINE

Transforming the Cash Culture and the Bill Payment System in Saudi Arabia

KHALID AL-YAHYA

IN MARCH 2002, a team from Saudi Arabia's Ministry of Finance and Central Bank, the Saudi Arabia Monetary Agency (SAMA), contemplated a future plan to reform the cash-based bill payment and revenue collection system in the country. The team—led by Mohammed al-Jasser, who was then the vice governor of SAMA, and Abdulmalik al-Asheikh, director of SAMA Banking Technology—was charged with overhauling the management of the government's revenue streams. At the time, the fragmented payment and collection situation was agonizing to the government, consumers, and private sector alike. Authorities estimated that government was losing between 10 and 15 percent of revenues annually due to human error, fraud, and delays associated with the manual, cash-based system. Consumers of basic services such as utilities and telecommunications were becoming increasingly impatient about the long lines at crowded banks and the service interruptions borne of delayed bank payments to government and private sector billers. Financial institutions incurred high transaction costs as they tried to manage the high volume of cash coming in through their branches from the thousands of customers queuing to pay their bills daily.

For several years, this situation was a major concern for the MOF, led by Ibrahim Al-Assaf. Al-Assaf felt the need to develop an efficient and

reliable system that would improve service delivery to disconcerted customers, enhancing financial operations for both the government and private sector. Moreover, he wanted to make Saudi Arabia a regional leader
in government-led innovation in e-service technologies. In doing so, the
SAMA team had many challenges at hand: reducing cash use in financial
transactions; developing standardized, efficient bill payment operations;
creating a robust information technology backbone; building consumer
trust in electronic bill payment; increasing competitiveness among public
and private billers to provide convenient and efficient electronic payment
options; and increasing transparency and accountability in government
finances. Any successful reform of the system would depend on reversing the "cash culture" in Saudi Arabia, which would be possible only by
"adopting innovation in service delivery as the driver for such change,"
al-Jasser explained.[1]

Al-Jasser, who holds a Ph.D. in economics from the University of Cali-
fornia, served as an executive director at the International Monetary Fund
from 1990 to 1995 and was a key member of the negotiation team during
the successful accession of Saudi Arabia to the World Trade Organization
(WTO). He had a clear vision for a competitive and well-functioning financial system in Saudi. He noted that previous attempts to fix the system
had ended with mixed results, more often than not with unintended and
undesirable consequences. Al-Jasser and Deputy Minister of Finance for
Revenues Saad Al-Hamdan, who later championed the reform idea within
public bureaucracy, believed there was a clear need for a creative solution
to modernize the bill payment and collection system in a way that not
only would satisfy the needs of consumers, streamline government revenue
collection, and address the deficiencies in bill payment nationally but also
increase the economy's overall competitiveness internationally.

This press to modernize the country's financial system came about
within a larger context of economic and institutional reform within Saudi
Arabia. As the largest economy in the Middle East, the top oil producer in
the world, and a member in the G20, Saudi Arabia needed a solid modern
infrastructure for handling financial transactions. At the turn of the twenty-
first century, the Saudi leadership was increasingly convinced of the need
to modernize the country's financial and economic institutions. Reforms
were, indeed, necessary to sustain growth and to benefit from greater integration with the global community. This conviction was evident in the
kingdom's decision to initiate the process of joining the WTO, which it
finalized in 2005.[2]

The early 2000s brought sweeping changes. Saudi Arabia began to take some steps toward economic reforms in the areas of privatization, foreign direct investment, trade liberalization, and diversification. King Abdullah accelerated the pace and scope of reform by making large public investments in the areas of education, health, communication and information technology, finance, and transportation infrastructure. In the area of service delivery, the government initiated a national e-government program called Yesser in 2003. The vision behind Yesser was that "by the end of 2010, everyone in the kingdom will be able to enjoy—from anywhere and at any time—world-class government services offered in a seamless, user-friendly and secure way by utilizing a variety of electronic means."[3]

SAMA was by no means certain about what changes would work to solve bill payment and revenue collection problems in Saudi Arabia. The officials were convinced, however, that they had to be something that fit the needs of government and the market. Moreover, they needed to meet the growing expectations placed on the country as a regional economic and political leader.

The task of generating solutions to the financial system's deficiencies was headed by al-Asheikh, a forty-year-old engineer who had spent eighteen years in SAMA and was credited with introducing several innovations and improvements in government and banking service delivery. He was the first to draw attention to the real scope of the problem in 2000, and thus was seen as the right person to lead the efforts to fix it. "I was aware of the increasing magnitude and complexity of the problem in recent years and had to raise the issue to al-Jasser." Al-Asheikh did not have a clear idea about what the end solution would look like but needed to "move quite quickly, because first, the situation was getting out of control, and second, I had the full support and commitment of the top leadership. I was very close to al-Jasser during the development period, updating him on all bureaucratic and technical obstacles we were facing," al-Asheikh recalled.[4]

A History of Financial Reform Efforts in Saudi Arabia

In the thirty years leading to 2002, bill payment and revenue collection in Saudi Arabia had gone through a series of experiments and rapid changes. Originally, fees for government services were paid in cash by customers at the premises of the agency providing the service. Such payments were collected by the *amin al-sanduq* (caretaker of agency revenues) assigned to each agency. This official was then responsible for depositing the revenues generated from provided services into the agency's account at one of the local banks. In turn, the local bank would transfer the deposited funds to the MOF account in SAMA (often after holding the deposited funds for a few days or even weeks). "The *amin al-sanduq* is an iconic figure in every organization. He collects and holds the money and pays salaries to all employees in cash; without him everything stops," said an official in the MOF.[5]

In some cases, the *amin al-sanduq* had to leave his post early in the afternoon to deposit the cash at the bank. When this happened, customers who came in to pay their fees were not able to do so. This meant additional trips were required by customers, many of whom would leave their jobs and spend hours or even days paying bills. This often caused delays in payment, with customers facing occasional interruptions in basic services such as water and electricity or incurring late fees in the cases of car registrations, labor permits, and traffic violations. Using cash as a method of payment allowed room for human error, the loss of revenues, or the use of counterfeit money. There were also security risks associated with the *amin al-sanduq* physically transporting large amounts of cash to banks; a few cases of theft and robbery were reported. Moreover, with an increasing number of customers and newly introduced services and charges, this way of paying bills and collecting revenues proved increasingly ineffective and unmanageable.

To reduce the use of cash and the dependence on the *amin al-sanduq*, different initiatives were introduced during the 1980s and 1990s. SAMA's banking technology unit, headed by al-Asheikh, introduced the program to transfer government payroll electronically. This eliminated the need for millions of public sector employees to stand in queues waiting for the *amin al-sanduq* to hand in their salary in cash.

The Ministry of Interior (MOI) and affiliated agencies that provided services with fixed fees (like those applied to the issuance of passports, drivers' licenses, and residency cards for foreign laborers) also began issuing prepaid coupons with a fixed monetary value that could be bought from designated banks and used to pay for services. Although the coupon system provided relief from the burdens of carrying and paying in cash, it created fertile ground for fraud with the use of counterfeit coupons. The process of purchasing coupons from banks also required customers to wait in long queues to purchase coupons. This, in turn, led to a black market for coupons: individual vendors would buy stacks of coupons from banks (or counterfeit them) and then sell these coupons to customers in the streets outside the agency providing the service. These coupon vendors also charged a "transaction fee" on top of the actual coupon value, causing widespread resentment among customers who had no choice but to pay the fee to get their business done quickly. Moreover, the coupon system benefited only a few designated banks and a limited number of agencies. Many service fees were not fixed or predetermined, which meant that customers still needed to see the *amin al-sanduq* for the exact amount to be paid.

The MOI and other affiliated service providers stopped using coupons as a method of payment in the mid-1990s and started experimenting with new solutions. The passport and traffic departments, for instance, succeeded in signing bilateral agreements with two banks that accepted payments on their behalf. In the context of this relationship, the agencies and banks shared databases, enabling customers to transfer fees directly from their bank accounts to their agency accounts using their bank's automatic teller machine (ATM). As part of the arrangement, the banks would hold the payments—in excess of US$267 million per month—for a month before transferring the revenues to the MOF.

There were problems with these arrangements, as well. The only customers who could benefit from these services were those who had accounts with the two banks. This created an uncompetitive market wherein intermediaries who held an account in these banks would take a fee (about 10 to 15 percent of the amount to be transferred) to pay the bills and added other charges if a customer did not have an account in either bank. Eventually, consumer complaints increased about the unlawful extra charges levied by intermediaries and about having to queue at the branches and ATMs of these two banks. Other banks joined in the protest, citing the potential loss of customers and the lack of fair entry to this bill payment market. Once the arrangement began, most customers opened alternative accounts in the two banks linked with the MOI just to use those accounts for paying bills to the ministry, quickly making the two banks the largest in Saudi Arabia in terms of number of accounts. Moreover, the MOF resented the practice of banks holding on to payments, because it slowed the flow of revenues into the country's treasury.

In later stages, some government agencies with better financial and technical capacities had their partner banks install point-of-sale (POS) machines, allowing customers to pay bills at the agency using their debit cards. This, too, was problematic. Not all banks benefited from placing their POS machines, and not all government agencies had the capacity to install the machines and synchronize their systems with the network. Furthermore, the cash-based system had to remain in place as many customers did not have debit cards. In some rural areas in Saudi Arabia, people often do not have bank accounts; their savings and commercial transactions are in cash. There were also system overloads on a daily basis, with downtime for the POS network increasing as the volume of payments increased. Banks also disapproved of the POS system, as government regulations prevented them from charging commission on either billers or customers.

SAMA's Mandate and Its Unintended Consequences

One contributing factor to the bill payment problems experienced in Saudi Arabia was a decision by SAMA in the early 1980s that had unintended consequences on the bill market. At the time, SAMA mandated that all Saudi Arabian banks should accept bill payments on behalf of utilities (electricity, telecommunications, and water) at no charge, whether the payer was a customer of the bank where the bill was being paid or not. In return, banks recovered a small portion of the collection costs through float income. Banks held onto the cash deposits for anywhere from seven to thirty days after the payment was received, during which time service providers received no confirmation of payment. This often resulted in the disconnection of services to customers due to delays in bill processing and reconcilement with service providers. The manual reconcilement between banks and billers was another reason for delays. An official in the Ministry of Electricity and Water described the process:

> Bill payment collectors from the 13 regional electricity companies in the country's 13 provinces used to stop by each bank in different cities and villages everyday to collect bill receipts of the previous day and brought back large boxes loaded with thousands of bills to our facility where we had an army of workers entering each bill manually into the system. The process was also a duplication of what the banks did after they collected payments. Government billers, like the water and police departments, had even more duplications, as other parties were involved, like MOF and SAMA. So, with all this duplication and manual collection and reconcilement, the process of completely settling payment sometimes took more than a month.[6]

At the time the SAMA mandate was issued, the number of bill payments processed by banks was limited and manageable. This changed dramatically in the mid-1990s with the introduction (and then the privatization) of mobile telecommunications services. In 2004, the number of mobile subscribers surpassed landline and electricity subscribers, growing at an annual rate of 67 percent. Furthermore, the population of Saudi Arabia itself was growing at a rapid rate. In fact, it tripled over thirty years to nearly 26 million in 2007. Presently, 60 percent of the population is under the age of twenty, suggesting the number of subscribers will continue to rise substantially in the next years.

The mandate by SAMA placed a particular burden on banks. Some 60 to 70 percent of all bills were paid in cash at bank branches, and 30 percent of customers visiting bank branches were there to pay their bills. The traffic resulted in high costs for banks in terms of front-office operations, payment processing, IT integration, and reconciliation. The incremental cost to the average bank for one bill payment transaction within a branch was estimated at 12 to 15 Saudi riyals (US$3.21 to US$4.01); it was even higher in smaller banks (up to US$10).[7] Additionally, consumers incurred a high cost as a result of long queue times at banks; it was estimated that customers spent a combined 12 to 15 million collective hours annually waiting at banks to pay bills. Bill presentation and collection was largely paper-based and conducted manually, creating significant inefficiencies and overhead costs for billers and banks alike, while also allowing room for human error and fraud. In the words of one of the bank's executives:

> By forcing banks to accept bill payment at no charge, SAMA effectively created a subsidy to billers at the expense of banks. The subsidy to billers like Saudi Telecommunication Company (STC) and Saudi Electricity Company (SEC) was estimated at a combined US$71.47 million in 2003. This transaction cost incurred in handling payments to banks increased to reach US$96 million in 2005. As SAMA became aware of the unintended impact of its decision on banks, it realized the need for a major change in service delivery that could achieve a more equitable sharing of costs and benefits between billers and banks.

Customer complaints of long waits at bank branches and delays in reconciling their bills with billers also continued. A survey conducted by SAMA in late 2003 found that the top customer complaints regarding bill payment were that the manual cash-based process was time-consuming and that postage delays, lost bills, and bill processing delays resulted in the disconnection of vital services like electricity and water. The situation was worse in small and remote towns as "citizens had to travel to the bank branch in another town to pay, and often were faced by unwelcoming banks that tried to find any reason to reject bill payment as branches were overwhelmed by the crowds preventing them from selling more profitable products and serving their own clients," said al-Asheikh.[8]

The Spaghetti Model

As the situation continued affecting bank and biller operations alike, some utilities, led by the communication and electricity companies (mainly STC and SEC), and a few banks took the matter into their own hands, independently introducing electronic bill payment through the use of ATMs, then later using other channels like the internet and phone banking. In the mid-1990s, utilities and big banks established bilateral agreements, developing direct electronic links with each other to process bill payment. This system enabled customers to use their banks' electronic channels to view and pay bills.

The new system required direct links to be created between each utility company and each bank in Saudi Arabia. This model, termed the "spaghetti problem" because of the messy collection of individual institutional links, was complicated and difficult to sustain. The problem was exacerbated as the number of bills increased as the population grew from 9 million in 1980 to 27 million in 2007 and as the mobile telecommunications market was opened to competition and new mobile operators started operating. Other sectors' payments also grew; by 2002, over 120 million payments were being made through the system annually in sectors like government, airlines, insurance, finance, real estate, and education. With the number of billers increasing, continuing the "spaghetti model" would mean hundreds of direct links between banks and billers. Ahmad Al-Hasan, an engineer working with the SAMA team, stated:

> If you have 12 banks with five billers, it is 60 connections, and if you have 20 billers, it is 240 connections, each with different IT standards and capabilities and duplicated investments due to the proliferation of non-standard multiple interfaces. In this case, banks will have large teams dealing with a different accounting process for each biller. Also, billers will deal with accounts in each bank, and it would be a nightmare for the billers' treasurers.[9]

While big billers were successful in getting linked with major banks, smaller billers who came later were not so successful. Banks began to reject new billers as it became clear that additional links, especially with government providers, would overwhelm their systems and individual bank branches with no significant economic return. Ultimately, those who failed to sign agreements with banks (mostly government agencies) to use bank channels complained to SAMA about the uncooperative banks.

For SAMA, the process for electronic bill payment was inefficient and ineffective, and there was no forum to bring all the banks and billers together to resolve problems jointly. According to SAMA, the problems with the spaghetti model were many:

- Banks kept deposited funds for seven sixty-day periods before transferring them to the relevant agency.

- Processes between banks and billers were complicated and confusing.

- Billers had to link separately with each bank, requiring a large support team on both sides. This work had to be duplicated with each new bank, and each link required different integration systems due to the lack of set standards.

- Billers undertook reconciliation and settlement with each bank individually, increasing time and financial costs.

- There was no real-time notification of payment. The biller needed to collect payment data from each bank and enter it manually at the end of each day.

- Billers and customers had limited confidence in each other due to information asymmetries, reinforced by the limited payment information provided by the intermediary bank in the absence of rules regulating access to information.

- Bill payment processes differed between banks, and each bank provided a different customer experience.

- Billers faced difficulty in adding new products and services since the systems were not designed for such an upgrade or flexibility.

- Each biller and bank provided an individual effort to promote electronic payment.

- Consumers had to physically go to their bank and queue at the ATM to pay their bills.

- Bill details were presented only on paper.

- Banks had no capacity to support additional billers.

- E-government initiatives were not being supported.

In government circles, particularly at the MOF, there was growing concern about the failing revenue collection in more than 200 government entities scattered across a country larger than Western Europe. The government structure in Saudi Arabia is highly centralized, and all revenues collected by public agencies in all regions in the country have to go through the MOF.

The ministry thought it was no longer possible for the government to ignore the need to push for a more reliable and transparent system that not only served consumers and private billers but also enabled government to collect revenues; minimized the fraud and corruption occurring in manual transactions; and provided an audit trail and data reporting for each transaction electronically. Modernizing the system was not a matter of luxury for the ministry. It needed to ensure effective supervision and accountability of its sister ministries and agencies.

How to Proceed?

At SAMA, al-Jasser and al-Asheikh had to mull over thorny questions: What kind of payment and revenue collection system should it be? Would it be feasible to have one automated system to serve both government and corporate firms representing different industries and sectors? Who should build it? Who should manage it? If developed by SAMA, would strong government ministries give up their independent systems and their control over revenue collection to a unified system run by a smaller semi-independent agency? Would powerful banks, utilities, and telecom companies change their existing systems after they had invested so heavily in developing elaborate networks that distinguished them from their competitors?

As a broader policy issue, should government be involved, especially in a period when everyone was talking about privatization and limiting the role and size of government? Many services, like water, electricity, and communications, that used to be in the hands of government were being privatized. Bill payment systems would normally be left to the market players to develop. There were also questions about whether the immature and fragmented private sector would be able to solve the problem without government leadership and huge financial commitments. Even if it was built by market forces, would it have the credibility and security needed to market and sustain the system in Saudi Arabia?

Moving Toward Implementation

Given his familiarity with bill payment problems as the head of the banking technology unit at SAMA, al-Asheikh shared his thoughts about the potential solution with his boss, al-Jasser, in early 2002. Both shared the view that the solution to the failing bill payment and revenue collection models in Saudi Arabia should be some form of electronic bill payment and presentment (EBPP) system. Such a system could be based in a networked governance structure.

The vision behind the proposed EBPP (or, the SADAD Payment System, as it has since been named officially) was to build a national, unified electronic platform to streamline bill payment transactions, one that served as a trusted intermediary between billers (government and nongovernment) and banks, and which was supported by cutting-edge technology so as to provide efficient and effective customer service to citizens and residents of Saudi Arabia.

There was also agreement among representatives of SAMA and the MOF, led by al-Jasser and Al-Hamdan (of the MOF), that government should lead the way and put up the necessary investment to set up such infrastructure. Although a firm believer in the free market and its ability to respond to new demands and opportunities, al-Jasser was a supporter of the role of government in promoting modernization and economic development. Given the idiosyncrasies of the Saudi Arabian market, it was obvious to him that the immature and fragmented market players would not work together to make the necessary investment to build a universal third-party system, at least not in the near future.

He believed government should take the lead in setting up such a strategic project in consultation with the private sector:

> As a government, we are forced into developing in place of the private sector because we want to move forward faster and at a large scale. The private sector could have done it, but not with the speed and scale that we desired. I believe we would be ten years behind if

we left all of these strategic developments to the private sector . . . There was a high level of uncertainty and risk, and these ventures were not profitable in the beginning. There were risks we expected the private sector to shy away from.[10]

Al-Jasser asserted that Saudi Arabia had become the largest and most competitive economy in the Middle East largely due to government leadership that pushed forward innovation and modernization in both public and private sectors. He also believed that developing a networked system would enhance business-to-business transactions in addition to business-to-government transactions. In this regard, the government's role in developing a payment system was in line with recent government policy efforts to expand the role of the private sector in aiding social and economic development, relieving government from some of the burden of service provision. This emphasis on supporting the private sector by enacting policies, including adoption of modern technologies and innovation, was reflected in Saudi Arabia's Eighth Development Plan (2005–2009).

A push toward a joined-up e-government was gaining momentum in the country, both to increase efficiency and productivity in the public sector and to improve customer service to individuals and businesses. In September 2003, a royal decree was issued directing the Ministry of Communications and Information Technology to devise a plan for providing government services and related transactions electronically. This brought about the development of Yesser, the national e-government initiative in Saudi Arabia. Although the conceptualization of a new EBPP took place independently before the e-government initiative was launched, al-Jasser envisioned that an advanced EBPP system would be a central requirement for completing the overall e-service infrastructure. In addition to serving the private sector, the new system could be the payment system for all e-government programs.

All this coincided with a broad movement aspiring to propel Saudi Arabia toward greater integration with the global community, as evident in a series of new policies to promote foreign investment and economic diversification. Saudi Arabia "is a regional economic and political leader, and a world-class financial infrastructure backed by leading technologies is a must to improve service delivery to our citizens and streamline and enhance the operations of government and market firms delivering these services," said al-Jasser. "Once we see the system running on its feet, we then could spin it off as an IPO."[11]

Building SADAD

Given the needed support from al-Jasser, al-Asheikh put together a small team and began the process of finding a new integrative model for Saudi Arabia. Al-Asheikh's strategy was to study Saudi Arabia's market needs and learn about EBPP systems in other countries, including the United Kingdom, Norway, Sweden, South Africa, and the United States. The purpose of this exploration was to develop a unique approach that fit the Saudi Arabian context. One of the most important pieces of advice al-Jasser gave al-Asheikh early on was, "Do not build a bridge in the middle of the desert," warning that whatever solution is chosen had to have the following success factors: "providing public value, economically viable, and has high impact and appeal in the Saudi market."[12]

To assess the current needs and success factors, the first step al-Asheikh took was to conduct a survey of a large random sample of bill payers in different areas (urban and rural) to find out more about existing problems, identifying obstacles to instituting the EBPP system for consumers. The survey revealed that approximately 30 percent of customer visits to bank branches were primarily for bill payment, and that bank branches and biller collection centers were the predominant channels for bill payment. Customers complained about lost time and the inconvenience of current arrangements for bill payment. Cost was also a common concern among respondents who received electricity or telephone bills (80 percent), as these bills accounted for 93 percent of the cost of the bills they received.

Over 70 percent of respondents stated that they were likely to use a service for paying bills through electronic channels, with acceptance being higher in larger cities. Those surveyed stated that ATM and phone banking were the preferred alternative channels to visiting bank branches for bill payment. As for their concerns, potential customers stated that they were worried about the confidentiality of their personal information, the accuracy of the bill and payment information, and control over their money.

Feedback was also solicited from major billers and banks through a series of meetings and workshops held before proceeding with high-level design of the bill payment and collection system. The findings gleaned from these events provided useful insights on what kind of system would be adopted. Furthermore, they also cultivated buy-in attitudes among stakeholders for future services to be provided by the system.

In searching for a suitable EBPP system, al-Asheikh called on a range of international experts and consultants to mull over a system that fit the

Saudi Arabian context. They solicited ideas and proposals by presenting a business case to the consultants, suggesting the development of a business-to-business and a government-to-business EBPP provider, wherein a consortium of potential users would be formed to facilitate buy-in behavior, including commercial banks, central banks, and large purchasers (for example, Saudi Aramco, the national oil company).

Al-Asheikh was not impressed with the consultants' proposals. "The consultants came back with a very rosy picture, describing the development of such a provider to be far easier than had been expected. Most ideas presented were borrowed from existing bill payment systems in other countries based on business-to-consumer models that focus on reducing costs mainly by eliminating paper bills."[13] Al-Asheikh and his team remained skeptical of the consultants' ideas, believing their suggestions simply were not feasible in Saudi Arabia. None of the ideas proposed could efficiently withstand the complexities of the Saudi Arabian banking system, the nuances of the country's social and commercial culture, and the size of the total population.

At this stage, the idea of SADAD crystallized: a trusted intermediary for bill payments that results in a "win-win situation" for billers and banks, while providing reliable and efficient service to customers. SADAD became a one-stop, back-end payment system focused on government-to-consumer and business-to-consumer transactions. It could be expanded in the future to cover government-to-business transactions and business-to-business transactions. The SADAD system that the SAMA team came up with was divided into two parts: operations and management. The service owner of SADAD was SAMA, while the service delivery or operational aspects and technical components were outsourced and handled by Atos Origin Middle East Group.[14]

How SADAD Works

As a national EBPP system, SADAD works according to the following process. First, government and private sector billers send bill information to SADAD on a predetermined schedule. SADAD validates this information, uploads it into its database, and checks for discrepancies. Then the customer requests the bill information through one of the five channels (bank branch, phone, internet, ATM, or mobile phone). The bank forwards this request electronically to SADAD, and SADAD instantly retrieves the information from its database and forwards it to the bank, which in turn provides it to the customer via one of the five channels. The customer selects each bill they want to pay and the amount to be paid, and the bank then debits the customer's account and sends the confirmation to SADAD. This process takes the same time it takes customers to withdraw cash from an ATM. SADAD updates its database and notifies the biller in real time once the bank has confirmed the transaction. At the end of the day, SADAD begins settlement instructions using the Saudi Arabian Riyal Interbank Express (SARIE), which enables banks to electronically redistribute collected money to billers' bank accounts. Billers then receive reconciliation reports from SADAD showing a breakdown of all transactions processed by SADAD. SADAD is then updated to reflect the bill status as settled in the same day.

The SADAD system has many notable features, including:

- SADAD can automatically show bills to customers by linking them with the customer's national ID number, as registered with the customer's bank, without the customer having to key-in any additional account number information.

- Customers have the ability (based on biller specifications) to pay bills partially, overpay them, or even pay before a bill has been issued.

- Billers know when their customers pay in real time, allowing them to continue providing the service, or even to reactivate the service after disconnection. This increases overall service usage by the customer, meaning more revenue for billers.

- SADAD has introduced a refund mechanism to allow billers to give money back to customers for services not provided or any other reason.

- In the case of a biller or bank system failure, SADAD provides access to all transaction records through an easy-to-use internet portal.

- The MOF now has real-time online access to all government agency transactions. In the past, it had to request these records from each agency, which often took months or even years to collect.

- The SADAD business model was based on a transparent value-pricing scheme that uses average volume and value of bills per each biller, which avoids the provision of any subsidy to billers.

Organization and Management Model

The SADAD designers had to think creatively about the best organization and management system that would fit its new roles and responsibilities. SADAD would have to serve and satisfy not only government entities but also private firms and individual consumers with different needs and expectations in a very dynamic environment. To gain wide confidence and deliver results, the new entity had to function professionally and efficiently. "Mr. al-Jasser and I envisioned an organization that promotes and values innovation, talent, and quick execution. This meant the new entity ought to have a semi-independent status from the conventional government bureaucracy structure, a team of qualified, empowered and motivated individuals, a progressive and participative culture, a flat non-hierarchal organizational structure, and open and flexible communication and information system," according to al-Asheikh.[15]

To provide effective in-house management and to attract needed local talent, SADAD's semi-independent agency model enabled it to avoid the conventional government management and reward system. SADAD created its own flexible recruitment, compensation, and retention systems that were different from the employment and human resources system used in the public bureaucracy. Positions and rewards were linked to competence and performance instead of considerations such as seniority or longevity. "SADAD, with the exception of very few senior positions that required certain experience, focused largely on hiring young local talent, especially females, and on creating the right environment for them to develop and operate."[16]

Finding the right implementation model was as challenging as developing the concept itself. The government sector did not have many implementation models to follow. On this, al-Asheikh stated: "SADAD had to have a maximum possible agility to maneuver. Therefore, if SAMA wanted to implement and operate the system, it had to change itself to resolve some issues that usually exist in government agencies, like decision-making speed, budgeting, hiring and firing, etc. A special process for staffing was created, and a carefully designed outsourcing model was developed."[17]

System Built, But Who Will Use It?

After building the system, the most critical task was to make sure everyone used it. "My boss's [al-Jasser] warning, 'Don't build a bridge in the middle of the desert,' was ringing in my ears throughout the process but more so when we came to launch and promote the system." al-Asheikh spent a lot of time contemplating the best way to proceed.[18]

Al-Jasser suggested they would have to get the biggest billers to use the system first to establish SADAD's credibility and visibility. This meant getting large government agencies and major private firms like STC and SEC to use SADAD from the start. "Once awareness and trust were built, and big billers and banks start using it, others would follow suit and would link to SADAD," al-Asheikh remarked.[19]

Following his boss's advice, al-Asheikh engaged big players in the planning stages by setting up the SADAD Steering Committee, which included senior management from the government sector, several powerful ministries, and major billers and banks, including STC, SEC, Al Rajhi Bank, National Commercial Bank, Arab National Bank, and Riyadh Bank. They were involved in the planning, development, and governance of SADAD. Al-Asheikh had to navigate on multiple different fronts:

> It was not easy to try to attend to and pull the different billers and banks into the same direction. I had to make sure all are engaged and informed about our plans. I needed to track all old and new initiatives by banks and billers that were not aligned with SADAD's vision and try to convince them not to go ahead with these initiatives and instead see the value of the new system. Up until we started operating, banks and billers continued to devise different plans to develop their own networks and differentiate their models for service delivery. Sometimes information about these plans is confidential and thus you don't really know what is happening or what people are really thinking.[20]

The SADAD strategy to first engage influential stakeholders worked. In May 2005, the Arab National Bank began using SADAD, followed by the National Commercial Bank. More joined over the next couple of years, with STC signing on in July 2006 and SEC in June 2007. In the year prior to STC joining, only four billers had been using SADAD as pilot billers.

In the year following STC joining SADAD, the number of billers rose to sixteen. After SEC joined, the number of participating billers rose rapidly.

Courting Public Bureaucracy

In the public sector, SADAD faced one of its toughest challenges: convincing government billers to change to the new system. There was resistance to delegating collection methods to an outside party due to fears of losing control over the process, the tremendous effort associated with developing new processes, and concerns about job loss. To mitigate this, the MOF, one of the most powerful ministries in Saudi Arabia, was called in to help.

Saad Al-Hamdan, the deputy minister for financial revenues at the MOF, was an avid supporter of the SADAD system from the outset. As the key person responsible for government revenue collection, he knew by heart all the problems inherent in the existing system: citizen dissatisfaction, delays, fraud, corruption, the black market for coupons, and the high transaction costs associated with the cash-based bill payment and collection system. Realizing the benefits of integrating revenue-generating agencies into SADAD to ensure proper supervision over government revenue collection and ease bill and fee payments for citizens, he raised the matter to Minister of Finance Ibrahim Al-Assaf. The minister's backing was politically necessary in anticipation of major resistance from some government billers. Al-Hamdan and al-Asheikh drafted a detailed letter laying out the multiple problems of bill and fee payment in Saudi Arabia, along with a comparison between the current system and the proposed SADAD system.

It did not take long for the minister to endorse SADAD as the sole national payment gateway, agreeing to use his influence and resources to persuade government agencies to join. "The minister and I shared the same sense of urgency to fix the problem and create public value by making it easy for citizens to pay for services they need and enjoy and for government to ensure efficiency, transparency and accountability when it comes to handling of public money," Al-Hamdan said.[21]

Doubts about a unified electronic platform supervised by an external party emerged once SAMA started approaching government agencies to switch to the new system. Each ministry's ability to collect and keep funds had given them a sense of power and independence. It also provided opportunities for corruption, as some individuals used the system to serve their personal interests. For instance, knowing someone in the police and traffic department could eliminate or lower tickets for traffic violations.

Al-Asheikh understood that changing attitudes and practices in public bureaucracies was difficult and would take time: "We hoped that all government agencies would change the way they operate to fit new integrated models of doing business like SADAD. Some have a complex legacy and a mindset that is almost impossible to change. But you need to keep pushing gradually and that change is good even if it does not appear to be in your interest in the short term."[22]

In addition to resisting change, some government agencies rightly claimed they lacked financial resources and the technical capacity to link to the sophisticated SADAD system. A preliminary gap analysis conducted by the MOF/SADAD team, which measured billers' readiness to integrate with SADAD, revealed that only 5 percent of government agencies were technically fit to join.

Knowing that linking to SADAD would take time and financial and technical resources that many government agencies did not have, and that some would resist joining anyway, the MOF adopted SAMA's recommendation to create the Government On-Boarding (GOB) project. The MOF allocated a large budget to "pay for everything government agencies need in order to link to SADAD; all software, hardware, engineers, and IT staff. The [MOF] even decided to pay for the fees required from government billers to use SADAD. This is unheard of. So there was no excuse for government agencies not to join and use the system," stated Abdullah Al-Lohaidan, the GOB manager.[23]

The MOF backing was an immense boost for SADAD and a signal that government was serious about fixing the old system. Al-Hamdan commented: "The Ministry and the minister were determined to transfer all government collection to SADAD. It used all of its influence over other agencies to get them to use SADAD as their sole collection mechanism, and provided all the needed resources—financial, human, and technical—to ensure that all agencies came onboard and discontinued using all other collection channels."[24]

Some in the government claimed there was no complete understanding of government requirements when SADAD was initially developed. One key weakness in the original design of SADAD that made some reluctant to join was its failure to address the walk-in customer and real-time bill upload problems. This concern was especially prevalent in the government sector.

While the SADAD system worked well for post-service billers like telephone and electricity companies, many fees and charges within the government were assessed only at the time customers placed their orders at an agency. This was a major concern for the MOI, which assesses certain charges, like late fees on renewing residence visas, at the time the service order is placed.

Customers also were not always sure what they needed, and bills might change once the customer was at the service provider's premises. Moreover, government agencies tended to change procedures and fees depending on new government policies and priorities. For instance, business owners often ordered more labor visas from the Ministry of Labor than the ministry could issue due to laws restricting foreign labor visas in certain sectors. Thus, if a business owner asked and paid for forty visas, he might get only ten or twenty. This created additional problems requiring renegotiation and refunds.

Some agencies used point-of-sale machines connected to the Saudi Payment Network (SPAN) to resolve this issue, but SPAN payments did not go through SADAD.[25] This left a large portion of the payment collection market outside of SADAD. If a customer chose to pay a biller directly using a credit card or debit card through SPAN, it was not processed through SADAD. Eventually, SADAD was able to address the problem by upgrading its system and linking it to SPAN, proving SADAD's capability to adapt and respond to new needs. According to al-Asheikh, SADAD's "innovative strength and robustness" emanated from its "scalability, agility, and adaptability."[26]

Approaching Billers and Banks

Changing the landscape of bill payment in Saudi Arabia without introducing a major shift in billers' attitudes was a challenge. SADAD required billers to pay for the service after they had enjoyed nearly free services from banks for years. Nezar Al-Mugren, SADAD manager for development who led some of the negotiations, described how they succeeded in convincing some billers:

> We had to cooperate with and engage them from the beginning on a top management level to align goals and interests of all parties by inviting their executives to be part of the steering committee planning and implementing SADAD. Another factor to achieve this was by communicating the advantages of the new system in terms of

superior services and functions compared to the current situation. We developed a very detailed cost-benefit analysis for utilities that clearly showed that SADAD was the right choice by developing a framework for quantifying the benefits to billers. It was estimated that each utility company would gain a one-time benefit of US$4.3 million and recurring benefits of US$23.5 million.[27]

With regard to the banks, the primary challenge was getting them to use one universal system despite their large investments in previous electronic channels. Under the pre-SADAD system, banks took pride in their individual electronic links with billers and worked hard to differentiate themselves from others to attract customers. Banks felt that SADAD would level the playing field for all banks to provide the same level of service. "When I presented SADAD's idea to the managing directors of banks, they were so worried to lose their technical advantages over other banks," al-Asheikh recalled.[28]

Al-Jasser understood banks' attitudes. "The Saudi market is not one where you often find cooperation between banks or companies as competition between them is imperative. To get banks to adopt a single system is not easy." He added, "Banks naturally thought about their own customers. As government, we had the interests of users of all the banks in mind and how all would enjoy equally good service."[29]

The SAMA team used a selling tactic that was persuasive to banks: cost savings and profit potential. SADAD made the case that banks would no longer bear the burden of subsidizing bill payments and attending to the long queues in their branches for free. Instead, they would be making money, as SADAD would share the fees it collected from billers with the banks. SADAD also gave statistics about the potential size of the market, which assured the banks of the economic benefits they would gain. SADAD's study showed that, with the switch, banks would gain a one-time benefit of US$4.3 million and recurring benefits of US$30.8 million.

In terms of users or bill payers, the critical issues were ensuring the confidentiality of personal information and trust in the system. These were challenges from the outset, and they continue to be issues to which SADAD must closely attend. Otherwise, it risked losing customers' faith in the EBPP and a reversion to a cash-based bill payment system. With regard to confidentiality, SADAD signed agreements with all contractors, vendors, consultants, and employees. On the other hand, the SADAD team believed that, given the government backing of the system, increased use of the internet, and growing awareness and confidence in e-government and other electronic services, society would develop the knowledge and trust needed for their system to succeed.

SADAD Today: Assessing the Impact

According to SAMA statistics and some government and market reports, SADAD has transformed financial service delivery in a significant way. The use of bank branches for bill payment decreased from 73 percent in 2003 to 0 percent in 2017. In the same period, the use of the internet for bill payment increased dramatically, from 1 percent to 85 percent. ATM payments were the channel of choice in 2010 for 41 percent of customers; by 2017, the figure went down to 4 percent of payments. In 2017, SADAD processed more than 18 million transactions a month, with each transaction being fully processed within two seconds. The result has been increased efficiency and convenience for customers, banks, and billers.

With SADAD, billers received funds for payments within one business day, instead of between seven and sixty days, as was the case previously in one bank. While billers did incur transaction fees as well as a cost for joining SADAD, they got many benefits in return: faster payment collection, IT integration cost savings, reconciliation cost savings, a reduction in service cuts, and fewer complaints and queries from dissatisfied customers. Small- and medium-size billers, who were previously rejected by banks, were able to utilize electronic channels to serve their customers. This eliminated the disadvantages of being a small firm, increasing competitiveness.

As for banks, they could no longer benefit from the float income generated by holding onto cash received for bill payment. However, benefits to banks included: reduced costs due to lower transaction volumes at branches, allowing banks to focus on their core customers; IT integration cost savings; reduced reconciliation (down by 60 to 70 percent) and settlement costs; and a reduction in customer complaints and queries.

The complexity of the bill payment system was drastically reduced. Under SADAD, there was one interface for electronic transactions with all seventeen banks, as opposed to multiple interfaces with each of the banks. Banks also got paid for each transaction: 58 percent of the SADAD transaction fee is given to banks. By addressing structural drivers, eliminating the direct links between banks and billers, and centralizing the EBPP system, SADAD reduced the overall costs associated with bill payment in Saudi Arabia by US$330,000 annually, or between 20 and 25 percent.

Most banks and billers seem to agree. By the end of 2017, seventeen Saudi banks had joined SADAD. On the billers' side, many of the major service organizations, including universities, municipalities, airlines, newspapers, insurance companies, telecommunications, and utilities, now use SADAD. Government officials, particularly those at the MOF, seem to be even more content. By providing real-time electronic payment services, SADAD has been able "to reduce manual cash handling and provide an audit trail and data reporting for each transaction, and ensure proper handling of public money," stated Saad Al-Hamdan.[30]

For SADAD and others, this growth is "a testament to both the serious need for an EBPP system in Saudi Arabia, as well as the good design and implementation of SADAD," stated Khalid Al-Romaih, the director of treasury at the Saudi Electricity Company.[31] The result in the case of SADAD was clear according to al-Asheikh:

We have a system that does not exist anywhere else: A system that can do Zakat, tax payment, customs payment, traffic violation, mobile, electricity, airlines, insurance, and prepaid. No other single system does all this. This emerging region needs a system like this. America and Europe are different markets, but in this region the government has a key role to create the infrastructure that everybody trusts and uses. We don't see every industry developing its own program. So instead of duplicating the system and infrastructure, we say build one strong infrastructure that is credible and backed by a strong trusted authority. In our case, it is the central bank [SAMA] and the MOF. SADAD made an impact in nurturing a new model, a third-party system.[32]

In international circles, SAMA's idea to build SADAD was well-received. In 2008, SADAD was awarded the United Nations Public Service Award as the best governmental project in the category of Service Improvement and Innovation. It also won the first place in the GCC E-Government Award in the e-economy category. Following these recognitions, SADAD received several enquiries about the system from other countries. Although al-Asheikh was willing to share the SADAD experience with others, he thought that every country ought "to develop a system based on its context needs and requirements and not to be inhibited to adapt and re-invent any borrowed innovation from other settings. Even in ours, we are always challenged by how to scale up the system, adding new services like e-invoicing and new clients like small businesses and international firms increasingly entering the Saudi Arabian market."[33]

Conclusion

In spite of the success of SADAD in improving the delivery of financial services in Saudi Arabia, it is still not certain whether the system will help ensure the highest standards of accountability and transparency in all government finances. As such, it is unclear if SADAD can eliminate corruption and fraud. Some in the private sector concerned about a government-led monopoly started asking whether SADAD should be spun off from government control. Will SADAD continue to be the only service provider in the e-payment and e-revenue market?

Al-Jasser, who was promoted to the top banker position as governor of SAMA in March 2009, seemed in no rush to make SADAD independent or privatize it as long as, "it is managed in the most professional and effective way. It is an evidence that government agencies and employees are capable of excellence and innovation and that they could do a job as good as or even better than their counterparts in the private sector."[34]

Al-Jasser reflected on SADAD as a symbol of a long-standing tradition of government and market working together in Saudi Arabia to serve the public interest. To him, it was made possible by the strong relationship between government and major players in the market. The government demonstrated a useful ability to leverage these partnerships in important national initiatives. In strategic matters, "the interests and goals of all ought to be aligned. Even if they are slightly misaligned, given the potent role and leadership of government in strategic development and modernization projects, the private sector is expected to adjust to and support government's broad policy priorities."[35]

Notes

1. Mohammed al-Jasser, former vice governor of the Saudi Arabia Monetary Agency (SAMA), interview with author, Riyadh at SAMA, June 18, 2012.

2. Khalid Alyahya, "Creating and Managing Economic Competitiveness: The Saudi Arabia General Investment Authority," Harvard Kennedy Case no. 1926.0., May 18, 2010.

3. In English, *Yesser* translates as *facilitate*. For more information, see www.yesser.gov.sa.

4. Abdulmalik Al-Asheikh (SADAD's president), interview with author, Riyadh at SAMA, May 16, 2012.

5. Ministry of Finance official, interview with the author.

6. Saudi Arabia is divided into thirteen administrative regions (*manatiq idāriyya*). Each region is divided into governorates (*muhafazat*), 118 in total. This number contains the regional capitals, which have a different status from municipalities (*amanah*) headed by mayors (*amin*). The governorates are further subdivided into subgovernorates (*markaz*). This interview was conducted in Riyadh at the Ministry of Electricity & Water, June 10, 2012.

7. US$1 = SR 3.7.

8. Al-Asheikh, interview with author.

9. Ahmad Al-Hasan, interview with author, Riyadh, June 13, 2012.

10. Al-Jasser, interview with author.

11. Ibid.

12. Ibid.

13. Ibid.

14. Atos Origin Middle East Group was bought by Hewlett Packard (HP) in 2007.

15. Al-Asheikh, interview with author.

16. Ibid.

17. Ibid.

18. Ibid.

19. Ibid.

20. Ibid.

21. Saad Al-Hamdan (deputy minister of finance), interview with author, Riyadh, June 20, 2012.

22. Al-Asheikh, interview with author.

23. Abdullah Al-Lohaidan, Government on Boarding (GOB) manager, interview with author.

24. Al-Hamdan, interview with author.

25. The Saudi Payments Network is the kingdom's automated payments network, which links all ATMs and point-of-sale terminals in the country to a central payment switch, which in turn processes the financial transactions to the card issuer, whether a bank, VISA, AMEX, or MasterCard. The network is also run by SAMA.

26. Al-Asheikh, interview with author.

27. Nezar Al-Mugren, interview with author, Riyadh, May 20, 2012.

28. Al-Asheikh, interview with author.

29. Al-Jasser, interview with author.

30. Al-Hamdan, interview with author.

31. Khalid Al-Romaih, the director of treasury at the Saudi Electricity Company, interview with author.

32. Al-Asheikh, interview with author, Riyadh, May 10, 2017.

33. Ibid.

34. Al-Jasser, interview with author.

35. Ibid.

TEN

Making Taxes Less Taxing

Overhauling Tax Policy and Administration in Egypt

FATEMA ALHASHEMI
KHALID ELASHMAWY

EGYPT IS LEGENDARY FOR a bureaucracy with roots extending over 5,000 years. According to one study by Suez Canal University, it takes each person an average of nine hours and 3.5 visits to a government office to complete a transaction like getting a building permit or a school transfer.[1] Bureaucratic inertia and resistance to change have been especially prevalent in revenue collection agencies, where income is hidden by those who manipulate the system for personal gain and others who use their authority to misreport tax liabilities and extract payment in the process, at the expense of the country's treasury.

Yet, in the late 1990s, tax and customs reform had become a pressing necessity for Egypt to put its finances on sound fiscal footing. After a series of economic and political shocks caused the growth momentum to slow, the government reacted by pursuing expansionary fiscal policies, which further undermined financial stability.[2] The budget deficit widened from 0.9 percent of GDP in 1997 to 3.9 percent in 1999–2000, and 6.1 percent in 2002–2003. By 2004, the budget deficit stood at LE 40 billion, 8.3 percent of GDP. Inefficiencies in the tax system led to a shortfall in tax revenues estimated at LE 3.2 to 3.5 billion.[3] It was generally accepted that the tax gap—actual revenue as a percent of potential collections—was more than 60 percent.

At around the same time, Egypt faced other pressing economic challenges, especially the need to increase investment rates to reduce high unemployment and absorb a growing labor force. Foreign investment had sharply declined since the 1980s, to less than 1 percent of GDP, and total private investment was stagnant at around 10 percent of GDP.[4] In 2005, a World Bank survey indicated that 60 percent of Egyptian domestic firms identified tax administration as a major constraint on doing business in the country.[5] As a result, stabilizing Egypt's public finances became intertwined with the need to improve the investment climate, and a simplified tax system that was efficient, transparent, and predictable became a prerequisite for fiscal stability, growth, and competitiveness.[6]

A Dysfunctional Tax System

Following a practice of administrative assessment, a tax collector evaluated the liability of taxpayers, as taxes were determined based on negotiations between the two parties. The tax collector was deeply distrustful of the taxpayer, convinced they were hiding or underreporting income. The taxpayer, in turn, believed the system was unfair and nontransparent. As a result, taxpayers attempted to either evade taxes or bribe tax collectors to lower their liability. The impact of this process was three-fold: it encouraged taxpayer dishonesty, promoted administrative corruption, and prevented government from collecting the taxes and revenues owed.[7] Specifically, there were a number of key problems in the existing system:

- Tax rates were excessive. Egypt charged a top rate of 32 to 40 percent on corporate income, more than twice the 15 percent top rate in Jordan and Lebanon.

- The tax law allowed for several exemptions and loopholes, which resulted in unequal treatment.

- Tax assessment was left to tax collectors, who were not obliged to abide by specific Egyptian or international accounting standards. The determination of taxable profit/income was fraught with imprecision and disputes.

- A taxpayer was allocated a specific inspector, and the relationship between the two to a large extent influenced the liability imposed on the taxpayer, opening the door for widespread corruption.

- The impartiality of tax committees, which looked at appeals from taxpayers, was questionable. Staff from the Egypt Tax Authority (ETA) were also members of the appeals committee, in essence playing the role of both defendant and judge.

- The environment was fraught with disputes. Often, taxpayers simply did not pay the taxes owed but, rather, opted to go through a lengthy appeals process (which included two internal reviews). As a result, the ETA had accumulated years of unpaid taxes amounting to LE 50 billion (around US$11.1 billion).

- Tax administration systems were not unified. There were three tax departments: Income Tax Department (ITD), Sales Tax Department (STD), and General Sales Tax and Real Estate Tax Department. Taxpayers could be subject to multiple audits from different departments in the same year and sometimes at the same time. The tax departments themselves had very poor relations.

The Beginning of Tax Reform

Some efforts toward tax modernization had been ongoing for twenty years, but these reforms were piecemeal, directed at specific administrative issues, and more serious reforms proved elusive. But in 2004, the tide shifted as three factors helped push reforms forward. The first was the appointment of a new reform-minded cabinet, which understood the need for reforms. The second was a committed leadership to directly oversee and implement the reforms. The third element was active support from committed external players who were prepared to provide the requisite technical assistance and financial support.

A pro-reform cabinet headed by Prime Minister Ahmed Nazif was appointed in July 2004, and the pace of economic reform gathered momentum. Privatization was accelerated, the government launched a comprehensive financial sector reform plan, and an interbank market was established. Emphasis was placed on creating an environment to promote foreign direct investment. Reforms encompassed several areas, including the exchange rate system, trade liberalization, modernization of the budget, and restructuring the banking system, among others.

It was within this context that reformers turned their attention to tackling the tax policy and administrative system. The newly appointed Minister of Finance Youssef Boutros-Ghali was tasked with leading the reform. Boutros-Ghali brought with him a solid technical background, political savvy, and extensive experience within the Egyptian government. After completing his Ph.D. in economics at the Massachusetts Institute of Technology, he joined the International Monetary Fund, where he worked for five years. He joined the Egyptian government in 1993, and held a range of senior positions in international cooperation, economic affairs, and foreign trade. He held the post of Minister of Foreign Trade just before his appointment as Minister of Finance in 2004. He was viewed as a determined leader with a pragmatic management style. Tax reform was an area in which he delegated major parts of the agenda to trusted experts, setting guidelines and milestones for others to meet. In the case of customs reform, he was quite "hands on."

Articulating the Vision for Reform

Boutros-Ghali, along with a core team of experts, identified the vision for reform early on. It encompassed several dimensions. The first focused on developing an appropriate policy and legislative framework to simplify and make transparent the tax law, which would create a more level playing field for investors and reduce the scope for corruption. The minister was convinced that a key facet of the new tax law should include reducing the tax rate to minimize dishonesty and tax evasion.

The second dimension involved transforming the relationship between the taxpayer and ETA. This meant moving from a system of administrative assessment to self-assessment of taxes, as well as changing the roles and accountability relationships between the taxpayer, accountants, and tax agency. It also meant establishing a relationship of trust where none had existed before.

The third dimension involved improving the efficiency of the tax administration. This entailed integration of two major bureaucracies, business process re-engineering, and structuring a new tax administration along specific segments of the taxpayer population. The integration of tax administration was seen to have several advantages, which included a single approach to taxpayer services, an integrated audit system, and an integrated approach to collection enforcement to ensure the taxpayer was treated as a single entity, among other factors.

Initiating Implementation

Boutros-Ghali built a team of reformers around him to manage the process. One of the key players he brought on board in 2005 was Ashraf Al-Arabi. Prior to joining the MOF, Al-Arabi had twenty-four years of experience in providing tax and business advisory services to local and multinational corporations. Al-Arabi's exposure to tax regimes around the world gave him extensive technical expertise on tax law and administration. In June 2005, he joined the government as the adviser to the Minister of Finance on tax policy, and he subsequently became deputy minister for tax policy and the new tax commissioner in 2007.

Beyond individual leaders, Boutros-Ghali recognized the need for committed internal reformers around him. He understood that the leadership's motivation alone would not be sufficient to negotiate with and maneuver through large bureaucracies, and that a strong base was required to implement the reforms. Elaborating on this idea, he stated, "We assume if political will is there to change, it will. But this is not true. What is needed is a critical mass of reformers. If I didn't have at least 50 people to do it, I couldn't have done the reforms. Technically I know what needs to be done. I lead autocratically. You need reformers at the lower levels to implement."[8]

Supporting the Egyptian reform leaders were key external actors. The IMF had a long-standing agreement with Egypt since 1991 on a range of economic programs. Working quietly within the MOF, the IMF helped draft tax policy reforms. On the administration side, a January 2005 IMF report, *Revenue Administration Modernization: Strategy and Priorities*, was accepted by Boutros-Ghali as a roadmap for tax administration reform. It also served as a guide for USAID and major international consulting firms. A full-fledged tax administration mission came back annually after that to update the roadmap and comment on progress. In addition, the IMF provided a senior tax administration expert for two weeks each quarter to follow up on and review all key tax administration reform issues.[9]

The minister also requested the support of USAID, which had been supporting tax reforms in Egypt for twenty years. USAID developed the Technical Assistance for Policy Reform II (TAPR II), a major contract designed to provide technical assistance and support for all government economic reforms. At the request of the minister, a substantial slice of this four-year program of assistance was focused on tax policy and administrative reforms. The total TAPR II project was valued at US$125 million; of this sum, US$25 million was allocated to tax administration and policy reform. In October 2005, USAID awarded the TAPR II contract to one prime contractor, BearingPoint, which was later integrated into Deloitte & Touche.

While Boutros-Ghali recognized the need for external expertise, he also believed their role needed to be carefully defined and managed. Fundamentally, he believed the success of reforms was contingent on local ownership, and that Egyptians needed to lead the process and implementation. In the words of the minister, "If you want to have deep reform, the last thing you want is overt interference of external players. The IMF worked here quietly. This is important to avoid the stigma of this having been done abroad. Critics will attack reforms as being imperialist." Hence, while international consultants and development agencies could be engaged in developing strategies and plans, they could not take the lead in implementation.

Internal Governance Structure

Boutros-Ghali, in consultation with BearingPoint-Deloitte & Touche, decided to establish a two-tier governance structure to oversee the reforms. It consisted of a high-level steering committee and a second-level design team. In addition, a project manager and project management office (PMO) were put in place.

The reformers tried to ensure that individuals within the Egyptian tax administration played a key role in the process. Accordingly, fifteen design teams were established, consisting of mid- and senior-level managers from the sales tax and income tax administrations. Those later transitioned into implementation teams. The teams were mandated to design a key element of the reform, specifically the integration of the two tax organizations, as well as to re-engineer business processes and make tax administration more efficient and effective. They undertook a comprehensive review of the operational processes and procedures in both departments and identified new integrated ones.[10] They then provided necessary information to the PMO for the latter to make informed decisions about the merger process.

Several features of the design teams are worth highlighting. They were constituted along functional lines to reflect the division of the new administration. This governance structure addressed one of the key goals throughout the reform—the need to work in parallel across functions. The phasing of reforms was also important. Reformers pursued a deliberate, methodological approach, particularly as the two authorities needed to be able to continue their activities during the period of reform. By bringing together staff from both the sales and income tax departments into one team, reformers addressed one of the key challenges of the integration—resistance to the merger from two organizations that did business very differently.

External consultants were co-housed with the PMO and design teams. Each of the design teams had an external advisor from BearingPoint who provided technical assistance. This collaboration between the external consultants and personnel of the ETA was done to ensure know-how could be exchanged while eliminating the perception that reform was being driven externally. Proposals from the design teams were shared with sector heads and senior management in the two bureaucracies to allow them the opportunity to provide feedback. This was crucial to gain buy-in and commitment to the process.

In the view of the reform leaders, one beneficial outcome of the creation of these teams has been a solid cadre of more than a hundred "champions" for change. Having worked daily with external advisers well-versed in best practice, they understood the need for reform and were able to effectively lead and communicate the operational changes down through the organizations. They became, in essence, agents of change.

Underlying Legal Reforms

The Minister of Finance kick-started the reform process by focusing on the legislative framework, with particular emphasis on revising the income tax law. In August 2004, he requested the assistance of the IMF to help draft the new law. He presented the law to the annual conference of the National Democratic Party in September, and by the end of 2004, the cabinet had approved the new unified corporate and income tax law. It was released in the *Official Gazette* in June 2005.

The new law envisioned several key changes, including:

- Improving transparency in the tax laws to facilitate investment by domestic and international businesses.

- Cutting rates for both personal and corporate income taxes as a key measure to minimize dishonesty and tax evasion. There was a 50 percent reduction in personal and corporate taxes, to a maximum rate of 20 percent. Income tax brackets were restructured into three categories, with tax rates of 10, 15, and 20 percent.

- Phasing out tax exemptions for newly established companies, and merging all income tax legislation into one law.

- Shifting assessment from administrative to self-assessment. The assessment of tax liability was no longer to be conducted by the tax collector but by the taxpayer. The tax collector had no power to make changes in the self-assessment unless it was in the context of a formal audit.

- Simplifying procedures and the application of tax law by specifying clear provisions, such as how taxable profit/income was to be calculated and measured, which eliminated scope for multiple interpretations and negotiation.

- Shifting from universal audits to risk-based audits, in which a sample of taxpayers was to be audited within five years of tax submission. High penalties for tax evasion and fraud were also introduced.

- Changing the makeup of the appeals committee to include a judge, two accountants representing taxpayers, and two members of the ETA.

By broadening the tax base and reducing the tax rates, reforms aimed to improve overall compliance and enhance revenues.[11] Confidence building measures for the business community were also incorporated. This was important to garner their support. Out-of-court settlements were introduced for existing court cases and unresolved disputes. The law granted a general amnesty for all taxpayers who had ongoing disputes with the ETA for disagreement on tax amounts that did not exceed LE 10,000.[12] Taxpayers were given the option of paying 20 to 40 percent of their liability, in return for the ETA closing all outstanding disputes.

The new tax legislation also contained provisions to encourage businesses to come into compliance with the law. This was done by offering a settlement process in tax evasion cases, if the concerned parties requested this, within one year of the issuance of the new tax law. The new tax policy sought to transform the relationship between the taxpayer, accountants, and the ETA by expanding accountability. According to Boutros-Ghali, "the point of the new law is to say what you want: whatever claim you make, we believe you, no questions asked, but you will be held criminally responsible and accountable for your claims."[13]

In the new system, accountability was extended to tax accountants. In the previous system, the accountants were not held legally liable for tax returns. They often acted as "middlemen" between the tax administration and taxpayer, waiting for disputes to arise between them and then intervening to help "solve" the dispute, thereby collecting handsome fees. Under the new measures, the accountant was held legally liable for false income tax statements along with the taxpayer. Accountants could be jailed for tax evasion and fined up to LE 10,000. This shifted the incentives of the accountant toward ensuring that all information was accurate. This legal liability drove up accounting fees, breaking the alliance between the accountant and the taxpayer. This helped the tax administration build a different relationship with accounting firms.

Generating Support from Business. The minister knew that support from key stakeholders was necessary to pass the new tax law through parliament. He, therefore, circulated the law to the private sector; held roundtables with business associations, accounting firms, and taxpayers; and attended Federation of Industry meetings. For example, business groups represented by the Federation for Industry tried to modify the laws significantly to satisfy their demands. Conversely, other private sector representatives that were advising the minister helped bridge the government to the business community, thereby successfully diffusing some of these demands.

Educating Taxpayers. The new tax law was passed in 2005 and implemented during the same year. A set of Executive Regulations (ER) for implementing the law were drafted, consisting of 146 articles contained in six books. It took five months to develop the regulations, which were published early in 2006. By delivering the tax law, as well as a clear interpretation of its obligations and all major tax forms, the government provided a complete and straightforward "how to" manual for compliance with the new tax system.

Given the scope of the change, a manual was necessary to translate legislation and executive regulations into concrete steps for public compliance. Al-Arabi's first task after joining the MOF was to oversee the development of this manual. Through the manual, Al-Arabi set out to balance the relationship between the taxpayer and ETA and "put them on the same page." The manual was structured "like a workbook"[14] to serve the purpose of making the new tax law easily accessible and understandable to the public. Another technique Al-Arabi used was to create sample tax returns, sequentially introducing provisions.

Additionally, an essential component of the move from administrative assessment to self-assessment was the education and awareness of taxpayers. Reformers embarked on a high-level public education campaign after the passage of the law in parliament. The campaign was driven with two objectives in mind: 1) to introduce the self-assessment system to the public, and 2) to change the face of the administration. Moving to self-assessment was initially a very big cultural change, and many Egyptians did not understand the concept. Through a public campaign, taxpayers were educated about their rights under the new law and that they would not have to pay money to the tax collector. To assist in the public media campaign, a consulting firm was hired.

Reforming Tax Administration

One of the greatest challenges was the integration of the two major tax bureaucracies, the ITD and the STD, whose combined employees numbered nearly 60,000. Integration meant bringing together two rivalrous organizations that had significantly different bureaucratic cultures, staff profiles, and incentive and compensation structures. Integration entailed dramatically changing the organizational structure in the new organization. These specific challenges were accompanied by more general issues—a huge underpaid bureaucracy, poorly skilled staff, and (in the perception of many) agencies riddled with corruption. Hence, beyond the technical issues involved in such a merger, resistance by entrenched bureaucrats was a major issue for reformers to tackle.

There was a need to transform the culture within the new tax administration. Top and middle management in the existing bureaucracies used to deal with offices as if they were "their empire."[15] They demanded personal loyalty from employees and held considerable influence over them. Tax collectors had grown accustomed to existing appraisal systems and compensation systems in the bureaucracy that rewarded them for the smallest efforts. Moving from an administrative assessment to a self-assessment system meant they would be stripped of the powers they had over taxpayers and the privileges this generated. This meant an overhaul of the internal incentive systems.

Cognizant of the challenge that lay ahead, the leaders of the reform began by creating an internal governance structure that brought in mid-level and senior managers from the two bureaucracies. As described earlier, this was largely achieved through developing the design teams. The leaders delineated a reform process for integration in three phases.[16] The different phases of the reform were laid out clearly:

- **Phase I: Introduction and Preparation,** which commenced in July 2006. This involved the administrative set-up of the project and high-level design strategy. The governance structure was established at this time, including the design teams and the PMO.

- **Phase II: Design,** which commenced in September 2006 and continued until July 2007. Design teams had to review existing business practices in the two departments to identify commonalities and differences and to develop appropriate business processes for the new ETA. In addition, pilots for new integrated tax centers were undertaken.

- **Phase III: Implementation,** which ran from July 2007 to August 2011. Phase III consisted of the gradual rollout of the fully integrated and modernized ETA.

Distinct from this process, a Large Taxpayer Center (LTC) was established in mid-2005 as a partially independent entity, given the significance of large taxpayers to the revenue base. This initiative was in line with international best practices in tax administration. Later, it was to be fully brought into the new ETA.

Strategic Considerations for Administrative Reform

One of the most significant strategic and technical questions Boutros-Ghali had to address was whether this would be a merger of equals or the acquisition of one entity by another larger and more dominant organization. This question would affect the type of integration strategy and the implementation plan. The minister decided to view it as a merger of two equals.

The reform team also recognized upfront that the human resources component of the reform would be the most difficult, given the potential for resistance from the workforce. Among the most significant concerns was the potential for job losses, including the reduced prospects for promotion and privileges afforded by the existing system. Specifically, the merger would entail a rationalization of employees, reducing the staff levels from 60,000 to 40,000. Moreover, promotion prospects would be reduced—particularly at the higher levels—since an integrated organization meant that the number of such top-level positions would be reduced.

Since these staff concerns could generate significant resistance and thwart the reforms altogether, the reformers made a few strategic decisions upfront. Staff would not be laid off, and any downsizing would come from a process of natural attrition and the freezing of new recruitment. Staff hired on a contract basis would not be renewed, and vacancies would not be filled with new hires. Surplus staff would be redeployed to new centers that were to be established as part of the reform. Finally, the old guard in the bureaucracy, who were most resistant to change, would stay on until their retirement.

These considerations also affected the sequencing of the overall reform. Reformers decided not to tackle the HR component in the initial phase. Rather, they focused on those aspects that would enable staff to understand the core objectives of reform and slowly transform their mindset. Emphasis was given to the objective of transforming the relationship between the taxpayer and ETA, and changes in the organization structure were declared and phased in gradually. The rationale behind this approach was to make both employees and taxpayers experience the new system before embarking on more contentious reforms involving internal reorganization.

Moreover, the sequencing of integration itself was influenced by these considerations. With more traditional reforms, integration usually begins with the headquarters and then moves out to the regions. Reformers decided to reverse the approach. Knowing that sector heads in HQ would start counting the positions in the new organizational structure and compare them with positions in the new organization, they decided to start with pilot offices and then move on with integration at the district and regional levels. With the exception of some core support functions, HQ integration was left to the last step.

Major Elements of Tax Administration Reform

Taxpayer Segmentation. Consistent with advice received from the IMF and others, one of the first tasks was to segment the taxpayer base according to size. Reformers began by undertaking analysis of the 2006 tax year income and sales tax returns. The analysis showed that large taxpayers constituted

0.8 percent of the total taxpayers (approximately 2,000 taxpayers), but accounted for 80 percent of turnover as reported to ITD and 90 percent as reported to STD. Medium size taxpayers made up 2 percent of the taxpaying population and about one-third of total tax revenue. The remainder of the taxpayers accounted for only 5 percent of total tax revenues.[17]

Accordingly, the LTC was created for those whose turnover was over LE 50 million; a Medium Taxpayer Center for turnovers between LE 300K and LE 50 million; and a Small Taxpayer Center for those below these thresholds. The idea behind segmentation was to reflect the contribution and risk that each segment represented to the tax system and to respond to the different needs of each of these groups.

Establishing the LTC. Given the impact of the large taxpaying base on the tax revenue stream, priority was given to establishing a well-functioning LTC, which was done in five months, between April and September 2005. Establishing this center created success early on in the reform process. Because the LTC was established before the official merger of the two tax bureaucracies, it was initially created as a separate legal entity. This step was necessary because the legal structures of the two bureaucracies themselves differed.

The LTC was a merger of the large taxpayer units in the sales and income tax departments. This integrated office had responsibility for administrative control of the 2,000 largest taxpayers in all Egyptian provinces, and it became the large taxpayer's single point of contact. Functions included audit, collections, and taxpayer education, assistance, and advice. A front office was established where taxpayers submitted documents, which was physically separated from the back office where returns were processed. This physical layout supported the objectives of the reform to separate the taxpayer from the tax collector. An outside consultant was recruited to run the office and ensure that the new practices supported the vision of the reform.

One of the challenges in creating the LTC came from the fact that some offices did not want to release their large taxpayer files. Effectively, the large taxpayer files were seen as the cream of the office, and there was significant reluctance to hand them over to the new LTC. It took the management team nine months to gather all the files. In February 2009, three years after the formal merger of the income and sales tax departments, the LTC was brought back within the new integrated ETA.

Other Taxpayer Centers. As part of taxpayer segmentation, medium and small taxpayer centers were established. The reformers decided to initially undertake pilots with a view to perfecting the approach through lessons learned in the pilot phase.[18] A full network of centers was established after the implementation of a merged headquarter structure. Due to complexities in Cairo and to signal that the reforms were not simply centered in the capital, the reform team decided to make the rollouts in other governorates first.

The pilot approach proved instructive and led to a major change in the original plan. After implementing the pilots for the Medium Taxpayer Center (MTC), reformers observed that staff preferred to work in the LTC than the MTC, and the MTC in comparison to the STC. Staff were vying to be part of the "higher" tax centers believing that their benefits and compensation would be better and the position more prestigious. As a result, the reform team decided to develop integrated tax centers (ITCs), which coupled small and medium taxpayers in one center. To some extent, this distinction was merely one of labeling. While the taxpayers dealt with one center, the actual back office functions pertaining to audit and taxpayer services remained segmented based on the size of the taxpayer. This is one example where reformers needed to be flexible and change plans during implementation.

Audit Suspensions. Reformers also decided to stop all audits for four years after the new tax law took effect in 2005. This was done to give tax collectors the time to recognize that it was no longer business as usual and allow them to internalize the new changes. Stopping the audits prevented tax collectors from maintaining the old practice of extorting money from taxpayers. Internally, the move to a "no audit" approach, even on an interim basis, was quite controversial. The IMF strongly advocated the immediate implementation of risk-based audit with the very first self-assessment returns, and it continued to advocate the resumption of audit as soon as possible, even if audit would not be at the full steady-state level.

Unifying Tax Administration. The merger of Egypt's two tax administration agencies—ITD and STD—was among the most challenging aspects of reform. Integration was planned in phases and took two to three years. Regions were integrated, which entailed merging twenty-five regions from sales tax and thirty-nine from income tax into fifteen integrated regions. In this process, the total number of offices was to be reduced from 350 to 200.

There were several crucial differences between the two organizations that were core to the integration challenge. The ITD managed a registered taxpayer population of 6.3 million and had 39,000 staff. Staff were older and automation was limited. The STD had a registered sales tax population of 150,000 and a staff of 18,000. In general, the STD had a younger staff mix, more sophisticated IT, modern offices, and higher compensation packages than the ITD. Moreover, STD viewed itself as the "superior organization," and ITD clearly felt that it had been left behind in terms of compensation and facilities.[19] Finally, each of the departments had its own commissioner.

Due to these differences, there was resistance to the merger, including from the commissioner of sales tax. The reform team handled the matter with some delicacy. They waited for the retirement of the income tax commissioner in April 2006. In May of that year, a presidential decree to integrate the two departments was issued. The existing sales tax commissioner became the head of the new integrated ETA, and he retained this post until his term finished in August 2007. With his departure, Boutros-Ghali appointed Al-Arabi as commissioner of the ETA, who also maintained his role as deputy minister for tax policy.

Changing the Culture of Doing Business

While the integration of the bureaucracies was in progress, reformers also had to address the culture of doing business in the new ETA. The introduction of new internal incentives and the establishment of a communications strategy for staff and the public were key initiatives toward this end.

Internal Incentives. Reformers introduced a number of measures to change staff incentives and make them more congruent with the objectives and values of the new ETA. This encompassed changes in hiring and promotion practices, training, new appraisal systems, and performance-based financial incentives. The existing system did not offer sufficient incentives based on performance. Rather, all staff were receiving salary increases based on general cost of living increases, tenure-based promotions, and law/decree-based salary increases and bonuses. In Egypt, changes to employee base salaries were constrained by the Civil Service Law of 1978, but authorities had flexibility with variable pay. In the existing system, employees received twelve months variable pay (ten guaranteed, two performance-based). Reformers also contended with a culture where managers gave the majority of employees a score of "excellent."

The new ETA looked to increase the performance bonus to four months, with eight months at base pay. This increased performance-based pay from 15 percent of total pay to 31 percent. Reformers designed a new appraisal system and incentive package to differentiate between high performers and the rest of the workforce when distributing bonuses. Key performance indicators were developed for each position that were aligned to the objectives of the specific department and ETA to differentiate between good and bad performers.

As part of the new incentives, salaries were to be increased significantly. There were plans to increase salaries ten-fold, in which 6.75 percent of the increase would reflect an increase in the base salary and the rest would be performance-based. For example, if formerly an employee was earning 500 pounds, then total remuneration jumped to about 4,000 pounds, including all incentives. A number of these measures were piloted in the LTC.

Training was also a critical element in attempting to shift the organizational culture. Motivated by the belief that a genuine culture change required that the reform process was driven by employees, reformers emphasized the importance of creating internal leaders. Accordingly, they devised a three-tier leadership development program created by taking 300 employees from top management positions, 2,000 from mid-level, and 6,000 from lower-level posts. Each of the tiers had a number of training modules focusing on topics such as managing employee performance, effective project management, and strategies for managing workplace conflicts, among other areas.[20]

Educating the Public. To promote the new culture and educate the public about the new integrated organization, reformers recognized the need to build a new brand image. The communications function was reformed, and new policies and procedures were introduced. The communications department was to act as a hub for data dissemination and to receive feedback.

A number of techniques were utilized to target audiences both internally and externally. Public education/awareness was carried out through periodic publications, such as annual tax return printouts, forms, and manuals. There was also a regular and consistent media presence, through press releases, news articles, and press and television interviews featuring the Minister of Finance and the tax commissioner.

Frequent conferences were also held with chambers of commerce and industry, business associations, and diversified audiences, including professional service firms and taxpayer societies. Well-built advertising campaigns were created seasonally in parallel with major tax-related events.

Advertisements were prepared and aired through national and regional media channels, with the aim of altering the public perception of taxes to promote voluntary compliance and transform the prevailing culture.

Achievements and Challenges

The success of the new tax law was most directly reflected in the fact that tax filings, which capture tax compliance, increased in the wake of the reforms. In 2006, the tax base increased from 1.7 million to 2.8 million taxpayers. This included about 240,000 corporations and 2.4 million individuals. Following this initial jump in the tax base, there was a 10 percent annual increase in new taxpayers up through 2009. There was also a steady increase in the number of returns received. By the 2008 tax year, the active taxpayer population was 241,092 corporations and 2,348,666 individuals.

Both income and sales tax revenues increased following the implementation of the new law. Corporate tax revenues increased from LE 22 billion for 2004 to 36.6 billion for 2005. Personal income tax increased from LE 8.1 billion to 8.3 billion in 2005. As shown in tables 10-1 and 10-2, both income tax and sales tax receipts have subsequently steadily increased.[21]

TABLE 10-1. Receipts by Income Tax Authority

(in LE millions)	2005–2006	2006–2007	2007–2008	2008–2009
Individual	8,330	8,963	10,497	13,817
Corporate	36,611	48,660	55,539	66,164
Income Tax/GDP	9.0%	8.9%	8.5%	8.7%

Source: Ministry of Finance.

TABLE 10-2. Receipts by Sales Tax Authority

(in LE millions)	2005–2006	2006–2007	2007–2008	2008–2009
Total Sales Tax	27,490	30,611	39,725	51,081
Sales Tax/GDP	4.6%	4.5%	4.1%	4.4%

Source: Ministry of Finance.

International measures on the ease of paying taxes also improved, although less dramatically. Egypt's ranking in the World Bank's *Doing Business Report* moved up from 152 in 2007 to 144 in 2009. There was also evidence from World Bank investment climate surveys that the burden of tax administration on businesses declined substantially. Between 2004 and 2008, tax inspections and related requests for bribes dropped dramatically according to surveys of Egyptian businesses. Problems in tax administration fell from the fourth leading constraint to the ninth, while tax rates fell from being the top constraint to the sixth (see table 10-3).

Reformers believed they were able to establish the foundation for reform within the ETA. An internal culture shift was underway. Staff recognized the changes within the organization and were beginning to view themselves as part of one organization—ETA—rather than two separate tax departments. According to the PMO, "to have staff accept that there is now one organization instead of two is a remarkable change."[22] Moreover, staff came to recognize that most of the changes in business practice would be to their benefit. Additionally, the reformers succeeded in creating internal champions from the design teams. Members "grew from ordinary tax middle-managers to real ambassadors for change and modernization."

These achievements did not come without challenges along the way.

TABLE 10-3. Leading Constraints on Business in Egypt

2004	2006	2008
Tax rates	Macroeconomic uncertainty	Macroeconomic uncertainty
Macroeconomic uncertainty	Illegal/informal competition	Informal sector competition
Regulatory policy uncertainty	Corruption	Regulatory policy uncertainty
Tax administration	Regulatory policy uncertainty	Workers skills
Illegal/informal competition	Tax rates	Corruption
Corruption	Cost of financing	Tax rates
Cost of financing	Tax administration	Cost of financing

Source: World Bank Enterprise Survey (various years).

Foremost, the minister and his team have had to deal with internal staff resistance due to concerns about losing jobs, positions, and privileges. Boutros-Ghali explained: "Bureaucracy will resist change. They fight back. They will trip you—often successfully . . . As head of large bureaucracy, you are not really in control of these organizations. You are there for too short a period to really affect it. You are told by deputies 'it's done, it's done.' It's only when I started checking, I knew it was not true."[23]

As in any major set of reforms, compromises were inevitable. When reformers initially developed the organizational structure for the new ETA, they decided to have sixteen sector heads based on a functional division. But when they had to get approval for this change from the Central Agency for Organization and Administration, they had to increase this number to twenty-three to satisfy political demands. They decided not to immediately launch the revised organizational structure but, rather, began by focusing on the district offices as well as the overall change to self-assessment and voluntary compliance.

Reformers also had to contend with the existing HR culture in which recruitment and hiring were based on nepotism and promotions were based on a seniority system. They addressed this by instilling a new culture, where hiring practices changed dramatically, and by management demonstrating that it was serious about the new HR culture. To some extent, they had to make compromises extending the timeline for implementation. They also adopted a strategy of waiting for some of the more senior sector heads, the "old guard," to retire out of the bureaucracy.

In addition to internal staff resistance, the civil service law also posed challenges. Replicating the success of the LTC to the rest of the income and sales tax departments was more difficult. The HR component of reform attempted to modernize the system and provide incentives for workers. But the civil service law placed restrictions on salary and incentive systems. It was one of the reasons the LTC was initially established outside the two bureaucracies, as this allowed it to be managed outside the civil service law structure. But the challenge for reformers then lay in how to implement the changes that were done within the LTC to another 60,000 employees whose terms of service fell within the civil service structure.

Two challenges specific to the reform process itself were also identified by the PMO. There was insufficient autonomy at lower levels for decision-making. Decisionmaking in the reform process tended to be more centralized, and signatures from top management were required for most issues. This led to a lengthy process for approvals. According to the PMO, sector heads had to be empowered, and there was a need to get them to accept responsibility. There was also no dedicated budget allocated to the PMO. Rather, it had to operate on a basis of ad hoc finance. All expenditures required approval from the minister, who controlled the budget. When money was required, it was received, but the process was viewed by many as lengthy and cumbersome.[24]

All in all, these challenges meant that the original time frame of two years for the administrative reforms could not be met. The minister acknowledged that "this resistance changed my time scale," and it needed to be dealt with in a step-by-step manner. Nevertheless, Boutros-Ghali and his team continued along the path of reform. They took the approach that it was important to confront the resistance and challenges early on and invest resources in setting the necessary foundations for reform. This meant being flexible with the sequencing and time frame for reform. The PMO director noted that the reforms "focused on success, not speed." Their hope was that with the main sources of resistance addressed, the process going forward would be "downhill."

The Post–Arab Spring Reform Agenda

The path of tax reform in the wake of the Arab Spring was neither simple nor straightforward. Boutros-Ghali was replaced as Minister of Finance on January 31, 2011, in the midst of the Tahir Square demonstrations. Just prior to President Mubarak's resignation, Boutros-Ghali and his wife flew to Lebanon. He was subsequently charged with corruption and the misuse of government property—charges that he disputed. He was tried in absentia, sentenced to thirty years in prison, and fined 60 million Egyptian pounds. He and his family were eventually granted political asylum in Britain.

The deteriorating financial situation in Egypt, which began during the global financial crisis of 2008, was further compounded by political instability and leadership turnover during the turmoil of the Arab Spring and subsequent transition. Growth was depressed for a few years, while poverty and unemployment rose markedly. The fiscal deficit jumped from around 6.8 of GDP in 2007–2008 to 13.7 of GDP in 2012–2013, due in part to a sharp decline in tax revenues.[25] Against this background, the long-term changes in administrative culture and organizational structure pursued by the first wave of tax reforms became secondary to the more immediate fiscal priorities.

A second wave of tax and customs reforms began after President El-Sisi assumed power in 2014. The real estate tax was amended in 2014, yet it continues to face challenges in valuation and collection procedures. A capital gains tax of 10 percent was imposed in 2014 but suspended twice, most recently in 2017 for a period of three years. The top income tax rate for companies and individuals was cut in 2015, and parliamentary consideration of the value-added tax was delayed to 2016. Replacing the 10 percent general sales tax with a 13 percent tax rate in September 2016, the Value-Added Tax (VAT) Law no. 67 represented renewed efforts to improve the tax code. Reforms carried through to 2017, with a substantial amendment to the income tax law designed to cushion the lowest income earners from rising prices.

With administrative efficiency in mind and to terminate paper-based processing within three years, Egypt introduced an electronic system for filing tax returns in February 2018, replacing paper-based cards and examinations with an electronic version. Egypt's finance minister took steps to achieve complete automation across ETA processes, which would entail a unification of electronic databases for taxpayer information. As part of a broader reorganization and restructuring effort, administrative reforms also aim to reduce bureaucratic inefficiencies by downsizing the ETA to fourteen departments from a current total of twenty-three.[26]

These scattered efforts, taken in the context of fiscal and political crises and with only partial implementation, have begun to show signs of success. Current tax and customs measures, announced by the government and supported by its international partners, that tackle persistent administrative inefficiencies will help sustain domestic revenue mobilization in the medium term. Nevertheless, the principle objectives of the initial reform efforts pursued by Boutros-Ghali and his team of reformers remain relevant today, including reducing corruption and tax evasion and transforming the culture and norms within the bureaucracy.

Notes

This case was initially drafted for the World Bank in 2010 and revised and updated subsequently by Fatema Alhashemi and Khalid Elashmawy in 2016–2018. The authors would like to express their gratitude to Nithya Nagarajan for her excellent and extensive inputs into earlier versions of this case.

1. Statement by former Minister for Administrative Development Ahmed Darwish, drawn from "Egyptian E-Government Initiative Moving Forward," Balancing Act: Telecoms, Internet and Broadcast in Africa, no. 174.

2. Among the key shocks were the international financial crisis of 1997–1999, the attacks in Luxor in 1997, and a domestic financial scandal in 1998–1999. The post-9/11 geopolitical insecurity following the U.S. invasion of Iraq in 2003 created further policy uncertainty. See Sufyan Alissa, "The Political Economy of Reform in Egypt: Understanding the Role of Institutions," *Carnegie Papers*, October 2007.

3. Amina Ghanem, Abdelmonem Lotfy, and Doaa Hamdy, "Overview of the Egyptian Economy and Business Environment," Ministry of Finance, 2010, www .mof.gov.eg/MOFGallerySource/English/OverviewoftheEgyptianEconomyand BusinessEnvironment.pdf.

4. See Andrew Stone and Adele Barzelay, chapter 8, in this volume.

5. The World Bank's *Egypt Investment Climate Assessment* in 2005 noted that 80 percent of firms identified "tax rates" as a major or very severe constraint in the survey, while 60 percent identified "tax administration" as a major or very severe constraint.

6. Egypt Tax Authority, "Administrative Tax Reform: Arab Republic of Egypt," Working Paper, 5th AITAC Technical Conference, October 2008.

7. Hazem Hassan (KPMG chair) and Halim Amin Samy (senior tax and business adviser at KPMG), interview with author, November 2009.

8. Boutros-Ghali, interview with author, December 2009.

9. This section draws heavily on correspondence with William Crandall in June 2010, who was heavily engaged in Egypt's tax reforms for the IMF.

10. Extract from Egypt Tax Authority (2008).

11. In other areas as well, some tax policy reform went forward. In 2006, the Stamp Duty Tax was comprehensively overhauled. In addition, in 2008 a new property tax law was enacted. Other areas left outstanding, for which work is in progress, were introducing a simplified tax regime for small and micro-enterprises and transformation of the sales tax to a full VAT, which later occurred in 2016. See Egypt Tax Authority, 2008.

12. Ghanem, Lotfy, and Hamdy, "Overview of the Egyptian Economy and Business Environment."

13. Rita Ramalho, "Adding a Million Taxpayers," World Bank Doing Business Report, 2007.

14. Ashraf Al-Arabi, interview with Nagarajan, November 12, 2009.

15. Ibid.

16. Extract from Egypt Tax Authority, "Administrative Tax Reform."

17. Egypt Tax Authority, 2008.

18. Ibid.

19. Ibid.

20. Egypt Tax Authority, "ETA Modern Leadership Fundamentals," August 2009.

21. Information in both tables is from the MOF, "Receipts by Income Tax Authority," Fiscal Sector, *The Financial Monthly*, October 2009, www.mof.gov.eg/ MOFGallerySource/English/Reports/monthly/2009/Oct09/t13-a.pdf.

22. PMO correspondence, December 2009.

23. Boutros-Ghali, interview with author, December 2009.

24. PMO, interview with author and correspondence, December 2009.

25. World Bank, "Egypt Country Brief," 2010; IMF, "Arab Republic of Egypt: Staff Report for the 2014 Article IV Consultation," 2014.

26. "Introduction of Optional Online Tax Filing This Year," AlMasry AlYoum, 2018, www.almasryalyoum.com/news/details/1258229.

ELEVEN

Creating a "Citizen Friendly" Department

Document Processing in Jordan

DEEPA IYER

Princeton Innovations for Successful Society Program

IN LATE 2010, KHALAF THEIBAT, an aged Bedouin wearing traditional Arab robes and a red-checked headdress, stood in a familiar location under a makeshift tarpaulin stall outside the main Amman branch of the Civil Status and Passports Department (CSPD). For nearly twenty-five years, he had made a good living by steering frustrated Jordanians through the complex and time-consuming process of applying for passports and other required government documents. However, his business had slowed considerably since the old days. "The changes at this department are indescribable," Theibat said. "You can't find words to tell the story. I haven't had a citizen complain to me in ages now."

In the late 1980s, Jordanian citizens prepared themselves for an ordeal when setting out to obtain or renew an official document. The CSPD, responsible for issuing proof-of-identity documents, was notoriously disorganized and inefficient. Radio show hosts and newspaper cartoonists often parodied the trials faced by citizens who had to deal with the department.

A citizen who required department services encountered a series of roadblocks. "It was an obstacle course," recalled Shuhaiber Hamdan, a former director of administrative development at CSPD who worked there from 1968 to 2006. Lines of applicants wound around the main branch in Amman, and fistfights sometimes erupted between citizens jockeying for position. Employees often called the police to bring order and to settle quarrels. "The citizens, we were pieces in a very inconvenient game," recalled Bashir Khadra, a professor of administrative development at the University of Jordan.

Inside the main office, issuance and renewal processes were complex and labor intensive. Citizens and employees had to scramble between four floors to complete applications. Guaranteed tenure by civil service laws, department staff "acted very arrogantly and impolitely," said Zuhair Al-Kayed, former director of Jordan's Civil Service Bureau. "They didn't care about the job, and routinely abused their power. It had a negative effect on service delivery."

Citizens had to interrupt their work schedules over days, weeks, or months to return to the department and check the status of their applications. Enterprising middlemen like Theibat set up cramped stalls surrounding the main Amman branch, winning ready customers with vague offers of connections to expedite applications. "Everyone preferred to work through them, paying a fee, instead of working with department employees," said Khadra.

> You went through all this, and, if you were lucky, would be called to gather at 2 p.m. one afternoon many days later for delivery in an open area. Everyone, all at once. An employee would call the name of the document owner, and when the owner raised his hand and voice, the official would throw the document at the owner. Sometimes, the owner would catch it. Otherwise, it fell on the ground.

The CSPD's shortcomings were especially glaring because the department was central to the lives of Jordanians. It registered families and their demographics into the civil register, issuing personal identification cards, citizenship certificates, family books identifying each family unit's members, and certificates of birth, death, marriage, and divorce. The department issued, renewed, and extended Jordanian passports, pilgrimage permits, and temporary passports for West Bank and Gaza residents. It also was responsible for compiling demographic statistics for use by other arms of the government.

"This was the department with the largest amount of interaction with citizens. We have an impact on every detail in citizens' lives since birth. This is why it was such a trial," said Salman Qudah, a department employee since 1985. Civil status documents like national IDs, family books, birth certificates, and death certificates allowed citizens to access most state services and benefits. Jordanian citizens depended even more on their passports. Given Jordan's history as a regional melting pot, citizens of Palestinian, Lebanese, Syrian, and Iraqi expatriate origin frequently visited families in other parts of the Middle East. Students studying abroad and pilgrims going on the Hajj, made yearly by pious Muslims, also contributed to seasonal swings in passport demand. "People often had to postpone plans . . . by a student to study in Alexandria, by someone to go on the Hajj, by a Palestinian citizen to visit family in the West Bank, just because they could not get their passport on time. It was very hard on the citizen," said veteran employee Hamdan.

Public discontent grew. The media labeled a trip to the department as "The Path of Sorrows," an allusion to Jesus's journey before his crucifixion. The CSPD reached a breaking point when the 1990 Iraqi invasion of Kuwait triggered the Gulf War, releasing a torrent of 350,000 Jordanian returnees,[1] largely of Palestinian origin. The sudden spike in document demand inundated the already struggling CSPD. The Council of Ministers, Jordan's cabinet, decided that the department needed a firm hand to tackle inefficiencies. In June 1991, Minister of the Interior Jawdat Al Sbool called Nasouh Muhieddin Marzouqa, a retired Public Security Department official, to offer him the position. Traditionally, the cabinet offered director general roles in ministries' subdepartments to high-level public security officials with long track records of government service. Marzouqa had extensive policing experience, from directing the kingdom's criminal investigations unit to heading the Royal Police Academy.

Initially, Al Sbool offered Marzouqa a choice of two jobs: the socially prestigious governorship of Amman or director general of CSPD. While Al Sbool attempted to persuade him to accept the governorship, which involved frequent interaction with the king, Marzouqa's background in investigative and detective work led him to favor the CSPD position. As a public security officer who once worked in the West Bank, Marzouqa had witnessed border problems emerging from data-entry errors on citizens' passports. Unsuspecting and innocent citizens occasionally found themselves behind bars when their names matched those of criminals. Marzouqa enjoyed unraveling such puzzles. He had solved several high-profile murder cases while working with the Public Security Department. For him, the CSPD post offered a chance to further such investigative work, using different types of data to inform managerial techniques. Marzouqa's other motivation was his religion. "Serving citizens is my way of being a good Muslim," he said. "I had heard citizens complaining about the department very often."

In July 1991, the council appointed Marzouqa as director general, and he set about leading a department-wide turnaround. Constrained by stiff resistance from employees, rigid civil service regulations that limited hiring and firing, and a low budget, Marzouqa and his team devised several solutions to the department's problems. Internally driven, widespread reforms overhauled the department's organizational structure, removed steps that delayed processes, enhanced training, upgraded technology, and increased employees' productivity. "We couldn't afford a consulting company, so we did it ourselves," Marzouqa said. By the end of his tenure in 1996, the average time it took to get or renew a passport or a civil status document had shrunk to just two hours.[2]

The Challenge

After the founding of the Transjordan Emirate in 1921, the Jordanian army, initially under British supervision, managed the issuance and renewal of passports. Civil status documents—birth and death certificates, family books, and personal ID cards—were handled by several different ministries until the Council of Ministers created the Department of Civil Status in 1968. In January 1988, the council decided to merge the two operations into a new Civil Status and Passports Department within the Ministry of Interior, led by a single director general. "Both civil status and passports are documents used to identify citizens," said former CSPD official Hamdan. "Both functions worked according to the stipulations of the Jordanian Law of Nationality—they required the same application inputs. Merging them made sense to the Council of Ministers at the time for accuracy of data across functions."

Following the merger, the new department's performance stagnated. Issa Omari, another former Public Security Department colleague who directed the department immediately after the merger from 1988 to 1991, said, "We were unsure how, exactly, the two entities should be merged. The two halves were competing with each other. There was uncertainty about how the new department should function. It was a mess."

Inconsistent and inconvenient service delivery emerged from organizational deficiencies in four areas: processes, employee and workload distribution, employee performance and motivation, and technology use.

Problematic Processes. Processes were labor intensive, and implementation was erratic. For example, passport issuance and renewal, the most complicated processes, took twelve manual steps performed by ten different employees. In the main branch in Amman, which processed the most applications daily, an average of 300 to 400 application files moved daily between four floors, traveling hand-to-hand between the archives in the basement, the accountants on the ground and third floors, the office manager and receptionists on the second floor, the printers on the first floor, and the director general on the fourth.

Delays were common at every step of every process. Complex application forms requiring unnecessary details confused both citizens and employees. The archives were disorganized, with bulky files "lying open, scattered all over, and even rats running around," recalled Omari. Additionally, every passport issued required the signature of the director general. Regardless of the time of completion, employees distributed all completed passports at 1 p.m. because the director general (or branch director) traditionally signed applications at 12:30. Crowds would assemble by the department at this time, and employees would toss passports at them. Accountants could not keep more than fifty Jordanian dinars (approximately US$70) in their cash registers, according to government regulations. They routinely left at 1 p.m. to deposit money at the bank, leaving citizens who needed to pay fees after that time in limbo. "Each step in the process could sometimes take more than an entire day," said Hamdan. A backlog developed as employees left applications incomplete at every stage of the process.

Workload Worries. The merged department retained separate civil status and passport wings, and each had a manager whose job was to coordinate matters of policy. Rigidities in the system hampered the department's ability to deal with seasonal swings in demand for various documents. During summer, demand for new and renewal passports increased as families vacationed, expatriates returned, and Palestinians visited the West Bank. Work volume also expanded sharply during the Hajj and Umrah pilgrimage seasons and at the end of the school year when the college application process required students to get official documents certified by the CSPD.

Most employees could perform only the document processes for which they had training. Employees trained to produce birth or death certificates could not produce passports, and vice versa. Hiring new employees to cope with short-term demand fluctuations was not an option because the Civil Service Bureau maintained strict annual quotas on hiring. The department needed a solution to address seasonal shifts in the volume of applications.

A second work-distribution problem involved staffing of department branches. In several regions, citizens traveled nearly 200 kilometers to access a branch, or simply went to the main branch in Amman. Because the department had no way of tracking branches' application traffic, no system existed to allocate the workforce according to the workload. Allocation did not consider employee competencies, population density in a branch's area, or a branch's volume of applications. "Branches in rural regions received merely two to three applications daily, while in urban branches like Amman, Irbid, or Aqaba, hundreds of applications came in," Marzouqa said.

Unmotivated Employees. Department employees lacked professionalism. Marzouqa recalled employees "lounging around, gossiping, reading newspapers, drinking tea and coffee by the gallon." Mothers would often bring their children to work. "Babies crawled around and got under peoples' feet; the women running the printers would just stand around and gossip; people would leave to eat or pray at all times of the day," he said. Employees frequently went home by 2 p.m.

In dealings with citizens, staff were "impatient, impolite, arrogant, and generally unhelpful," said Al-Kayed, the former director of the Civil Service Bureau. In Jordan, government employees traditionally operated in a culture of privilege, and the CSPD was no exception. Employees purposefully delayed processing for applicants whose behavior irked them, leaving unfinished applications on desks for days. Additionally, because Jordanian surnames indicated nearly everything about an applicant's social, ethnic, and tribal status, department employees could easily discriminate against certain groups by delaying applications, and they did so often. Extortion was commonplace, and employees often used their jobs to conduct side businesses, such as selling used postage stamps from old applications. Long-time CSPD employee Qudah added, "Citizens used connections and bribes because there was no other way of getting the job done."

Technological Hurdles. Although computers had existed in the department since 1983, many were unused, and few employees had computer-related skills. Many of the machines lacked the processing power and memory to handle the large quantities of data handled by the CSPD.

Computer equipment was distributed unevenly among branch offices, and as a result most branches had no connection with the department's main server in Amman. Branches mailed applications to Amman for archiving, adding to the disorganization in the central office. "Mailed materials from branches were often misplaced, left lying around, or lost in the mail," Hamdan said. "We could only call them on the phone to communicate. It took hours to check sometimes."

Employees continued to write data into ledgers despite the availability of computers. Without proper verification, this manual process contributed to a high number of errors. Similarities between names contributed to these mistakes. For instance, the name Mohammad could be spelled in several different ways in Arabic script. Spelling was left to the discretion of the employee. Other names could apply to males or females, and many employees arbitrarily assigned a gender when trying to verify records. Department employees inadvertently issued duplicate documents when previous records under a specific spelling did not surface in the archives, or when citizens recorded different spellings in applications. Inconsistent surnames meant invalid documentation and normally required an extra trip to a courtroom to legally standardize surname spelling.

Hamdan, whom fellow employees called the department's "encyclopedia" because of the extensive knowledge he had gained from nearly four decades at the CSPD, summarized the problems: "Every single thing took so long that nothing was happening."

Framing a Response

When he became director general in July 1991, Marzouqa set about tackling these challenges. The heavy migration flows induced by the Gulf crisis and the ensuing spate of applications for new and renewal passports required quick action. By the end of the year, Marzouqa set several measures in place to manage a concerted turnaround strategy.

As a newcomer to the department, Marzouqa recognized that he first needed information to identify and prioritize key issues. In his early months on the job, he consulted with department veterans and lower-level managers to learn the intricacies of the document issuance processes.

Concurrently, he met with people who had expertise in administrative development—such as Khadra at the University of Jordan and Al-Kayed, who was director of the Committee on Administrative Development at the time—to speak about the delays and how they could be addressed. "Within one week, you could say, he had grasped the problems at the department. After that, he was talking to as many people as possible to try to pair problems with solutions," said Qudah.

Marzouqa required all managers to produce daily, weekly, and monthly reports containing data on application volumes, daily tasks, problematic employees, and process delays. For two months, Marzouqa, Hamdan, and other managers sat for hours daily at the department's service counters, keeping detailed notes on processes and employees' interactions with citizens. In these reports, officials identified key problem areas. "It was a very consultative process," Marzouqa said. "We tried to ask as many people as possible for problems and ideas, from professors and experts to our own employees to the citizens themselves."

Marzouqa also initiated an open-door policy that allowed citizens to walk in without appointments to air complaints about processes or employee behavior. He kept track of complaints and looked for trends. He formed a Committee on Citizen Complaints, comprised of three senior employees, to meet with citizens and compile reports on application-related mishaps on a case-by-case basis. Previously, citizens who wanted to address mistakes in applications had to file lawsuits, a process that could take years. Now, citizens' complaints could be resolved swiftly.

To formalize the employee-observation process, Marzouqa formed the Development, Training, and Modernization Committee, which later became the Department of Administrative Development and Training, and appointed Hamdan, the CSPD veteran, to lead it. The committee measured employees' training levels and identified steps that delayed processes. Conducting a survey and tracking the records of employees, they found that fewer than 3 percent had attended training courses and that veteran employees rarely trained new ones on the job.

Marzouqa and Hamdan drafted a list of "citizen friendly" objectives, based on their observations at the service counters, and presented the list to department submanagers. The list included completing applications as quickly as possible without compromising quality, changing CSPD's image from that of a "favor provider" into one of a "service provider," changing employees' attitudes toward the public, and training employees to improve skills, facilitate intra-department transfers, and promote computer usage.

The managerial team widely publicized these objectives among department staff, holding meetings and posting the objectives on notice boards. They also hung posters containing all the information needed for each process. To facilitate implementation, Marzouqa created rules of thumb for employees to follow. While observing processes at the counter, he and Hamdan had used stopwatches to determine how long certain procedures took, and they used the findings to calculate average time requirements. Using these motion studies, Marzouqa set two service delivery goals: First, citizens should receive newly issued documents on the same day they submit their applications; second, citizens should receive document renewals within two hours.

Marzouqa knew that achieving these objectives would require an overhaul of the CSPD's organizational structure. The division of the civil-status operation from the passports wing, with separate staffs, managers, and budgets for each, did not make sense. "Employees could not perform the job of the department as a whole. I wanted the whole department to have a single vision: being as citizen-friendly as possible. This required integrating the department better," he said. Marzouqa set about the overhaul by forming committees to examine particular areas. These committees eventually translated into departments, while separate manager positions—one for civil status and one for passports—were eliminated.

The Development, Training, and Modernization Committee eventually became the Department of Administrative Development and Training, headed by Hamdan from 1992 to 2002. The Committee on Laws and Legislations, formed by Marzouqa to compile a book of all the laws covering the department's activities, became the Legal Affairs Unit. The Employee Affairs Committee, a forum to examine citizens' complaints against specific employees, became the Central Inspection Office. Its mandate expanded to include human resources and monitoring employees.

Marzouqa established the existing backlogs and dealing with all security-sensitive applications related to Gulf Crisis returnees as top priorities, extending the workday to 7 p.m. He stayed at the department until the last employee left, to make it clear that work rules applied to everyone, including the boss. In a further move to clear the backlog, Marzouqa simplified processes for Gulf-related applications. Because of security concerns linked to Palestinian militant organizations, the CSPD had to get clearance from the Public Security Department for all returnees' documentation, a requirement that could take weeks. Leveraging contacts he had made during his work at the Public Security Department, Marzouqa received permission for the CSPD to issue temporary clearances. These actions cleared a bottleneck, and the backlog disappeared within weeks.

Hamdan said the initial changes in Marzouqa's first year "really set the stage for what was to come later. When I first entered the department in 1968, one of the managers told me that 'Before any story of the land can be told, it is the priority of the state to know the numbers of its people and their demographics.' Finally, this was starting to happen here in Jordan."

Getting Down to Work

While setting up a long-term infrastructure to manage changes, Marzouqa began revising processes, implementing use of the national number into procedures, emphasizing employee training, increasing branch breadth, and monitoring employee performance.

Streamlining Processes. Marzouqa and his team condensed procedures for all documents, from passports and national IDs to birth certificates and death certificates. They first focused on the passport issuance and renewal process, which was the most complicated. After observing and timing processes, Marzouqa and his team cut this twelve-step, ten-person process down to four steps by four employees at the same counter. First, an employee checked application inputs, entered data into a computer, and approved the application. Second, the applicant went to the accountant (next in line at the counter), who accepted and processed payments. During this time, another employee printed the new or renewed passport in the printing office. Within two hours, a manager (also at the counter) signed the application, after which the citizen received the completed passport.

Before the reforms, office assistants had to double-check application inputs manually with documents in the archives. Employees worked to organize the previously chaotic archives alphabetically, with files arranged by family. Data-entry employees entered the archives' information into the computer system. Eventually, computer algorithms double-checked application inputs as the archives were entered electronically. This process, started under Marzouqa, reached completion under his successor.

Marzouqa personally supervised a construction team in late 1991 that reconfigured workspace to accommodate the new processes and increase accessibility for citizens. He had workers remove the walls between offices on the ground floor and add counter space. He then moved all employees directly involved in the process (data-entry specialists, accountants, printing workers, and managers) behind the same counter. Support staff such as typists worked in the same hall, visible to the citizens. "I feel that this worked because employees were directly witnessed by the citizen; they could no longer shirk their duties," Marzouqa said.

Implementing the National Number. To address the problem of data-entry errors from spelling inconsistencies, Marzouqa decided to use citizens' national numbers as a key element in issuance and renewal processes. The government had used national numbers since 1983 for social security purposes. Each ten-digit number indicated a citizen's year of birth, gender, and number in the registration queue. Before the merger, the Department of Civil Status had asked citizens to submit their numbers with all applications, but the numbers were never actively used for processing.

Before national numbers could be incorporated into processes, however, technical equipment and support services had to be improved. Marzouqa forged a partnership with the Royal Scientific Society, Jordan's largest technical research organization. The society assessed the department's information technology (IT) equipment and found the system didn't have the power to hold data on the entire Jordanian population. Additionally, key support equipment was missing, including photocopying machines and generators for use during power outages.

Marzouqa approached the leaders of the Royal Jordanian Air Force, who were friends from his past work at the Public Security Department, on the recommendation of the scientific society. They formed a joint technical committee and looked deeper into the department's computer problems. The air force sent eight staff members to train department employees on data entry, verification, and IT use for two years. In 1995, IT staff connected twenty branches to the main servers in Amman, so that branch employees could easily look up information. The department installed a generator system to deal with power outages. On the whole, however, equipment was hard to come by. "Because of low budgets, we could not afford to buy new devices," Marzouqa said. "We could only update what we had and learn to use it better."

The Committee on Development, Training, and Administration assigned employees to compare name entries in manual files with those in computer databases. If a duplication existed (for example, two people with precisely the same name) and if all other data matched (date and place of birth, mother's maiden name, etc.), they would cancel one of the files.

They then linked national number data, using a computer search program, to the citizens' electronic files.

All newly issued documents were stamped with citizens' national numbers. Documents that came in for renewal after expiration also received stamps, which allowed all documents in circulation to eventually carry the numbers. The department focused first on civil status documents like birth and death certificates, and in 1996 began issuing national IDs and passports with national numbers. With unique numbers on official documents, cases of mistaken identity at border crossings, an especially irksome problem, were nearly eliminated.

Productivity Training. Training programs instituted during Marzouqa's tenure served two purposes: to facilitate employee transfers and to improve employee skill levels. To facilitate transfers and meet seasonal demand fluctuations, the CSPD trained employees to perform issuance and renewal procedures for all types of documents. "We created a comprehensive employee: one who could be shifted from task to task based on what the citizens needed," said Hamdan. Marzouqa used the weekly and monthly reports submitted by submanagers to assess application volumes and allocate employees and equipment according to need to specific processes in branches.

To improve employee skills, Marzouqa sent assistant managers and managers to training and certification courses at the Jordan Institute of Public Administration and the Royal Scientific Society. Staff members from the society taught computer courses at the department. The training team circulated among employees a book on laws covering the department that had been produced by the Legal Affairs Unit.

Decentralization. Broadening citizens' access to its services in rural areas, the CSPD expanded its branch network by nearly two-thirds during Marzouqa's tenure, lifting the total number from forty-five in 1991 to seventy-four in 1996. Marzouqa's team worked directly with municipalities to open branches, taking variables like population density, demographics, and potential application volume into account. Enthusiastic municipalities often would offer buildings as office space to the department, alleviating the constraints of a low budget. To staff the branches, Marzouqa negotiated with the Civil Service Bureau for an increase in the department's headcount. Employee numbers rose from 870 in 1991 to 978 in 1996, an increase of 12 percent.

Evaluating Employee Performance. In 1992, Marzouqa internalized the monitoring of employee performance by forming the Central Inspection Office. Initially, the office consisted of four staff members who assessed every aspect of the department's daily work. Each staff member was responsible for analyzing a particular issue—either finances, computers, administration, or processes. They dropped in, unannounced, to perform informal audits in each of these fields, submitting weekly reports on employee productivity (for example, for a document employee, the number of applications completed daily, or the person's manner of interacting with citizens). If a shortcoming was identified, submanagers summoned the employee to discuss the reports and urge improved performance.

Managers and the director general met twice a year to discuss the findings of the inspection office. In addition to these reports, employees' direct supervisors evaluated them, as well as the directors of their branches. Evaluations were based on thirty criteria in six categories: abiding by working hours, interactions with citizens, interactions with colleagues, accuracy, the extent to which the employee completed daily tasks, and the employee's qualifications.

Budgetary limitations constrained Marzouqa's efforts to motivate employees and improve performance. Because raising salaries was not an immediate option, Marzouqa loosened up the rigid bonus system. At the end of each working year, every employee in the department received a bonus based on an equal portion of a pool allocated by the Ministry of Finance. Typically, each employee received a bonus of about ten Jordanian dinars per year (approximately US$20). Marzouqa changed the bonus structure, linking the same pool of bonuses to performance, based on inspection office reports. Employees who performed well received a larger percentage of the pool, while poor performers received less.

Marzouqa also informally changed promotion procedures within the department. Upon entering the department and observing its workings, he promoted several experienced staff members, including Hamdan and Qudah, to senior positions. He continued this policy throughout his tenure. Previously, promotions had hinged on seniority. "He made it clear that staying around a long time was not the incentive for career development in his department. Rather, performing well was," Hamdan said.

Overcoming Obstacles

"At every single step of the process, there was someone pushing back. Resistance, resistance, resistance," Marzouqa said in describing the key hurdle he faced. Al Kayed echoed the sentiment: "They faced so much opposition, so much inertia from employees to change the status quo."

To improve employee behavior and build a more client-friendly attitude among workers, Marzouqa used management techniques drawn from his work in the police service. "He never left the office until the last person left," recalled Salman Qudah. "It seemed like he was always there." Hamdan agreed, saying, "He couldn't increase salaries, but still, the employees for the first time felt respected. He knew each of them and would drive someone home if they needed a ride."

Marzouqa faced opposition not only from lower-level employees but also from his submanagers. When he was observing processes at the counter, for example, they "would complain of aches and pains, and tried to make excuses to go back to their offices, even though I was a much older gentleman than any of them," Marzouqa recalled. "They felt like they were losing their prestige in front of the citizens."

The success of many of Marzouqa's reforms depended on his ability to get his employees to recognize that they were not above the citizens they served.[3] Doing this required staffers to understand that government employees were not superior to regular citizens, and that citizens had the right to challenge civil servants who were not doing their jobs well. Marzouqa led by example. His open-door policy for citizens sent a strong message to department employees, and he frequently visited branches to keep an eye on things. These recurrent surprise visits to observe processes in branches—occasionally with Marzouqa in disguise—made it clear that top management held employees accountable for their actions.

Marzouqa personally rebuked errant employees. When he visited a branch in disguise and found employees misbehaving, he would call the employees in question to his office and say, "You treated a certain veiled old man very badly when he came to get services from your branch. Is this really the image you want to give of yourself and our department?" In one instance, Marzouqa received several complaints against a branch manager who kept citizens waiting outside his office for days. After speaking with him once about it, Marzouqa expected the problem to cease. When it did not, he called the employee to an urgent meeting at the main office in Amman. When the employee arrived, Marzouqa purposefully left him in his waiting room for hours. The employee became agitated, pacing around the room and irritating the secretaries. When he finally called the branch manager in, Marzouqa calmly said, "At least you had coffee and tea, as well as a seat to sit, in my waiting room. Many of the citizens who you subject to this treatment don't even have that." The employee changed his ways, Marzouqa said.

In other cases, Marzouqa would take pains to carefully explain the department's objectives. For example, in his second week on the job, he called a meeting of all the senior submanagers and floated the idea for the list of objectives, saying that eventually a passport should be renewed within one hour. The submanagers objected, and one senior official made the case that, if this were done, citizens would not value their passports and instances of loss or damage would rise drastically. Marzouqa persuaded the managers that this would not happen because the procedures for getting a new passport after an instance of loss or damage involved higher fees and a longer waiting period.

Some cases required sterner measures, even though people employed under strict civil service labor laws could not be fired unless they committed a felony. At the beginning of his tenure, Marzouqa had six submanagers who, despite his overtures, would not cooperate with his reform vision. After a few months, he approached the Council of Ministers and requested their dismissal, as this was the only way he could proceed, given civil service regulations. When the council twice postponed addressing his request, he issued an ultimatum, saying, "Either they go or I go. If you want things to happen, we cannot have such poor leadership in managerial positions." Given Marzouqa's long tenure at the Public Security Department and his respected judgment, the Council of Ministers acquiesced.

Another constraint on Marzouqa's reform momentum was a lack of political will. Although he had tacit support from King Hussein, who facilitated his appointment in 1991, frequent cabinet turnover meant that expressions of political support from ministers were fleeting. "The government would only give us financial resources after we demonstrated results," said Marzouqa.

A critical turning point was the 1994 election. Marzouqa suggested using the national number to identify people in election lists. The department spearheaded the election registration effort, helping to reduce problems of ghost voters and people who voted multiple times. "Marzouqa used this to convince the government of the importance of reforming CSPD. The state started supporting and believing in our reforms," said Hamdan.

During Marzouqa's tenure, the department's budget rose 31 percent, to 3,660,000 dinars. "Towards the end, we could pressure the government to give us the needed finances because we were doing a good job," Marzouqa asserted.

Assessing Results

Before reforms, the department had no system for collecting data on processing times. Several employees, however, agreed that document processing times varied widely, ranging from as long as two years to as short as four or five hours. In 1996, at the end of Marzouqa's tenure, department data systematically measured processing times and indicated that the average time to process a passport or a civil status document was just two hours. Because fees were set by law and the MOF allocated the department budget, citizens did not face an increase in fees paid despite improved services.

Streamlining processes did not compromise quality. The department implemented several measures designed to prevent forgery and fraud, from fingerprinting and specialized barcodes to holographic stamps that yielded special images when held under a flame. As a result, Jordanian passports became compliant with International Civil Aviation Organization standards. According to department data, the number of cases related to illegal fabrication fell annually, starting in 1991 with Marzouqa's tenure. After 1999, no cases of fabrication were reported.

Employee motivation was important in the absence of the ability to hire and fire. During Marzouqa's tenure, employee performance improved as employees were held more accountable through informal audits, enhanced training, and restructured offices that made them more visible to citizens. Interviewees mentioned that corruption lessened because applications changed hands fewer times as procedures became increasingly streamlined. Bribes to speed up applications became superfluous as delivery times shrank. According to some of the middlemen occupying stalls outside the Amman branch, demand for their services fell. The department even opened a free help desk.

According to Sawsan Gharaibeh, a governance analyst for the United Nations Development Program in Jordan, issuance and renewal processes became more equitable. It was no longer possible for employees to delay applications based on applicants' last names, especially after national numbers came into use. "I think that this was an inadvertent outcome of the reforms. As the processes became more standardized and transparent, and employees were held more accountable, the general public began to realize that there is little room for discrimination or favoritism, and this all led to increasing the trust in the department," she said.

Previously, service delivery lacked consistency and convenience. Hamdan attributed public dissatisfaction to these factors. The middlemen standing outside the Amman branch echoed this sentiment and told stories about citizens' impatience. Despite this perceived impatience, between 1992 and 1996 complaints against the department fell. According to Marzouqa and other employees, the Committee on Citizen Complaints, which received an influx of complaints between 1991 and 1993, received none by 1995–1996. According to many interviewees, fewer citizens called in to citizen activists' radio shows to criticize the department. Instead, they were likely to praise the department on these shows and send in letters of appreciation.[4]

Continuing Progress with Awni Yarvas

Shuhaiber Hamdan, who worked at the CSPD for forty years and directed its Department of Administrative Development, said, "Even after Marzouqa's time, the department still had room for progress to achieve full efficiency and perfect service delivery. There was always room for progress." Four key areas required attention.

First, the department lacked trained staff who could maximize the use of its computers. Many employees frequently found manual ways to get things done, bypassing computers and making processes unnecessarily labor intensive and more prone to corruption and error. Computer use in processes required standardization. Second, the training regime required restructuring to become an integrated and coherent system. Under Marzouqa's training program, every employee could perform every process, but computer use was not part of the pedagogy. Third, performance management required a systematic policy framework. Although Marzouqa had promoted individuals based on qualifications rather than seniority and had linked bonuses to performance, his efforts were largely ad hoc. Fourth, data-entry errors remained a significant problem. Department employees estimated that at least 40 percent of the system's data contained some sort of inaccuracy. Although Marzouqa had used Jordan's national number to sharply reduce errors stemming from similar names, the problem of input errors by employees remained unaddressed.

In addition to correcting these internal deficiencies, Marzouqa's successor had to sustain the department's initial reforms. In April 1996, the Council of Ministers appointed Awni Yarvas, a former major general in the General Intelligence department, as director general of the CSPD. According to Hamdan, Yarvas "had an eye for detail and the capacity to keep his eyes on everything happening in the department. I think that this, and, of course, good performance in his previous position, led to his appointment."

During his decade-long tenure as head of the CSPD, Yarvas built upon Marzouqa's initial reforms by standardizing training and performance-management systems for the department's nearly 1,000 employees; promoting the use of technology in production processes; and correcting data-entry errors. Salman Qudah, a department employee of twenty-six years, said, "Marzouqa's era involved achieving manual efficiency, while Yarvas's era involved achieving technical efficiency. Yarvas brought the department into the modern era."

This portion of the case study demonstrates how a manager can boost efficiency and service delivery by using a predecessor's achievements as a springboard. By 2005, efficiency at the CSPD reached a maintainable peak, as processing times for all documents were cut to thirty to forty-five minutes without compromising quality. These changes earned the recognition of Jordanian political commentators, government officials, citizens, and international documentation organizations. At the time of the interviews in late 2010, government officials and citizens alike rated the CSPD as Jordan's most efficient and improved public service department. Interviewees attributed the persistence of the department's reforms to continuity of leadership, which contrasted with frequent top-level turnover in other Jordanian government operations.

Picking Up Where Marzouqa Left Off

When he joined the CSPD, Yarvas spent his early weeks closely studying the department's inner workings to learn "the daily procedures, processes, people—the nature of the job itself." He knew that processes could always use simplification to maximize efficiency and eliminate delays. Khaled Taha, a long-time department employee who in December 2010 was assistant director of administrative development, agreed that process evaluation was crucial: "This department is all about processes. Every single thing is a process, or a sub-process, or a process within a process." Within a month, Yarvas had identified key interrelated focal points for promoting progress.

The department's technical inefficiencies affected citizens in different ways. Because citizens' civil files were kept only at their local branch offices, residents of Zarqa, for instance, could get their documents only at the Zarqa branch. If they moved to Aqaba, they had to return to Zarqa for all document-related transactions because their files remained in their former hometown. Although Marzouqa had connected some branches' computer servers to the department's main Amman server that employees in different locations accessed to run programs, the process was incomplete, leaving branches unconnected. The department had to make it possible for any citizen to receive any service at any of the seventy-four branches throughout the country.

CSPD also made inefficient use of its computer resources. Marzouqa had revised manual processes and trained employees in all types of document issuance and renewal procedures. Although many workers gradually began to use computers for data entry, computer skills varied greatly among employees, processes, and branches. Recognizing what he called the "link between the machines and the people who work them," Yarvas knew he had to ensure that employee capacity kept pace with technological gains. Doing so required the creation of a comprehensive training system, because no in-house training program existed for all department employees.

Data-entry error posed an additional problem. Qudah said, "There was little assurance of quality. I would estimate that around 40% of the data previously entered was incorrect somehow, possibly even more." To address errors stemming from similar names and inconsistent spelling, Marzouqa had begun using national numbers. However, he had not instituted a system for verifying the entered data. Such mistakes were costly for both the department and citizens, causing document duplication and requiring court cases to verify documents.

Finally, Yarvas wanted to strengthen incentives for employee performance. Marzouqa had created the Central Inspection Office, which monitored individual employee performance in several ways, including the number of applications handled, the quality of interaction with citizens and colleagues, accuracy, and the completion of assigned tasks. He had allocated bonuses based on these criteria. Yarvas wanted to build on this system by standardizing its use across all branches and employees, adding additional criteria for setting bonuses.

Framing a Response

Yarvas quickly realized that pre-reform capacity building was critical prior to undertaking any large-scale changes in production methods, training, or performance management. Working with a team of senior employees, he charted the department's potential for technical and personnel development, collecting information to identify opportunities for improvement.

Yarvas knew that the successful implementation of technical changes in processes and data entry hinged on the skills of his staff. "First, I needed to know who was qualified, because machines can't do the job on their own," he said. Yarvas formed a human resources committee composed of senior Central Inspection Office staff to survey the department's 978 employees. The survey asked department employees about attendance at computer training courses at private institutions, degree qualifications in programming or computer administration, and use of computers in daily work.

The study found that many employees still did not use computers, mainly because of a low level of training. Results indicated that only 30 percent of department employees had attended training courses. A related problem was that many department employees who did have computer training often were in positions that required mainly manual functions. "They had the qualifications but still operated manually because the entire department was more comfortable with manual when it came to producing documents," Yarvas said. "We identified two linked steps on how to proceed: exploiting the machines by integrating technology into production processes, and training people to handle this change."

Because computers were used and distributed unevenly across employees and processes, Yarvas believed that standardizing their use would improve speed, accuracy, and, ultimately, service delivery. Upgrading and repairing the CSPD's aging IT equipment was imperative. Yarvas continued the advisory partnership with the Royal Scientific Society that had been initiated by Marzouqa. Consultants from the society, working with the department's technology unit, assessed the capacity of the main server in Amman and added crucial memory to the system. The group also had the Ministry of Communication organize telephone and internet cables, built special office storage for technical equipment, and installed generators to maintain power during electrical outages.

Getting Down to Work

Yarvas started by focusing on short-term staffing requirements. Working with the Royal Scientific Society, senior employees of the Central Inspection Office analyzed staffing needs. Establishing goals for different processes and subprocesses, they listed the baseline degrees and qualifications required for each task. They estimated and tallied the numbers of different types of employees required for different functions, matched this to the department's existing capacity, and worked on closing the short-term capacity gap via training. Based on this initial analysis, Yarvas had employees within each category take external training courses to kick-start initial changes. For instance, fifty employees might be trained in data entry, or twenty might be trained in programming, according to department demand for these skills. Relying largely on promises of higher annual bonuses to encourage cooperation, the department, in October 1996, began to roll out orchestrated reforms.

Extending Training. During his tenure, Marzouqa had sent assistant managers to training programs at institutions such as the Royal Scientific Society and the Jordan Institute of Public Administration. He occasionally brought their specialists to CSPD offices to conduct training. Veteran employees sometimes trained new ones, but that decision was often left to individual discretion. Yarvas continued Marzouqa's policy of training all employees in all procedures, creating a "comprehensive" employee who could switch tasks easily to meet seasonal shifts in document demand. Additionally, under Yarvas, the department started training employees systematically to deal with increased computer use in processes. Yarvas chose the experienced Hamdan to develop and manage a cohesive in-house training program for all employees.

Hamdan set a high bar for his trainees. Under his system, all new employees underwent an intensive, month-long course in Amman on computer use and the laws that applied to the department. At the end of the course, employees took two written tests: one on computer use and one on laws. To pass the training, employees had to score at least 90 percent on the computer-use test and at least 80 percent on the legal one. Failing to do so meant they had to retake the training and examinations. "We set the baseline score so high to make it clear that our employees had to know everything about their jobs," Hamdan said. To ensure consistency in staff capacity, veteran employees had to pass the same written tests, although they did not necessarily have to take the same one-month training course. "Even if they had 20 to 25 years of experience within the department, they were still tested," Hamdan asserted.

Systematizing Performance Management. New employees had an incentive to perform well in the training because their exam grades at the end of the course determined their qualifications and placed them on distinct career paths. Although exam grades determined the positions assigned to new employees, subsequent promotions depended on additional criteria from the employee performance reports compiled by the Central Inspection Office.

Yarvas, like Marzouqa, linked bonuses to performance, but with some important changes that formalized and added criteria to the award system. The department distributed annual bonuses from a pool specially allocated by the MOF. Previously, application output had been the main factor used to calculate bonuses, but Yarvas added variables such as the number of applications an employee's branch received, volume of workflow, population density served by the branch, and the type of employee. "Quite a few employees, upon noticing these financial incentives, willingly expressed their desire to attend training and improve their skills," recounted Yarvas. Because rigid civil service constraints applied mainly to hiring and firing, Yarvas had the latitude to change procedures and requirements involving employee training and performance.

Technical Changes. While creating a training regimen that would facilitate technical change, Yarvas focused on expanding computer use in data entry and retrieval and better integrating technologies into all document-production processes.

Yarvas finished linking all branches to the main Amman server and to one another. This effort required the creation of a central data repository in Amman that was then made available to all branches. When the department had operated manually, citizens had two files at the department archives: one for passports and one for civil status. Employees had to cross-check both against information that was submitted on applications, a tedious and time-consuming process. Linking branches to the main server meant that any citizen's files were electronically available at any branch.

Importantly, connecting branch computers to the main server allowed Yarvas to get a faster, more accurate picture of application volumes and outputs across branches and processes. Marzouqa had collected this kind of information from daily reports that had to be compiled by branch managers. The changes improved the flow of information and saved managers' time.

Increased digitization of production processes officially began in October 1996 with birth certificates. This process was the simplest and most affordable, as it required only data entry, data verification, and printing onto a single sheet of paper. Employees entered data into the computer system by using the national numbers of the newborn's parents, verified the information electronically, and automatically printed the document.

By December 1996, the department had expanded automation to other civil status documents, including death and divorce certificates. By May 1997, national identification cards were computerized, and by 1999 production of all documents, including passports, had fully incorporated computerization. Expanded training programs and performance management systems facilitated the staff's adjustment to revised processes.

Data Accuracy. According to long-time department employees Qudah, Hamdan, and others, 40 percent or more of the information entered into the computers was incorrect in some way at the start of Yarvas's tenure. Data entry errors that resulted in duplicate documents were a significant problem because citizens had to go to the courts to get their documents fixed.

Yarvas launched an accuracy drive, stressing to department employees that quality of data entry was critical. "It was not optional. It had to be 100% correct," he said. Validating the system required correcting existing errors as well as preventing future mistakes. To correct erroneous data in the system, employees were assigned to double-check applications that came in for issuance or renewals with the department's records and with the citizens who presented the applications. Citizens who had errors in their documentation due to data entry mistakes received free renewals and corrections at the department.

To prevent future mistakes, Yarvas changed the system. Previously, each employee assigned to data entry had to enter 200 families daily into the computer. Because this approach emphasized quantity over quality, employees often made mistakes. Shifting the emphasis to quality rather than quantity, Yarvas began fining employees who made data entry mistakes. When a mistake was discovered—often by an inconvenienced citizen—supervisors traced it back to the responsible employee, who would be fined through a pay deduction. In cases of repeated mistakes, where fining did not work as a form of prevention, Yarvas instructed managers to bring employees responsible for the errors face-to-face with the citizens affected by the mistakes. If mistakes continued, the employee received an administrative punishment—a fine divided among his colleagues within his subunit and a lower annual bonus. These measures worked to prevent mistakes, and data entry errors became rare. If an employee continued to make errors, supervisors transferred the person to manual functions, as civil service regulations all but precluded firings.

Improving Processes. Yarvas constantly searched for ways to improve processes. For example, he decided to issue all department documents in both Arabic and English to simplify international use of documents for students studying abroad and other traveling citizens. Previously, the department had issued documents only in Arabic. To allow for consistent translations from Arabic into English, Yarvas had a committee within the department compile a dictionary of common Arabic names with standardized English translations. He then contacted the Ministry of Education, which kept an English database of the names of all students taking secondary school examinations. The CSPD used the database to link Arabic names to standardized English spellings.

Yarvas also relieved a bottleneck caused by work requirements for branch accountants, the employees who collected and recorded fees. By law, accountants had to fill out three separate sheets of paper containing the name of each citizen, the citizen's national number, application input information, and his or her application fee. The accountant kept one copy in his receipt book, gave one to the applicant, and kept a third in the citizen's archival files.

Yarvas was unable to hire more accountants due to stringent civil service regulations and budget limitations. With the approval of the MOF, he instituted a program under which accountants received books of tickets each morning that indicated the fees required for all types of documents. Each citizen who came to pay a fee received a ticket. When the citizen paid the amount indicated on the ticket, the accountant simply attached a second ticket copy to the citizen's application file. Then the ticket number was entered into the computer and added to the citizen's electronic files. Instead of writing detailed receipt and application information down, accountants merely issued tickets and entered ticket numbers into the computer.

The ticket system also worked to emphasize accountability and reduce corruption. Because each book held a specific number of tickets and each document had a specific fee, employees had no excuse if the total sum of money in their registers did not match the simple arithmetic of multiplying the number of tickets issued by their respective fees. "It worked to lower corruption because the documentation was shortened," Yarvas said. The ticket system also saved the department money, as ticket books cost 1,200 Jordanian dinars (about US$1,700) a year, a small fraction of the three-copy system's annual cost of 14,000 dinars.

Overcoming Obstacles

Yarvas ran into the same obstacles that his predecessor had encountered. "Employees naturally were afraid of new changes," said Yarvas. Many employees were unwilling or unable to adapt to the technological changes within the department, engendering resentment between older employees and their younger, more tech-savvy counterparts.

Again, Yarvas's response was systematic. He observed that his employees could be divided into three groups. First, those who already had computer qualifications and were performing tasks unrelated to their degrees. They were largely enthusiastic about their transfers to relevant departments and did not pose a problem. The second group lacked qualifications and initially resisted change, but these workers later became enthusiastic when they learned that they would be trained. The third group was the key problem: employees who resented all changes and did not take to training. Some of these employees could be enticed by annual bonuses that now depended on their performance. Because firing was not an option under labor regulations, employees who would not accept changes and training were transferred to manual functions such as filing archives.

Yarvas faced another key obstacle related to the budgetary constraints of acquiring updated equipment. Updated or new equipment for processes— whether computers or printers—required money. Additionally, with new technologies constantly emerging, machines became obsolescent quickly. Given a limited budget, at the start of his tenure Yarvas had consultants from the Royal Scientific Society initially map the lifespan of all department machinery, allotting money to machines that required immediate updating for processes to continue at a steady pace.

Yarvas and the Royal Scientific Society conducted detailed analyses of processes and procedures, keeping a close eye on which machines were obsolete. These machines were replaced subject to the department's budget, with Yarvas frequently requesting extra funding from the MOF. Yarvas's team also applied for and received grants from the United Nations Development Program to further develop technical elements such as electronic archiving and backup disaster-recovery systems.

Assessing Yarvas's Results

Yarvas's multipronged efforts bore fruit. By 2005, at the end of his tenure, the time required to issue and renew all documents had fallen from around two hours to fifteen to forty-five minutes. The department maintained that performance level into 2010. Reduced processing times corresponded to streamlined processes and increased employee productivity during the 1990s and early 2000s. Accuracy also improved vastly during Yarvas's tenure. According to Hamdan and other department employees, the department corrected all previously existing errors in the electronic system and archives. At the same time, practices instituted for preventing mistakes—improved training, cohesive performance management, and employee fines—proved effective.

The CSPD's successes drew recognition. King Abdullah, visiting the department in disguise toward the end of Yarvas's tenure, noted the department's ease of operation and positive interactions with citizens. International conferences hosted panel sessions on the department's efficiency and effectiveness. Citizens' blogs cited interactions with the department as positive government transactions. Citizens also offered ready praise to the department in radio talk shows and through letters. In 2005, the Council of Ministers recognized Yarvas's achievements at CSPD by appointing him to head the Interior Ministry.

Reflections

Several interviewees described Nasouh Marzouqa's tenure as a period that jolted the department out of lethargy, setting the stage for further reforms under his successor, Awni Yarvas. The stability of leadership at the department—Marzouqa from 1991 to 1996 and Yarvas from 1996 to 2005—was a crucial determinant of the turnaround's success. In Jordan, with its history of frequent cabinet turnover, reform momentum was rarely sustained: "Frequent ministerial changes in the cabinet meant that director generals of departments within ministries faced yearly changes in the ministries' policy and management, so how could anything happen? CSPD was the sole exception to this Achilles' heel," said Zuhair Al-Kayed, former director of Jordan's Civil Service Bureau.

Department veteran Shuhaiber Hamdan seems to agree, saying, "This was very unusual in Jordan. CSPD is, perhaps, the only department where one leader was humble enough to build off another's work while instituting his own reforms as well." Awni Yarvas, who served as director general from 1996 to 2005, agreed that his strategy was to expand and bolster the reforms of his predecessor rather than to tear down and start over: "When you start at a department, you don't start from zero," Yarvas said.

Marzouqa's management style—which involved identifying problems through extensive consultation and observation—"was really what got the job done," said Bashir Khadra, professor of administrative development at the University of Jordan. Longtime department employee Salman Qudah added, "He really put himself into the shoes of the employee, and the shoes of the citizen, to solve problems and devise solutions. In this sense, it was not just reform. It was revolution."

Notably, reforms placed a premium on increasing convenience for citizens, who have better things to do than stand in line for government documents. Yarvas expressed confidence that the Jordanian public was pleased with his work. "The citizen felt the impact of this reform," he said. "Ask any citizen in the street." Raghda Butros, a prominent citizen activist, wrote enthusiastically on her blog in September 2010, "Whoever is behind the process at CSPD and other departments that perform this well—be it the person or people who develop the system or the people who run and execute it—deserve recognition, praise and gratitude."[5]

Notes

Deepa Iyer compiled this case study based on interviews conducted in Amman, Jordan, in November 2010. It was produced under the Innovations for Successful Societies program at Princeton University, Princeton, NJ, and is used by permission. We have integrated a separate ISS case in this chapter as well, "People and Machines—Building Operational Efficiency," which focuses on the department from 1996 to 2005 under Marzouqa's successor, Awni Yarvas.

1. Oroub Al Abed, "Palestinian Refugees in Jordan," *Forced Migration Research Guide*, February 2004.

2. Civil Status and Passports Department, Department of Administrative Development, Civil Status and Passports Datasheet, 1989–2009.

3. See, for example, famous Jordanian cartoonist Imad Hajjaj's comic strip

parodying this bureaucratic culture at www.mahjoob.com/en/archives/view.php?car toonid=1624.

4. See, for example, several citizens' blogs praising the department, www.7iber .com/2010/09/positive-government-transaction/ and www.black-iris.com/2010/10/ 03/renewing-a-canadian-passport-in-amman-is-tougher-than-renewing-a-jordanian -one/.

5. Raghda Butros, "A Positive Government Transaction," September 19, 2010, www.7iber.com/2010/09/positive-government-transaction/.

TWELVE

Conclusion: Making Sense of It All

The Lessons from Experience

ROBERT P. BESCHEL JR.
TARIK M. YOUSEF

ARE THERE GENERAL TRENDS that can be identified across these various cases, or are the experiences too diverse and the epistemological hurdles too great to draw any robust conclusions? The methodological challenges are not insignificant. The number of cases involved is modest and represents only a subset of public sector reform efforts attempted in the Middle East and North Africa (MENA) throughout this period. There are eleven in all, or thirteen if one counts earlier failed reform efforts in the Morocco voluntary retirement program and Egypt one-stop shop examples.[1] Reform objectives and political environments differed, as did the ways in which these reforms were implemented. Selection bias could have arguably factored into the choice of cases or in interpreting the results.[2]

On the positive side, the cases selected are among the most interesting from within the MENA region over the last two decades. Substantively, they cover a broad spectrum of public sector challenges. Most are technocratic in nature, in that they sought to reform government systems and processes to improve the quality of decisionmaking, the regulatory environment, the effectiveness of service delivery, or the mobilization of financial and human resources. One focused on improving transparency to enhance accountability. They also cover a range of countries at different stages of development with differing political and administrative traditions.[3] Each represents a serious, real-life effort in which significant resources were dedicated toward improving existing practices. Considerable political capital was invested, reputations were won or lost, and, in some cases, careers were made or ended.

Through the prism of these case studies, this chapter reflects on MENA's broader experience with governance and public management reform during the last two decades. We consider which types of reforms have tended to work and why. We review the qualitative lessons from implementation, and the ways in which the reforms were identified and moved forward. We also ponder the extent to which the lessons from these reforms are likely to be of use downstream.

How Successful Were the MENA Reforms?

Box 12-1 breaks down the criteria used for evaluating the success of various reforms, which were arrayed along a five-point spectrum that ranges from "clear success" to "unsuccessful."[4] The actual results are presented in box 12-2. The cases are well-documented, and their ranking is relatively straightforward. There was no internal disagreement about where to place them on this spectrum. To facilitate comparison, we have assigned each ranking a number on a straight ordinal scale from 1 to 5, with 5 representing the "clear success" ranking.

BOX 12-1. Criteria for Evaluating Successful Public Sector Reforms

CLEAR SUCCESS: The reform achieved all or the vast majority of its intended results. Outcomes were unambiguously better in terms of efficiency, effectiveness, transparency, and quality of customer service.

MOSTLY SUCCESSFUL: The reform achieved the majority of its intended results. Outcomes would be viewed by most impartial observers as a significant improvement over the original state of affairs.

MIXED SUCCESS: The reform achieved one or two of its primary results. Outcomes were generally better than the alternative. However, there were some problems, trade-offs, or areas where the reform agenda remained incomplete.

MODERATELY UNSUCCESSFUL: The reform may have encouraged some modest improvements, but it did not attain its principle objectives or result in many enduring changes.

UNSUCCESSFUL: The reform's objectives were not attained, and the intervention ultimately made little or no difference to existing bureaucratic performance or practices.

BOX 12-2. Assessing the Relative Success and/or Failure of Various Reforms

(5) CLEAR SUCCESS

Advancing e-Governance in Dubai

The Dubai e-government initiative transformed public sector culture and operations. Significant productivity gains were achieved in many services. UAE ranks high on various global indices of e-governance.

One-Stop Shops in Cairo (Second Attempt)

The second attempt was a clear success. GAFI became a true one-stop shop; the number of procedures was cut from nineteen to three; and processing times were reduced from thirty-four days or more to only three days. There was also a significant increase in businesses registered after 2004.

Bill Payment in Saudi Arabia

The SADAD case was a success. The traditional use of banks for bill payments decreased from 73 percent in 2003 to 6 percent in 2010. In 2010, SADAD processed more than 9 million transactions in a month. These transactions were fully processed within two seconds, resulting in increased efficiency and dramatically enhanced service delivery.

Document Processing in Jordan: Part 2 (1996–2005)

The time required for issuing passports and IDs dropped from two hours to 15–45 minutes. Errors in data entry decreased substantially. Service delivery and customer satisfaction increased.

(4) MOSTLY SUCCESSFUL

Reforms in Public Financial Management in the West Bank and Gaza

The PA managed to centralize the flow of revenues; improve expenditure controls; inject greater transparency in the management of public enterprises; and reduce corruption in the payment of salaries to security services. Challenges remained in the role of audit and the lack of alignment of the budget with policy priorities.

Implementing an RTI Regime in Tunisia

In the wake of the revolution, the Tunisian government was able to put in place very strong RTI legislation, and many government entities have taken important steps toward proactive disclosure. Yet considerable work remains to fully implement the legislation, and the law remains underutilized by the broader public.

Overhauling Tax Policy and Administration in Egypt

A new tax law was successfully implemented, which made the process easier and more straightforward. The reform resulted in higher rates of tax filing, including an annual increase of 10 percent. Both income and sales tax revenues increased substantially. Corporate tax increased from LE 22 billion in 2004 to 36.6 billion in 2005. However, implementation was slower than anticipated and significant overstaffing remains.

Document Processing in Jordan: Part 1 (1991–1996)

Processing time for passports decreased from two years to two hours. Corruption decreased, and the quality of service delivery improved. However, the process still suffered from inefficiencies and high rates of data inaccuracy.

(3) MIXED SUCCESS

Civil Service Rightsizing in Morocco (Second Attempt)

The second VRP resulted in significant financial and economic gains. Approximately 38,600 public servants retired, and the wage bill was reduced from an average of 11.8 percent in 2005 to 10.2 percent in 2010. However, problems of adverse selection resulted in a loss of the most talented civil servants, which negatively affected the public sector's capacity and performance.

(2) MODERATELY UNSUCCESSFUL

Reforming Cabinet Structures in Jordan

The reform of cabinet decision procedures was not fully achieved. The process generated a White Paper (which was embedded within the broader National Agenda), some excellent analytic work, a revised cabinet manual, modest improvements in by-laws that reduced the administrative burden on the cabinet, and some changes in organizational structures. However, a sustained restructuring that addressed many of the fundamental challenges flagged in the case was not forthcoming. Furthermore, some of the major institutional reforms that were implemented initially—such as upgrading the status of the Ministry of Administrative Development and placing it under the prime minister's office—were later reversed.

(1) UNSUCCESSFUL

Civil Service Rightsizing in Morocco (First Attempt)

The first attempt was a failure, since only 696 public employees left instead of the 20,000 targeted. There was no noticeable reduction in the wage bill.

Strengthening Human Resource Management in Lebanon

The newly proposed hiring system was rejected from the beginning since it was lengthy, complex, and directly challenged entrenched political interests.

One-Stop Shops in Cairo (First Attempt)

The first attempt was a failure due to the lack of clarity in procedures, and investors still needed to go to various agencies to get their approvals. No significant change was made in the procedures for establishing a business in Egypt.

Four cases were unequivocal success stories, including advancing e-governance in Dubai; the one-stop shop in Egypt; the SADAD payment system in Saudi Arabia; and the second document processing case in Jordan. Four cases were mostly successful, including the public financial management (PFM) reforms in the West Bank and Gaza; right-to-information (RTI) legislation in post-revolutionary Tunisia; tax administration overhauls in Egypt; and the first document processing case in Jordan.

At the other end of the spectrum, the first attempt at civil service rationalization in Morocco; the Lebanon human resource management reforms; and the first Egypt one-stop shop attempt were clear failures. Morocco's second VRP effort was considered a mixed success. Jordan's cabinet reforms were viewed as moderately unsuccessful, although the country has subsequently continued to press forward with several reforms in this area.

This put the notional success rate—here defined as reforms that were a clear success, mostly successful, or a mixed success—at around 70 percent. It is important to note that one should not read too much into this number because the cases were not chosen to form a statistically random sample. And yet, interestingly, this number does not markedly diverge from the success rate of comparable public sector reform efforts supported by institutions such as the World Bank. An assessment by the World Bank's Independent Evaluation Group (IEG) in 2008 found that, on average, 74 percent of the bank's public sector reform projects were either highly satisfactory, satisfactory, or moderately satisfactory, with considerable variation across regions and reforms.[5] While more data is required, a safe working hypothesis would be that public sector reforms in MENA are not unique, and they are no more likely to succeed or fail than those attempted in other regions.

Analyzing Specific Types of Reforms

We have broken the MENA case studies into five substantive categories: 1) center of government (COG) reforms; 2) PFM, including reforms in both revenue collection and expenditure; 3) administrative and civil service reforms (CSR), including reforms in civil service pay and employment and HRM; 4) reforms in service delivery, including business process reengineering and other efforts to improve the quality of services provided to the public; and 5) transparency and social accountability.

Of the cases explored in this volume, PFM cases were clearly the most successful. CSR cases were the least successful, with most being either unsuccessful or achieving only modest success. Service delivery and transparency reforms fell somewhere in the middle. The experiences of public sector reform profiled in this book are consistent with reviews of World Bank public sector reform projects, at least with regard to the PFM and CSR results, where projects focusing on the latter set of reforms have historically been more difficult to implement successfully than those focusing on PFM reforms.[6]

Center of Government Reforms. In advancing reforms to its policy process, Jordan was actually ahead of the curve in implementing measures to improve coordination—a chronic problem in governments throughout the MENA region and beyond. While the Jordan case was largely unsuccessful, COG reforms have continued to move forward throughout the MENA region. Kuwait, for example, invested heavily in a major set of reforms to the prime minister's office in 2010–2012. The reforms marked an ambitious effort to move forward with an integrated reform package addressing policy, strategy, delivery, and communications—all areas where improvements were needed. It failed for a variety of reasons, but the principal causes were the unfavorable political environment and the general lack of support from the country's political and bureaucratic leadership.[7]

Elsewhere, the jury is still out, although momentum for COG reforms continues to accelerate. Tunisia established a delivery unit in 2014. Drawing on the experience of Malaysia's Performance Management and Delivery Unit (PEMANDU), Oman launched its Implementation Support and Follow-Up unit in 2016.[8] Morocco created a delivery unit, and Egypt is contemplating similar reforms. Qatar has worked on designing a whole-of-government monitoring and evaluation system to oversee the implementation of its National Development Strategy. Saudi Arabia has embarked on one of the most ambitious sets of COG reforms, including the creation of a number of units to oversee the implementation of Vision 2030. They include the Strategic Management office for translating Vision 2030 into action plans and implementation programs and the National Center for Performance Monitoring, or Adaa, to measure progress in implementation. Saudi Arabia also initially created a delivery unit, the Delivery and Rapid Intervention Center (DARIC), but it had a relatively short shelf-life.

Many of these reforms focus heavily on improving service delivery in selected areas, or in tracking progress across whole-of-government in association with national development strategies or vision documents, which are useful. But streamlining the machinery of government and improving interagency coordination remain the areas where reforms are most desperately needed. Beneath the façade of an authoritarian state, many MENA governments are administratively fragmented with poorly developed mechanisms for interministerial coordination.[9] Agency and ministerial mandates are imprecise and overlapping, and functional duplication and mission creep are commonplace. Information flows are tightly guarded and almost exclusively vertical in nature. Coordination mechanisms are often ineffective, and these countries lack the dense network of interagency working groups often found in OECD governments.

Public Financial Management. Many MENA countries have pursued a variety of PFM reforms over the past decade with varying degrees of success, quite a few of which remain ongoing.[10] In particular, three types of reforms have tended to enjoy the most success: 1) budget classification; 2) budget transparency; and 3) tax and customs. The first is relatively technical and can be implemented without encountering too much political and bureaucratic resistance. The second is neither particularly demanding technically nor contentious politically, and it can serve as a modest step toward greater social accountability. The third is more contentious but also more valuable for governments that are chronically in need of additional revenues and private sector investment. At the other end of the spectrum, efforts to implement medium-term sector strategies; to improve budget scope and coverage; to introduce performance metrics; to reform procurement; or to implement large financial management information systems have tended to be more problematic. Another set of reforms has enjoyed mixed success, including those targeting budget integration, commitment control, and payroll management.

There are several reasons for the relative success of PFM reforms vis-à-vis those in other areas. Such reforms tend to be more technocratic in nature and fall primarily under the domain of the Ministry of Finance or the Ministry of Planning, which tend to be more powerful than Ministries of Administrative Development or Civil Service. A body of practice exists that is better developed and more integrated, along with an increasingly well-established set of indices in the Public Expenditure and Financial Accountability (PEFA) indicators. Typically, civil service reforms directly impact the welfare of tens or hundreds of thousands of employees, and as such are subject to tremendous scrutiny and resistance, whereas PFM reforms are viewed as more instrumental in nature and, thus, inherently less threatening. It is one thing to try to introduce greater consistency with international experience in budget classification; it is quite another to try to reduce a bloated civil service or to prune back opportunities that have historically flowed to certain groups or individuals.

Yet these reforms are still attempted because they offer clear, tangible, and valued benefits—in terms of providing access to additional funding or curtailing unnecessary expenditure. Salam Fayyad's PFM reforms in Palestine and Egypt's tax reforms are broadly consistent with this experience. Both sets of reforms were complex and technical in nature, and both tackled powerful vested interests with a stake in the status quo. They were undertaken as essential steps toward enhanced fiscal sustainability and, as such, had strong political backing from their champions.

Service Delivery and Business Process Reengineering. MENA has also been home to relatively successful reforms targeting the quality of service delivery. Most, such as the Cairo one-stop shop case, the Jordan document processing cases, the Saudi SADAD case, and the Dubai e-governance case, involve the redesign or reengineering of business processes, often with the aid of information technology. Such efforts can deliver benefits on multiple levels: services become much faster, more transparent, and more citizen-friendly; user satisfaction rises; corruption decreases; and, in many cases, revenue collection increases. After an initial capital outlay, the cost of providing these services often declined.

Again, there are a number of reasons why such cases were successful. First, the bar was often set low. Although many nations have witnessed improvements in recent years in areas such as business licensing, MENA countries have traditionally been among the most bureaucratic in the world. Prior to the reforms, Jordan's document processing involved twelve manual steps performed by ten different employees. It took an average of twenty-five visits to obtain a business license in Egypt. Processes were labor intensive, and implementation was uneven and ad hoc. Delays were common at every step of the process. Under such circumstances, far-reaching reform efforts of the type covered in this volume were able to contribute to major increases in productivity and user satisfaction.

Second, it is less politically problematic to eliminate unnecessary steps. Such efforts may encounter bureaucratic resistance from employees who are uncomfortable with the new procedures or, more perniciously, view them as a threat to their power or livelihood. But they are popular with the public, and administrative friction can be overcome through determined efforts at implementation. Furthermore, many procedures accumulate over time and become antiquated or unnecessary, so their elimination poses no great risk. By 2006, for example, Egypt's General Authority for Investment and Free Zones managed to eliminate more than forty different startup procedures that were no longer administratively or socially relevant.

While reengineering efforts may be politically popular, their implementation is often remarkably complex, with administrative implications that typically run far beyond the initial streamlining effort.[11] In the words of Ziad Bahaa El-Din, who oversaw the Cairo one-stop shop effort, the redesign of procedures is "plumbing work—the details are what kill." Procedures need to be carefully mapped and understood; legal and regulatory changes need to be introduced; electronic transactions need to be made legally binding; new hardware and software needs to be integrated with legacy systems; revised organizational structures and innovative ways of motivating staff need to be developed; and the question of what to do with redundant staff needs to be addressed. The failures of earlier efforts to reform bill payment in Saudi Arabia or to create a one-stop shop in Cairo demonstrate why hurried or half-hearted reengineering efforts seldom deliver as promised.

Organizational Restructuring. Most core and line department reforms involve organizational restructuring at some point. Such efforts typically come in two varieties. The first are centrally driven efforts at reform, and restructure the machinery of government as a whole.[12] These initiatives are often overseen by either the prime minister's office or by a ministry of administrative development. Organizational reviews are conducted, and a blueprint is developed for restructuring the entire public sector. At the same time, teams work with individual line ministries and departments—or a subset of them—to develop restructuring plans for these organizations, which are then fed into the broader restructuring effort.

With the possible exception of small city-states in the Gulf Cooperation Council, efforts to restructure government as a whole have not worked in MENA. They are too complex and politically problematic, and the central agencies tasked with developing plans for restructuring seldom have the gravitas to oversee their implementation. By contrast, the internally driven reorganization of individual ministries, agencies, and departments has been a more promising task. A number of cases in this volume offer successful examples, including Jordan's document processing cases, the one-stop shop and tax administration cases in Egypt, and Salam Fayyad's efforts to restructure the MOF in the WBG.[13] In such cases, reorganiza-

tion was almost always undertaken as an adjunct to a broader set of reforms rather than an end in itself. In Jordan, it was necessary to end a
relatively meaningless division and reduce redundancies between two sets
of functions that had resulted from an earlier imperfect merger. In Palestine, the restructuring of the MOF along the functional lines of revenue
and treasury administration came relatively late in the reform process, as
Fayyad's first priority was to consolidate and centralize PA revenues and
expenditures.

Pay and Employment. The MENA region is, on average, home to some of
the largest public sectors in the developing world, and long-term sustainability of the wage bill is a challenge even in major oil exporters such as
Saudi Arabia and Kuwait. Yet pay and employment reforms have seldom
been high on the agenda for political economy reasons.[14] Morocco deserves credit for being one of the few countries to tackle this problem directly. Its VRP displayed many of the strengths and weaknesses common
in exercises of this type. It was effective in containing wage bill costs, at
least for a time. The program may have had positive economic returns, in
that a number of those who participated may have gone on to start businesses and engage in pursuits that brought higher value-added to the Moroccan economy as a whole. However, the best and the brightest also left
the public sector, resulting in skills gaps and some short-term problems
with service delivery. The program also illustrates the difficulty inherent in
coordinating large public sector reform efforts.

Most other reforms deliberately steered away from both targeted and
voluntary staff reductions as too contentious. Some governments, such as
Lebanon, applied hiring freezes. To bypass the hiring freeze and bring in
needed talent, the government resorted to recruiting contractual labor in
all but the highest levels of the civil service. Compared to tenured staff,
many of these workers were better skilled, more efficient, and more willing
to work longer hours. However, their salaries were much higher, which led
to tensions with existing civil servants and strained the budget even further.
Such practices created a parallel administration of qualified but largely unregulated employees whose lines of accountability were not clearly defined
and whose hiring and performance evaluations were ad hoc. As such, it
served as a poor substitute for an institutionalized and professional public
administration. Lebanon is hardly alone in this practice, as many governments in the region have used similar fixes to circumvent dysfunctional
recruitment and payment policies.

Reformers often employed innovative solutions to get around these constraints. To motivate GAFI staff, Ziad Bahaa El-Din took advantage of GAFI's autonomous financial structure to raise salaries by 30 percent across the board and to implement an incentive system of up to 20 percent of salary. To increase output and justify the higher salaries, he extended the workday by 1.5 hours. Other reformers also took advantage of bonus payments to work around existing salary rigidities. Because raising salaries was not an immediate option in Jordan, Nasouh Marzouqa loosened up the rigid bonus system. Previously, at the end of each working year, every employee received an identical bonus based on a pool allocated by the MOF. Marzouqa changed this bonus structure by linking the same pool to performance based on inspection office reports. Employees who performed well received a larger percentage of the pool, while poor performers received less.

Human Resource Management. If reforms in pay and employment were difficult, those involving HRM were almost impossible.[15] HRM problems are chronic throughout the region and go to the core of weak performance in many ministries and departments. They include antiquated civil service rules and regulations; recruitment that is formally based on merit but actually rife with *wasta* or connections; and massive overstaffing of employees exhibiting general administrative skills but lacking required skills and competencies.[16] They also include promotions awarded on the basis of seniority or connections instead of performance, as well as deficiencies in implementing rules regarding attendance and discipline.

A handful of public sectors have been able to instill a genuine performance ethos, such as those in Dubai and Abu Dhabi. Others, such as Saudi Arabia and Qatar, have managed to create "islands of excellence," largely by exempting key agencies from civil service terms and conditions. Relatively little progress has been made elsewhere despite the need for far-reaching reforms. At one level, the Lebanese effort to directly tackle HRM issues was commendable. At another level, however, it failed miserably when set against traditional networks of patronage and sinecure. Nor was Lebanon alone. Egypt's Ministry of Administrative Development tried for years, without success, to implement far more modest reforms to expand contract employment and strengthen administrative disciplinary procedures. Jordan's 2004 White Paper envisioned a variety of reforms to modernize HRM that never saw the light of day. Other states, including Bahrain, Morocco, and Tunisia, have adopted HRM reforms with more success, although the process is slow, and many of these efforts remain very much a work in progress.

Where possible, reformers sought to build a new agency from scratch. Staff could be brought in under a new administrative culture and terms and conditions, which allowed for a fresh start in terms of socialization and the inculcation of professional norms and values. This was the case in Saudi Arabia's SADAD system and Dubai's e-governance, and it can also be found in many of Saudi Arabia's recent COG reforms. This trend of establishing new task-specific, quasi-government agencies became a popular element of public management reforms pursued particularly within the GCC. It allows the new agencies to operate in a more efficient and flexible manner, as they can adopt different operational and managerial practices that include longer working hours and higher salaries. They can also terminate staff for poor performance. When this was not possible, reformers focused on developing their own management team through controlling promotions. In the Cairo one-stop shop case, nonperforming staff were made redundant or reassigned, and new heads of departments were appointed.

Transparency and Social Accountability. The transparency movement has been one of the most pronounced global governance trends over the past three decades, with the number of countries adopting RTI legislation, to cite one proxy, increasing from around fourteen in 1990 to 129 in 2020.[17] The movement toward greater transparency is closely linked with the struggle against corruption, another dominant theme across the globe. In MENA, only a few countries have formally adopted RTI legislation. However, it is promising that a handful of others are considering steps in this direction, and several countries, such as Egypt, have taken significant steps to enhance fiscal transparency. Given this background, the Tunisia case is at one level quite atypical for MENA. Against the odds, the country has produced one of the most far-reaching pieces of RTI legislation in the world.

Yet the Tunisia example also serves as both a beacon and a cautionary tale. It took over five years to finally pass the new RTI legislation. The fluid and shifting political environment made it a challenge to build stable coalitions to support the RTI effort and to keep them intact through frequent changes in government. The transparency effort drew on citizen support and on a growing network of local and international NGOs. Yet it was plagued by resistance within the career bureaucracy, indifference among

the general citizenry, a chronic lack of funds, and a host of other pressing demands on an overstretched leadership, including terrorism, crime,
and youth unemployment. Once established, political attention turned
elsewhere, and implementation lagged—a common feature of many RTI
regimes. Large portions of the bureaucracy remain fixed in traditional pat-
terns and habits, and public use remains tepid and underdeveloped. It will
take time to fully realize the promise within Tunisia's RTI effort.

Lessons from Public Sector Reform in MENA

MENA provides a variety of lessons on the strategy and tactics for approaching public sector reform. This section reviews several of the most
prominent, including the context and motivation for these reforms; how
reformers coped with resistance; the use of benchmarking and stretch targets; the importance of generating credibility early in the process; internal
and external communications; the effective use of oversight bodies and
consultants; and leadership and the importance of perseverance.

Context, Motivation, and Political Economy. Most treatises on public
sector reform begin or end with the importance of political will.[18] Its existence is cited to explain how successful reforms came to fruition; its absence is rolled out as a justification for lack of progress. Several of the cases
in this volume underscore the dangers of tackling the prevailing political
culture head on with agendas that are too broad or threatening, such as
the Lebanon HRM reforms, or in trying to take forward a far-reaching
reform program during a period when political agendas are rapidly shifting, such as the Jordan cabinet reforms. Conversely, several sets of reforms
clearly benefited from backing at the most senior levels, such as the Dubai
e-governance case or the Morocco VRP program.

Yet other cases also reveal that political backing need not be strong or
explicit. Marzouqa's reforms in Jordan benefited from the tacit support of
King Abdullah, and he was fortunately spared the short tenure that has
undermined other Jordanian reformers. But these reforms were not a top
national priority during this period. Most line department reforms were
consistent with broader national goals and objectives, and as such enjoyed
what could be called the "detached blessing" of national leaders. However,
few experienced strong and sustained support from the most senior levels
of government.

Perhaps the key lesson is that reforms within a particular department can survive on the talent and dynamism of their minister, provided they are consistent with broader national objectives, deliver concrete benefits, and do not create too many political problems. Those that require extensive coordination across multiple ministries are likely to be hostage to broader political developments. If the political environment remains stable, as was the case in Morocco, the reforms can proceed as intended. If it does not, as was the case with the Jordan cabinet reforms, they could very well become a casualty.

Coping with Opposition. As with similar efforts elsewhere in the world, reforms in MENA encountered opposition from various sources. Reformers employed a variety of strategies for dealing with resistance. A fortunate few who received strong backing and support at the highest levels were able to bully, push, persuade, and cajole their way forward. They had the mandate and often the resources necessary to compel recalcitrant units to fall in line. Staff who refused to cooperate could find themselves sidelined or even removed.

Those who were not so blessed needed to find other ways to accomplish their objectives. Under these circumstances, successful reformers moved in ways that were more analogous to streams than to high pressure hoses. They sought to flow around opposition and minimize its interference rather than taking it on directly and blasting it out of the way. This approach could be characterized as one of "strategic opportunism," or seizing the chances that present themselves in the context of a broader vision. Salam Fayyad characterized it as doing "what you can, wherever you can do it, as soon as you can do it."

A strategy often employed by leading reformers was to forge ahead in multiple directions at once, with the understanding that some agendas would likely stall but others could move forward. This approach had the virtue of keeping one's political and bureaucratic opponents off balance. Successful reformers also often combined an unfailing focus on their objectives with tactical flexibility in getting there. These were reforms that were bold in concept but cautious and careful in implementation.

There is often an organic quality to such reforms, which tend to proceed more by evolution and trial and error than by design. This phenomenon has been increasingly recognized within the literature on institutional development as "problem driven iterative adaptation."[19] Officials set out to solve a particular problem, such as controlling expenditure or streamlining business processes. They may experiment with several different approaches, carefully tracking progress to see what is working and what is not. They make progress, but then find that the ultimate resolution will depend on solving other problems, such as organizational design and employee training and motivation. A virtuous circle is established, in which some successful initial reforms build momentum for others downstream. Sometimes, they also open up unanticipated opportunities.

Benchmarking and Stretch Targets. The management principle of benchmarking and stretch targets was put to especially good use. In Jordan, Marzouqa set the goals that citizens should receive newly issued documents on the same day they submit their applications and that they should receive document renewals within two hours. Fayyad challenged his staff at the MOF to implement his public pledge that the ministry would never again issue a bad check. The process of issuing such challenges was typically a consultative one, in that such benchmarks were established only after senior managers first probed their achievability.

Perhaps no country went further toward the use of such targets and benchmarking than the city-state of Dubai. As noted, the Dubai government conducted a strategic audit and benchmarking exercise to define the existing gap between the objectives of the e-government initiative and the realities of its current administration. The exercise also analyzed successful e-government initiatives globally to identify key lessons. Both proved useful in helping articulate Dubai's own approach to e-government, as one of its early lessons was that there is no single "one size fits all" approach.[20] Following established private sector–based management approaches, a structured strategic management system was adopted that identified the Dubai e-government mission, core values, vision, strategy, initiatives, and the strategic progress measurement. Within this system, the government implemented a balanced scorecard–based strategic progress measurement system that included various e-services-related key performance indicators.

Tunisia's open government case offers a particularly interesting example of how reformers used an international organization, in this case the Open Government Partnership (OGP), to establish benchmarks and help lock in reforms domestically. OGP has minimum eligibility criteria that include four major dimensions: fiscal transparency, access to information, asset disclosure for public officials, and citizen engagement. Applicants are scored on a scale in which they need to get at least 75 percent of the applicable points for eligibility. Tunisia's decision to join the OGP in 2014 not only ensured that its transparency practices would adhere to standards that were consistent with global best practice, but also that there would be additional independent coordination and monitoring capacity.

Generating Credibility Early in the Process. Reformers face a host of different challenges with regard to garnering support for their efforts. In areas with a clear production function, such as passports and documents, progress was relatively easy for both officials and for the general public to measure. In other areas, such as PFM, the challenges were more difficult. As Fayyad notes, "people cannot eat reform," and the types of PFM changes he was seeking would typically have only an indirect impact on the general populace. Yet even in this case, Fayyad was able to generate some positive sentiment by putting the budget on the internet, thus enhancing transparency. He also sought to use limited PA funds to pay small suppliers first, thereby generating considerable good will among the broader populace.

Ease of implementation is often a critical concern in generating these early wins. Some reforms can be done with the stroke of a pen; others require major legal changes or convincing thousands of employees to perform their duties differently. Not surprisingly, many successful reformers started with "stroke of a pen" reforms and tackled more difficult and/or serious problems downstream. Fayyad's consolidation of PA accounts into a single treasury account typifies this approach. It is also interesting to note that, as was the case with Fayyad, some of these initial moves required quick maneuvering and fast-track implementation to be effective. Otherwise, they were likely to have become mired in bureaucratic resistance, and the prospects for a quick win would have been lost.[21]

Even programs that involve major systems upgrades, such as the Dubai e-government initiative, felt compelled to deliver results quickly. Dubai managed to strike a balance between medium-term requirements of systems development and near-term expectations of quick results by delivering waves of e-services in different stages, gradually leading to increased maturity over the years. Saudi Arabia's SADAD system targeted larger government and corporate users in the early stages on the assumption that if they could get them on board and using the system, others would follow.

A number of reformers modified the physical administrative environment to broadcast that larger reforms were underway. As part of his effort to instill more credibility and customer orientation in document processing in Jordan, Marzouqa reconfigured the workspace to accommodate new processes and to increase accessibility for citizens. He removed walls between offices and transitioned to a more open office concept, while simultaneously placing counters between employees and customers. He also placed support staff, such as typists, in a position where they would be visible to citizens. This made it more difficult for them to shirk their duties. GAFI implemented similar changes in Egypt.

Internal and External Communications. Another interesting feature of many of the more successful reforms is the premium placed on effective internal and external communication.[22] The Morocco VRP case is particularly illuminating in this regard. One of the reasons the first VRP effort failed was inadequate communication. The second program devoted considerable time and energy to rectifying this problem and was, ultimately, much more successful. However, even with the second program, the communications effort tailed off after the exercise was completed. This resulted in a lot of uncertainty, speculation, and miscommunication surrounding the ultimate efficacy of the operation.

Egypt's tax reforms also invested heavily in communications along multiple fronts, rolling out a differentiated communications effort with a number of target audiences. Extensive consultations were held with members of the business community and private sector representatives as well as roundtable discussions with business associations, accounting firms, and taxpayers. A high-level communications campaign was developed for taxpayers with the twin objectives of introducing self-assessment and of changing public perceptions regarding tax administration. Perhaps one of the most important and innovative efforts was an initiative to make the tax code much more accessible by developing a user-friendly manual. Dubai e-government also used integrated community outreach and marketing programs to boost the use of its services by the public and businesses. These programs were composed of several activities targeting different customer segments, including mass-marketing, events participation, informative sessions, campaigns, etc.

The case studies also contain examples of where ineffective communications have compromised the efficacy of the reform effort. Perhaps the most obvious example is Tunisia, whose openness campaign was, ironically, not accompanied by a major communications push commensurate with the task at hand. As a result, many Tunisian civil servants were unaware of their duties under the law and how to best execute them, and many members of the public were not aware of their new rights and privileges. Use of the new legislation has, therefore, been relatively modest. Tunisia is hardly unique in this area; research supported by the World Bank has indicated that similar problems have plagued the implementation of RTI efforts in many other contexts.[23]

Leadership. Turning to the oft-noted but frequently intangible role of leadership, our cases offer important insights and raise provocative questions. At a minimum, the three Jordan cases show the importance of a sustained hand at the tiller. Both Nasouh Marzouqa and Awni Yarvas from the two document processing cases enjoyed lengthy tenures at the helm of the Civil Status and Passport Department (five and nine years, respectively), whereas the Ministry of Administrative Development (and its successor, the Ministry for Public Sector Reform) witnessed no fewer than eight ministers at the helm between 1999 and 2006 while the cabinet reforms were taking place. In any public organization, such short tenures make it virtually impossible to implement lasting change, as employees know they merely have to "wait it out" for a few months or a year until a given minister's tenure is over.[24]

Successful leaders in MENA often embody identical talents and techniques used by effective leaders elsewhere. They led through example and modeled the types of behaviors they expected their staff to follow. Marzouqa stayed at the office until the last employee left, sending a message that the rules applied to everyone, including the boss. (In contrast, one of the less effective ministers in the cases under consideration was known primarily for insisting that no other staff ride the elevator when he was in it.) In Egypt, tax administration reformers put an end to nepotism and granting special favors to employees. They worked hard to send consistent signals and to ensure alignment between the formal and informal rules. While retaining their long-term strategic vision, successful leaders were also willing to get their hands dirty in the details when necessary. This was particularly true for reengineering efforts, whose success often depended on mastering the legal and procedural obstacles that were delaying applications.[25]

It should also be noted that leaders who created strong leadership teams were among the most successful. Former Egyptian finance minister Youssef Boutros-Ghali argued that a critical mass of reformers is especially necessary. If he did not have at least fifty people, he could not have been successful because proper implementation requires reformers working at lower levels. Some built their teams by recruiting largely from inside their organizations; others drew heavily on external expertise; and others utilized a combination of both. Several reformers had a strong "number two," such as Abdulmalik Al Asheikh in the SADAD case, who was immersed in the technical details of planning and implementation while his superior managed upward and outward within the broader administrative milieu.

It is difficult to envision the success of these reforms without the dynamic leadership of those who championed them. Yet the close linking of reforms to personalities is symptomatic of a broader problem that plagues public sectors throughout the region. It reflects the lack of effective institutions, norms, and mechanisms that can guarantee the continuity and sustainability of reform and ensure its long-term impact. There is a tendency to associate reform with individuals, and thus progress is contingent upon whether those officials and their networks remain in their posts. The Tunisia RTI case was a fortunate exception to this broader trend, and perhaps a sign that new approaches emphasizing coalition building can be successful, at least in a post–Arab Spring context. But in many cases—including a number presented in this volume—reforms slowed down or stopped once their champions left.

Conclusion

The lessons from these cases are instructive but not definitive, and it is our hope that this volume will encourage a more comprehensive study of public sector reforms within MENA. The need for reform is more urgent than ever. In the wake of the Arab Spring and the more recent protests of 2019, public expectations have been raised and ponderous bureaucracies are struggling to meet them. The Arab citizenry is less willing to accept the uneven quality of service delivery or the preferential treatment of large and well-connected firms. Citizens are increasingly recognizing and calling out corruption and cronyism.

The public sector challenges confronting the region over the next decade are both clear and massive. To cope with the demographic tsunami already underway, governments will need to simultaneously expand the scope and the quality of services they provide to their citizens, paying particular attention to lagging regions and underserved communities. They will need to educate the next generation to compete in a globalized workforce. They will need to serve as an attractive destination for capital, providing both the services and business environment that will facilitate foreign and domestic investment. And they will need to be agile enough to respond to a host of known and unknown threats, from climate change and water scarcity to pandemics and transitions in global energy markets.

Perhaps the most politically fraught challenge relates to the social contract, which trades political acquiesce for a job in the public sector. Governments must confront the reality that this is, ultimately, a Faustian bargain. The challenge is not merely one of fiscal sustainability—although that threat is palpable and intensifying rapidly. It is recognizing that this bargain undermines meritocracy and hinders the creation of the sort of high-performing public sectors that will be necessary to address these pressing economic and social problems. It also creates perverse incentives that undermine other critical objectives, such as economic and labor market diversification.

Yet the cases in this book provide hope and illustrate that transformative change is possible. They offer a rich and engaging set of examples about both the content of reforms and how successfully they were implemented, including issues of context and motivation; coping with opposition; and using a variety of tools and techniques to achieve the intended results. For better or for worse, the experiences captured within these cases reflect the conventional wisdom about what to do—and what not to do—with regard to public sector reform more generally. This may not align perfectly with global knowledge and practice, but neither is it entirely alien. To the extent that MENA countries differ, it is only in certain areas, and often more by degree than in kind.

The revolutionary social, political, technical, and economic changes now sweeping through the region have opened new possibilities while also creating new complexities. It is hoped that the lessons from this experience, both good and bad, will be of value to the next generation of Arab reformers as they embark on the critical task of ensuring that their governments and public sectors can respond to the pronounced developmental challenges they will be asked to address.

Notes

The authors would like to thank Khalid Al Yahya for his excellent input on the initial draft conclusions. In addition to the extensive material compiled by the authors of the individual case studies, we conducted interviews with the reformers from 2014 to 2019, from which we draw selected quotes in this chapter.

1. In this analysis, we have treated the Nasouh Marzouqa and Awni Yarvas cases from Jordan as two separate cases.

2. The question of selection bias is an important one. All cases in this analysis share a combination of visibility and accessibility. Many reform initiatives in MENA during this period never advanced beyond the initial design stage, which raises

questions about their ultimate relevance; see Shaun Goldfinch, Karl Derouen, and Paulina Pospieszna, "Flying Blind: Evidence for Good Governance Public Management Reform Agendas, Implementation and Outcomes in Low Income Countries," *Public Administration and Development* 33, issue 1 (2012), pp. 50–61. Researchers also needed to have access to the relevant decisionmakers and documents. As a result, the analysis does not incorporate reforms that took place in environments where the political, administrative, or logistical obstacles toward documenting them were problematic. While these omissions may have reduced the diversity of cases under consideration, it is unlikely that they systematically biased the outcomes in ways that would distort or misrepresent the findings.

3. The importance of local contextualization of public sector reform efforts to ensure success is now widely acknowledged within the development community. See Brian Levy, "Governance Reform: Getting the Fit Right," *Public Administration and Development* 35, no. 4 (2015), pp. 238–49.

4. We do not claim to present a scientific evaluation of reform efforts in this volume, a failing that has generated considerable criticism of public sector reforms in advanced and developing countries; see D. McTaggart and J. O'Flynn, "Public Service Reform," *Australian Journal of Public Administration* 74, issue 1 (2015), pp. 13–22. However, because we draw on the detailed findings of the case studies in this volume, we are able to present deeper insights than are typically offered in comparative analyses of public sector reforms. On the methodological challenges of evaluating public reforms, see Karen N. Breidahl, Gunnar Gjelstrup, Hanne Foss Hansen, and Morten Balle Hansen, "Evaluation of Large-Scale Public-Sector Reforms: A Comparative Analysis," *American Journal of Evaluation* 38, no. 2 (June 2017), pp. 226–45.

5. Independent Evaluation Group, World Bank, "Public Sector Reform: What Works and Why? An IEG Evaluation of World Bank Support," 2008, http://documents.worldbank.org/curated/en/311251468150314338/Public-sector-reform -what-works-and-why-An-IEG-evaluation-of-World-Bank-support. An evaluation of governance projects supported by the UK's Department of International Development in developing countries between 2005 and 2009 reported a performance score of 71 percent; see Department of International Development (DFID), "Governance Portfolio Review: Summary Review of DFID's Governance Portfolio, 2004–2009," London, 2011.

6. See IEA, "Public Sector Reform"; the same is true of DFID's 2011 governance portfolio, where PFM and tax reform projects scored higher on performance than other public sector reforms, including CSR projects.

7. In an interesting, broader analysis of the role of political support in shaping public sector reform efforts, a report by the Overseas Development Institute reviewed thirty-four cases of donor-supported public sector reforms and noted that such reforms perform best when both political and bureaucratic incentives are aligned. See Helen Tilley, Sierd Hadley, Cathal Long, and Jeremy Clarke, "Sustaining Public Sector Capability in Developing Countries," Overseas Development Institute, Working Paper 432, December 2015, www.odi.org/publications/10226-sustaining-public-sector-capability-developing-countries.

8. Delivery units have become a popular approach to improve service delivery in both advanced and developing countries. See Ray Shostak, Joanna Watkins, Ana Bellver, and Indu John-Abraham, "When Might the Introduction of a Delivery Unit Be the Right Intervention?" World Bank, Technical Note, June 2014.

9. In many advanced countries, organizational fragmentation and the resulting problems of coordination have been blamed in part on the transfer of central government authority to specialized agencies, prompting the subsequent emphasis on a "whole-of government" approach to ensure integration across the public sector. See Mark Robinson, "From Old Public Administration to the New Public Service Implications for Public Sector Reform in Developing Countries," UNDP Global Centre for Public Excellence, 2015; and Christopher Pollitt and Geert Bouckaert, *Public Management Reform: A Comparative Analysis—New Public Management, Governance, and the Neo-Weberian State* (Oxford University Press, 2011).

10. For a comprehensive analysis of PFM reforms in MENA, see Robert Beschel and Mark Ahern, "Public Financial Management Reforms in the Middle East and North Africa: An Overview of Regional Experience," World Bank, 2010, http://documents.worldbank.org/curated/en/769021468036251773/Public-financial-management-reform-in-the-Middle-East-and-North-Africa-an-overview-of-regional-experience.

11. On the broader challenges facing reengineering reforms, see Marlene C. Jurisch, Christian Ikas, Wolfgang Palka, Petra Wolf, and Helmut Krcmar, "A Review of Success Factors and Challenges of Public Sector BPR Implementations," 2012 45th Hawaii International Conference on System Sciences, Maui, Hawaii, 2012, pp. 2603–12.

12. These efforts in MENA started in the late 1970s and lasted through the 1990s in response to a series of economic crises driven by commodity price shocks and structural rigidities. They aimed to implement Washington Consensus-style reforms to curb the dominant role of the public sector. See Tarik Yousef, "Development, Growth and Policy Reform in the Middle East and North Africa Since 1950," *Journal of Economic Perspectives* 18, no. 3 (2004), pp. 91–116.

13. Reflecting their perceived success, over eighty countries have introduced one-stop shops that offer government-to-business/citizen services with external support from donors and development agencies. See Aziza Umarova, Kimberly D. Johns, and Jana Kunicova, "Re-Inventing Service Delivery through One-Stop Shops: Proceedings from an International Workshop, May 3–5, 2017, Singapore-Johor Bahru, Malaysia," World Bank, 2017, http://documents.worldbank.org/curated/en/141471507703727123/Re-inventing-service-delivery-through-one-stop-shops-proceedings-from-an-international-workshop-3-to-5-May-2017-Singapore-Johor-Bahru-Malaysia.

14. Even as subsidies and other welfare benefits receded in the last decade in the face of growing fiscal pressures, public sector jobs have retained their primacy as a vehicle for distributing government patronage and welfare, as well as for managing political dissent. See Robert Beschel and Tarik Yousef, "Public Sector Reform," in *The Middle East Economies in Times of Transition*, edited by Ishac Diwan and Ahmed Galal (London: Palgrave Macmillan, 2016), pp. 259–78.

15. By and large, civil service reforms in developing countries including HRM efforts have been viewed as largely unsuccessful and have scored lowest in evaluations (see IEA, "Public Sector Reform" and DFID, "Governance Portfolio Review"). For a summary of the underlying reasons, see Sarah Repucci, "Designing Civil Service Reform: Lessons from Past Experience," *Public Administration and Development* 34, issue 3 (2014), pp. 207–18.

16. There is growing survey and empirical evidence showing the widespread use of *wasta*, not only in obtaining government jobs but also in accessing government services, which has further weakened trust in government. See Hana Brixi, Ellen Marie Lust, and Michael Woolcock, "Trust, Voice, and Incentives: Learning from Local Success Stories in Service Delivery in the Middle East and North Africa – Overview," World Bank, 2015, http://documents.worldbank.org/curated/en/88940 1468051843544/Trust-voice-and-incentives-learning-from-local-success-stories-in -service-delivery-in-the-Middle-East-and-North-Africa-overview; and Amaney A. Jamal and Michael Robbins, "Social Justice and the Arab Uprisings," Issam Fares Institute for Public Policy and International Affairs, April 2015, www.daleel-madani .org/sites/default/files/Resources/20150401_sjau.pdf.

17. For information on the historic spread of RTI legislation, see the Center for Law and Democracy, "Global Right to Information Rating Map," www.rti-rating. org/.

18. Recent political economy conceptualizations of "political will" recognize the critical importance of creating alignment between reform objectives, institutional contexts, and political incentives to implement reforms. See World Bank, "World Development Report: Governance and the Law: Main Report," 2017, http://documents.worldbank.org/curated/en/774441485783404216/Main-report   for the adoption of this framework to analyze governance and service delivery in developing countries. For a broad conceptual and practical perspective, see Matt Andrews, Lant Pritchett, and Michael Woolcock, *Building State Capability: Evidence, Analysis, Action* (Oxford University Press, 2017).

19. See Matt Andrews, Lant Pritchett, and Michael Woolcock, "Escaping Capability Traps through Problem Driven Iterative Adaptation (PDIA)," Center for Global Development Working Paper 299, June 2012, www.cgdev.org/publication/ escaping-capability-traps-through-problem-driven-iterative-adaptation-pdia -working-paper; and Matt Andrews, *The Limits of Institutional Reform in Development: Changing Rules for Realistic Solutions* (Cambridge University Press, 2013).

20. Thomas Ahrens, "Assembling the Dubai Government Excellence Program: A Motivational Approach to Improving Public Service Governance in a Monarchical Context," *International Journal of Public Sector Management* 26, no. 7 (2013), pp. 576–92.

21. This finding mirrors international evidence indicating that "quick wins" may not generate sustained reforms over time, especially when government commitment is weak to begin with and reformers are not strategic leaders. See Simone Bunse and Verena Fritz, "Making Public Sector Reforms Work: Political and Economic Contexts, Incentives, and Strategies," World Bank, Policy Research Working Paper,

WPS 617, http://documents.worldbank.org/curated/en/649411468328580569/Making -public-sector-reforms-work-political-and-economic-contexts-incentives-and-strat egies.

22. This is especially relevant for future reforms with the revolution in information and communication technologies and the growing reliance of publics in MENA on social media; see Fadi Salem, "Social Media and the Internet of Things: Towards Data-Driven Policymaking in the Arab World," vol. 7, Mohammed bin Rashid School of Government, 2017, www.mbrsg.ae/getattachment/1383b88a -6eb9-476a-bae4-61903688099b/Arab-Social-Media-Report-2017.

23. Toby Daniel Mendel, "Designing Right to Information Laws for Effective Implementation," Right to Information Working Paper no. 3, World Bank Group, January 2015, http://documents.worldbank.org/curated/en/204481468188355311/ Designing-right-to-information-laws-for-effective-implementation.

24. On this, see Sergio Fernandez and Hal G. Rainey, "Managing Successful Organizational Change in the Public Service," *Public Administration Review* 66, no. 2 (March-April 2006), pp. 168–76. In Jordan, high government turnover rates have also acted as a disincentive for reformers to pursue costly or controversial reforms. See Sufyan Alissa, "Rethinking Economic Reform in Jordan: Confronting Socioeconomic Realities," Carnegie Endowment, Carnegie Papers, no. 4, July 2007, https://carnegieendowment.org/files/cmec4_alissa_jordan_final.pdf.

25. In this sense, they were effective policy entrepreneurs with significant indi-vidual agency and the ability to motivate others to advance reform objectives as ob-served in other developing countries. See Clare Cummings, "Fostering Innovation and Entrepreneurialism in Public Sector Reform," *Public Administration and Devel-opment* 35, issue 4 (2015), pp. 315–28. Several of the reformers in our case studies could be classified as "Diaspora-Immigrants," which may have further enhanced their impact; see Jennifer M. Brinkerhoff, *Institutional Reform and Diaspora Entre-preneurs: The In-Between Advantage* (Oxford University Press, 2016).

Contributors

Mark Eugene Ahern is the program leader for economic issues with the World Bank office in West Bank and Gaza. He works on economic issues, governance, and private sector development. Previously, he was a lead public sector specialist with the World Bank Jakarta office, working on public financial management. Mark worked with the IMF for eight years in several developing and in-transition countries, and prior to that with the New Zealand Treasury for fifteen years. He holds a Master of Commerce degree from the University of Canterbury.

Fatema Alhashemi was a research assistant with Brookings Doha Center. She is currently pursuing an M.P.A. in development practice and an M.A. in quantitative methods in social sciences at Columbia University. She is specializing in economic development policies, with a focus on unemployment and economic marginalization. Fatema has conducted program evaluations in Morocco, India, and Uganda, mostly on programs geared toward entrepreneurship ecosystem development. She is the coauthor of *Resource Regionalism in the Middle East and North Africa: Rich Lands, Neglected People* (Brookings Doha Center, 2018).

Khalid Elashmawy is a consultant with the World Bank's Governance Global Practice in the Middle East and North Africa region. Previously, he worked with the Egypt Network for Integrated Development, a United Nations project promoting sustainable development in Upper Egypt. He holds an M.A. degree in economics and international development from the American University in Cairo. Khalid was awarded the Model Arab League Graduate Fellowship.

Adele Barzelay is an analyst with the World Bank's Global Governance Practice (MENA). Her research interests include public sector reforms in MENA, data governance, and tech regulations. Previously, she worked in international law and human rights in London and political risk in Washington, DC. She has advised companies on human rights risks. She is a member of the New York Bar Association, having obtained her law degree from the University of Oxford. Adele holds an M.A. in international economics and Middle East studies from Johns Hopkins School of Advanced International Studies. She is currently developing a specialization in the digital transformation of government, focusing on data governance and the regulation of tech.

Robert P. Beschel Jr. is the acting practice manager for the World Bank's Governance Practice in the Middle East and North Africa region. His research focuses on policy coordination, public financial management, anti-corruption, governance, civil service and administrative reform, and public sector reform in the Middle East and other regions. He was previously the World Bank's global lead for the Center of Government Reforms and headed the Bank's Governance and Anticorruption Secretariat. Robert holds a Ph.D. in political science from Harvard University. He was the principal author of the Asian Development Bank's anticorruption strategy and, from 2010 to 2012, served as director of the policy unit in the Amiri Diwan in Kuwait.

Mhamed Biygautane is a research fellow with Monash University, Australia, specializing in public management within the MENA region. His research interests include privatization, knowledge management, and public sector reform. Previously, he was a research associate with the Dubai School of Government. He holds a Ph.D. in public-private partnerships from Monash University. He is the coauthor of various publications, including "The Prospect of Infrastructure Public-Private Partnerships in Kuwait, Saudi Arabia, and Qatar: Transforming Challenges into Opportunities," *Thunderbird International Business Review* (2018) and "Do PPP's

Work? What and How Have We been Learning So Far?" *Public Management Review* (2018).

Tristan Dreisbach is a public policy consultant with Innovations for Successful Societies at Princeton University and the World Bank's Global Delivery Initiative. He has conducted health policy research in South Asia with Harvard University's Global Health Delivery Project. Tristan spent two years as a journalist based in Tunisia, where he was the managing editor of *Tunisia Live*. He studied state building and peacebuilding in transitioning states at New York University's Center on International Cooperation. Tristan holds an M.A. degree in politics from New York University.

Khalid El Massnaoui is a senior economist with the macroeconomics, trade, and investment department of the World Bank. He is based in Morocco and works at the World Bank's Rabat office. His research focuses on macroeconomics, fiscal and public sector management, poverty, and development economics. Previously, he worked at the Moroccan Ministry of Planning. He holds an M.A. degree in applied economics from the University of Michigan. He is the coauthor of *An Evaluation of the 2014 Subsidy Reforms in Morocco and a Simulation of Further Reform* (World Bank, 2015).

Okan Geray is a management consultant and is the co-chair of the Data Economy Impact, Commercialization and Monetization Working Group in the ITU Focus Group on Data Processing and Management. He has consulted for several organizations in the Netherlands, France, Italy, Germany, South Africa, Turkey, and Dubai. Okan worked previously with A. T. Kearney Global Management Consulting Firm before joining the Dubai government as a strategic planning consultant. His responsibilities include strategic planning, strategic performance management, and policymaking. He holds a Ph.D. in systems and control engineering from the University of Massachusetts.

Tony Goldner is principal of Lyceum Advisory Partners, a public leadership and impact advisory firm, and a consultant with the global governance practice of the World Bank. For over a decade, he has advised a number of MENA governments on national economic reform strategy and center of government reform, governance, and institutional capability building programs. He is a former partner at the strategy consultancy, Monitor Deloitte, and prior to attending the Harvard Kennedy School, he worked in infrastructure project finance and diplomacy in Australia, Asia, and Africa.

Deepa Iyer is an associate at Luminate working on media investments globally. She previously worked at Draper Richards Kaplan Foundation to source, fund, and support high-growth social enterprises around the world, with a focus on innovative social ventures in South Asia and Africa. She also led engagements with governments and multilateral agencies in several countries as a senior researcher at Princeton University. Deepa holds an M.B.A. from the Wharton School, University of Pennsylvania, where she was the director of investment for the Wharton Social Venture Fund. She also holds an M.S. degree in development economics from the University of Oxford.

Fadi Salem is the director of research and advisory at the Mohammed Bin Rashid School of Government. He is also a senior research fellow with the Future Government Group at the same school. Earlier, he was a research associate with the Belfer Center for Science and International Affairs at Harvard Kennedy School. His research interests include digital governance, technology policy, and smart cities development. He is currently a Ph.D. candidate in public policy at the University of Oxford. Fadi is the author of several policy publications on social media and public engagement, "future of government" applications, and the impact of digital transformations in the Arab region, including the *Arab Social Media Report* series and the *Arab World Online* series.

Andrew Stone is an adviser for Sustainable, Financial, and Private Sector Development (PSD) in the Independent Evaluation Group. His analysis covers state-owned enterprises, SMEs, trade facilitation, carbon finance, rural nonfarm economy, urban transport, and financial inclusion. His research interests also include business transactions costs, business-government consultation, and assessment of business constraints. Previously, he was lead PSD specialist with the World Bank MENA, focusing on providing a comparable basis to guide private sector development strategy. He is the coauthor of *From Privilege to Competition: Unlocking Private-Led Growth in the Middle East and North Africa* (World Bank, 2009) and *Investment Climate Around the World* (World Bank, 2002).

Simonida Subotic is the deputy secretary for economic development with the New York State Executive Chamber. She has consulted on economic development and growth and change management across Asia, the Middle East, and North America. She served as a principal for the Boston Consulting Group and consulted for the World Bank and the United Nations. Simonida holds a Master of Public Policy, Political and Economic Development from the John F. Kennedy School of Government at Harvard University.

Khalid Al-Yahya is a governance reform and public policy expert. His research examines human capital utilization, institutional reform, innovation in government, labor and employment, knowledge management, and public-private partnership. He worked as a fellow at Harvard Kennedy School of Government and as an assistant professor at Arizona State University. Khalid has consulted for various government agencies in Saudi Arabia, UAE, Oman, and international organizations including the World bank, UNDP, OECD, and the Swedish International Development Agency. He holds a Ph.D. in comparative public policy and management from the University of Connecticut.

Tarik M. Yousef is senior fellow in global economy and development at the Brookings Institution and director of the Brookings Doha Center. His research focuses on the political economy of policy reform in the Arab world. He has authored numerous articles and co-edited several volumes, including *After the Spring: Economic Transition in the Arab World* (Oxford University Press, 2012) and *Young Generation Awakening: Economics, Society, and Policy on the Eve of the Arab Spring* (Oxford University Press, 2016). His policy experience includes working at the IMF, the World Bank, and the UN. He has a Ph.D. in economics from Harvard University.

Index

Surnames starting with "al-" are alphabetized by the following portion of the name.